Tying Dry Flies
Third Edition

For my mother,

Oda Kaufmann

*For having the insight to let me go at an early age,
allowing me to wander the American West in search of
adventure, wild trout, and myself. For being my
mentor and best friend and for making
so many things possible for me.*

*Oda Kaufmann,
Wawona, Yosemite National Park, California,
May 1995.*

Tying Dry Flies
Third Edition

Tie the World's Most Popular Dry Flies
With Speed, Ease and Efficiency

By Randall Kaufmann

Illustrations—Mike Stidham

Foreword—Jack Dennis

Western Fisherman's Press
2001

Books By
Randall Kaufmann

American Nymph Fly Tying Manual
Lake Fishing With A Fly
The Fly Tyers Nymph Manual
Tying Dry Flies
Bonefishing With A Fly
Tying Nymphs
Tying Dry Flies, Revised Edition
Fly Patterns Of Umpqua Feather Merchants
Fly Patterns Of Umpqua Feather Merchants, Second Edition
Tying Nymphs, Second Edition
Bonefishing!
Tying Dry Flies, Third Edition
Tying Nymphs, Third Edition
Fly Tying Made Easy
Fly Tying Made Easy For Beginners

© 1991 by Randall Kaufmann; Revised Edition, © 1995; Third Edition, © 2001

All rights reserved. No part of this book may be reproduced or utilized in any form or by any means, electronic or mechanical, including photocopying, recording, or by any information storage and retrieval system, without written permission from the publisher, except in the case of brief excerpts in critical reviews and articles.

All photos and flies by Randall Kaufmann unless otherwise noted.

Published by:
Western Fisherman's Press
P.O. Box 357
Moose, Wyoming 83012
www.westernfishermanspress.com
e-mail: westernfishermanspress@comcast.net
(971) 235-8390 phone
(866) 859-9592 fax

Printed in Thailand
10 9 8 7 6 5 4 3 2

Library of Congress Catalog Card Number: 94-061567

International Standard Book Number: 1-885212-17-8 (softcover)
                                     1-885212-18-6 (spiral hardcover)

Contents

Acknowledgments vi
Foreword vii
Part I: Getting Started—Basic Techniques
    1. Introduction 10
    2. Recent Dry Fly Evolution 12
    3. Tools 14
    4. Hooks 17
    5. Materials 20
    6. Parts of a Dry Fly 26
    7. Basic Tying Techniques 32
Part II: Tying Instruction
    8. Foam Beetle 42
    9. Proportions 45
    10. Sparkle Dun, Comparadun, and CDC Comparadun 46
    11. Hackle 50
    12. Griffith Gnat and Cluster Midge 60
    13. Hatching Midge 62
    14. California Mosquito 64
    15. Black Flying Ant 68
    16. Adams 70
    17. Light Cahill and Quill Gordon 72
    18. Blue Dun, Black Gnat, and Royal Coachman 76
    19. No Hackle 80
    20. CDC *Callibaetis* Spent Spinner 82
    21. Blue-Winged Olive Thorax 84
    22. Parachute Adams 88
    23. PMD Parachute 90
    24. Parachute Caddis 92
    25. Green Drake Paradrake 94
    26. E/C Caddis 96
    27. Braided Butt Damsel 98
    28. Elk Hair Caddis 100
    29. Stimulator 102
    30. Royal Wulff 106
    31. Irresistible 110
    32. Humpy 114
    33. MacSalmon 118
    34. Dave's Hopper 120
    35. Henry's Fork Hopper 122
    36. Tying With Speed and Efficiency 124
Part III: Pattern Directory
Pattern Directory 128
Untying Flies 137
Landing and Releasing Fish 138
Bibliography 139
Index 141

Acknowledgments

Thanks to Jim Black, Production Manager at Umpqua Feather Merchants, for fly samples and for advising me of the most popular dry flies.

Tony Capone, for photographing Mike Stidham's art.

Jack Dennis, who made time in his busy schedule to write the foreword, and for his early enthusiasm for this project.

Mary Erickson, for ideas, support, encouragement, proof reading, and, most of all, for keeping me laughing.

Lance and Oda Kaufmann, for attending to Kaufmann's Streamborn, Inc. while I completed this project.

Brian O'Keefe, for supplying fishing photos.

Bob Rector, for tirelessly and enthusiastically proofing and editing the many drafts and his unending attention to detail.

Mike Stidham, for the concise illustrations and oil paintings. Mike's understanding of fly tying, fly fishing and fish makes him a pleasure to work with.

Joyce Sherman, for typesetting, editing, formatting, and design advice.

Ian Templeton, for editing the final draft.

Ken Mitchell, for printing and press check advice.

The fly innovators who supplied detailed pattern information and flies and those who supplied historical information, including: Dennis Black, Ed Black, Pret Frazier, Renè Harrop, Gary LaFontaine, Mike Lawson, Craig Mathews, Terry Ring, Polly Rosborough, Ed Schroeder, Al Troth and the many angling authors whom I relied upon for information and ideas.

The fly tyers who supplied flies for the color photos: Jack Dennis, Pret Frazier, Renè Harrop, Mike Lawson, Craig Mathews, Ed Schroeder, Ken Shimazaki, Shane Stalcup, Al Troth, Dan Bailey Flies, Highland Flies, Riverborn Flies and Umpqua Feather Merchants.

Most important, thanks to my mother, Oda, for encouraging my early fly tying endeavors, tolerating my extended weekends away from school and my taking over the kitchen table with fur and feathers. For driving me on numerous fly selling trips before I was able to drive myself and for driving my friend, Steve Peeters, and me to North Lake for our first High Sierra backpack, returning the next week to pick us up at Pine Creek—1,000 miles of driving. For providing a home refuge from my early traveling mania. For understanding, but not necessarily agreeing, when I decided to pursue flyfishing full-time. For helping Kaufmann's Streamborn, Inc. get started and for continuing to help make it successful. For encouragement, wisdom, advice, and for being my special friend.

Foreword

Randall Kaufmann and I are similar in many ways. We are both fly fishermen who have owned fly fishing stores for the same amount of time and penned books on the subject of fly tying. We both learned to tie flies from studying books and were influenced by tyers like Wayne "Buz" Buszek and Roy Donnelly. Randall learned to tie flies to match the insects found in the mountain lakes and streams of the Sierras and Rockies. I learned about flies and fishing in the Wyoming Rockies and Jackson Hole. We have both had the pleasure and advantage of meeting many of the pioneering fly fishermen and tyers.

Both Randall and I went to school during the turbulent 1960s. This was a time of political and social change, and fly fishing was undergoing a renaissance. This renaissance increased demands for new products and improved angling and tying techniques. It was at this time that Randall Kaufmann, Dennis Black and I entered the field with the idea of making fly fishing a business.

I was a junior in high school when I met Randall and his brother, Lance. They walked into my father's liquor and sporting goods store in Lander, Wyoming looking for fishing information. They had driven from California during summer vacation and were anxious to fish the waters of the famous Wind River Mountains. From the moment we started to talk about fishing, I knew Randall and I would be lifelong friends. A couple of summers later I rounded up Randall, and we were off to Yellowstone on a tying and fishing adventure. We tied and fished our way from West Yellowstone to Jackson, where we ended up tying flies in Dick Boyer's Rod and Reel shop. We dreamed of having a fishing business of our own and talked about a partnership, but Randall left for sunny California when the first cold days of winter arrived.

During that same summer we became friends with Dennis Black. The first time we fished together was on a spring creek near Jackson. Dennis and I showed up with our fancy fly gear and vests full of Hardy reels and flies. Randall, always the practical joker, showed up with a spinning rod and bubble. He asked, "Isn't this the way you fly fish?" We laughed and told him we would show him how to fly fish. Randall said he would do just fine and proceeded to show us how it was done! He would drift a nymph under his bubble just like we would off the end of our leaders. It was Randall's choice of flies, his ability to read the water and drift the fly that proved so effective that day.

Throughout those early years the three of us kept in close contact. Randall's and Dennis' road trips were legendary; they would often visit me in Jackson unexpectedly. They always brought tying tools and materials. The three of us each had fly quotas to meet for Orvis and other dealers. It was during one of these drop-in visits that the infamous fly tying contest was spawned. The object was to tie the most flies in a given length of time. This was not only great fun, but a chance to learn from each other while increasing our tying speed, knowledge of materials, and technique.

A lot of proverbial water has flowed under the bridge since that day, and each of us has been fortunate to realize many of our dreams. Dennis Black developed Umpqua Feather Merchants, which is the largest commercial fly tying operation in the world. I have a fly fishing store in Jackson, Wyoming and have written two volumes of my *Western Fly Tying Manual* and *Tying Flies With Jack Dennis and Friends*. I have also enjoyed great success with my fly fishing video library. My dreams continue to manifest themselves.

Randall and Lance have realized many of their dreams with Kaufmann's Streamborn, Inc., a world-wide catalog business. Their stores in Tigard, Oregon, and Seattle and Bellevue, Washington are the finest in the Northwest. They helped shape the fishing evolution that began in the 1960s and have carried on the ethics of old and set new standards for today. In addition, Randall produced the classic fly tying book, *American Nymph Fly Tying Manual*. His *Lake Fishing With A Fly* and *Bonefishing!* are considered the best works on the subjects. Randall's *The Fly Tyers Nymph Manual* was recognized by the United Fly Tyers as the 1986 book of the year. A beautiful color version, entitled *Tying Nymphs*, was published in 1994.

In *Tying Dry Flies*, Randall simplifies the techniques of what many consider the most difficult patterns to tie and once again sets the standard for excellence. The instructional photos are incredibly concise, and the tying techniques are amazingly effective. Randall presents readers with flies that he has had experience with and that work. A couple of patterns are his own, some are contemporary, but most are time-proven throughout the fishing world. He presents them in a way I know you will understand and enjoy. His unique tying style will make all tyers more proficient at the vise.

Randall is a humble man and gives credit to those who have developed the various patterns. You will enjoy the historical perspective. Lastly, Randall has a unique writing style. It ranges from his witty jokes to his serious ethics about environmental concerns. He advocated the use of barbless hooks and catch and release long before it became fashionable. When you read Randall's books, you will feel the deep love and respect he has for fly fishing. This book is written by a good and caring person. I treasure his smile, his sometimes outrageous ways, and, most of all, his friendship.

Jack Dennis
February 2, 1995
Jackson, Wyoming

Part I:

Getting Started—
Basic Techniques

Tying your own dry flies and fishing the West is the best. The only thing better is fishing New Zealand or South America during their summer, which is opposite ours. Drifting big dry flies over steelhead-sized trout is only one of many attractions. This beautiful brown lives in Chile.

Part I explains how to get started and recommends books and videos. It presents a general overview of tools, hooks, materials and dry fly proportions. Basic tying techniques necessary to begin actual fly construction are discussed and demonstrated. It is suggested that you practice all the techniques presented and thoroughly understand them before progressing to Part II.

Chapter 1

Introduction

*D*ry fly is a general term that denotes a fly that is fished on top of the water or more in the air than in the water. The adult forms of caddisflies, stoneflies, damselflies, water beetles, terrestrials (grasshoppers, cicadas, ants, shore beetles); the hatching and adult forms of specific Diptera (chironomids, or midges, and mosquitoes); and the hatching, adult and spent spinner stages of mayflies are all commonly imitated with dry flies fished in the surface film or on the water's surface.

Of the many fly fishing methods, dry fly fishing is the easiest. One does not need to be an expert to hook fish on the dry fly, especially if a good hatch is in progress and fish are not too discriminating. This is true, in part, because surface currents are visible and relatively easy to read, and anglers can see fish attack their flies. This is not to say that dry fly fishing is always easy, quite the contrary. If one is *consistently* to hook fish feeding at the water's surface, both imitation and presentation must be precise. Tying dry flies is much like fishing them. By their very nature of balancing and floating on the water's surface, dry flies must be exact.

This dry fly manual begins with basic tying techniques, proceeds to the tying of easy dry flies, then progresses to the most difficult patterns. Patterns and instructions are presented in a logical sequence, which should be followed. When you have tied all the presentation patterns, you should be able to tie almost any dry fly.

Besides working through this manual, aspiring dry fly tyers who want to accelerate their progress should seek out the best tyers and watch them work. Local sport shows often showcase prominent tyers. The Federation of Fly Fishers conclave presents the best selection of tyers possible under one roof. Local fly fishing specialty stores are a convenient source of information. If they offer seminars or tying classes, take advantage of them. More serious aficionados might wish to take an intensive "on location" fly tying and fishing course where you tie flies and fish them under expert tutelage.

Throughout my fly tying career, I have been fortunate to watch, tie with, and exchange ideas with many of the best tyers. One fact has emerged: No one tyer has all the answers. My strategy has been to seek out and learn from the best innovators, selecting the most efficient and effective methods of each. This accumulation of knowledge is presented within these pages. This manual is the next best thing to having a master fly tyer stand over your shoulder. Fly tying is, after all, an incredible escape and wonderful therapy, second perhaps only to fly fishing, and I believe in making it *easy* and *fun.*

Angler-tyers are also urged to broaden their horizons with books and videos. Following is a list of some of the most useful currently available books and videos that relate to tying and fishing dry flies. Remember that someone else has already discovered and solved or explained many of the problems and frustrations that you may encounter. Don't reinvent the hook. Take advantage of available information; it contains many lifetimes of learning. Spend your energies elsewhere. Eventually you may be able to contribute and build upon fly tying and fly fishing knowledge. Read and fish all you can. There is no substitute for on-the-water experience. . .and what a pleasure it is!

Recommended Books
   Caddisflies, Gary LaFontaine.
   Lake Fishing With A Fly, Ron Cordes and Randall Kaufmann.
   Matching The Hatch, Ernest Schwiebert.
   Reading Trout Streams, Tom Rosenbauer.
   Selective Trout, Doug Swisher and Carl Richards.
   The Dry Fly, New Angles, Gary LaFontaine.

Recommended Videos
   Advanced Strategies For Selective Trout, Doug Swisher.
   Fly Fishing Made Easy, Bob Guard.
   Fly Fishing Tips From The Traveling Fishermen, Jack Dennis, Mike Lawson, Gary LaFontaine.
   Fly Tying Basics, Jack Dennis.
   Learning to Fly Fish for Trout, Jack Dennis.
   Strategies For Selective Trout, Doug Swisher.
   Tying And Fishing The Caddisfly, Jack Dennis, Mike Lawson, Gary LaFontaine.
   Tying Flies for Spring Creeks and Tailwaters, Jack Dennis.
   Tying Flies with CDC, Shane Stalcup.
   Tying Flies with Jack Dennis and Friends, Jack Dennis.
   Tying Western Dry Flies, Jack Dennis and Mike Lawson.
   Tying Western Trout Flies, Jack Dennis.
   Understand Fly Tying Materials, Jack Dennis with Scott Sanchez

Chapter 2

Recent Dry Fly Evolution

Gray Hackle Yellow and Pale Morning Dun are old and new PMD imitations.

Jack Horner and Royal Humpy, old and new "attractors," or multi-purpose flies.

Grizzly King and Extended Green Drake, old and new Green Drake imitations.

Bucktail Caddis and CDC Caddis, old and new caddis imitations.

E/C and Hot Butt™ Caddis, more recent imitations.

Engaging in a little nostalgia, I paged through my 1960s pattern "bible," a well-used edition of *Flies* by J. Edson Leonard. Patterns like the Pink Lady, Gray Hackle Yellow, Blue Bottle, Dusty Miller, Grizzly King, and Scarlet Ibis took me back. Comparing the patterns in *Flies* with those in this book, I found 30 that matched. I rummaged through an old suitcase and found a 1962 copy of Wayne (Buz) Buszek's fly fishing catalog; of 60 cataloged dry flies, 30 are listed in this book. Ray Bergman's classic book, *Trout*, revealed 28 flies in common, and, in a 1970 edition of Roy Patrick's *Pacific Northwest Fly Patterns*, I found 29 flies in common with this book. I checked the second Kaufmann's Streamborn catalog (1972) and counted 40, but some are seldom fished today, and only included for historical perspective.

The majority of today's popular patterns have been developed within the past 25 years, and most of these have evolved within the past 15 years. The survivors either closely resemble naturals (Cahill, Quill Gordon, Adams) or are effective fast water imitations (Humpy, Wulff, Irresistible).

Fly fishing boomed during the 1970s and 1980s, and a younger, less traditional generation of tyer-anglers renovated the sport, from the vise to the stream. Innovative tyers proliferated, and average angling skills soared. Old-time patterns succumbed to more realistic and specific imitations or were updated with new materials.

One such example is the standard Midge pattern, which consists of a tail, body, and hackle and was tied to imitate any small insect, whether it was a mayfly, caddis, or midge. Today, a midge is strictly and specifically referred to as a midge (chironomid), and each stage is represented by a particular pattern (Hatching Midge, Emerging Midge, Adult Midge, etc.) The standard midge pattern of yesterday still works, but it is limited in scope and is not nearly as effective as its many and varied offspring.

In the 1960s, the casual lake angler often fished a Gray Hackle Peacock (it used to be my favorite fly) or perhaps an Adams to represent "those speckled upwing flies." Today's angler would recognize this hatch as *Callibaetis*, and a full range of imitations, including nymphs, emergers, hatching duns, cripples, adult duns, and spent spinners would be in the fly box. This selection and knowledge of how and when to fish greatly expands productive angling time.

The 1971 publication of *Selective Trout* by Doug Swisher and Carl

Richards revived the match-the-hatch concept and brought the term "no hackle" to the vocabulary of every fly angler. Specific imitations became the rage and were eventually refined into No Hackles, Comparaduns, stillborns (cripples), hatching (emerging) duns, and spent spinners. This expansion and pattern refinement is still in progress.

The value of parachute-style flies has been recognized, and a plethora of effective patterns is currently in use. Downwing patterns have also proliferated (caddisfly, stonefly, midge), and terrestrials have undergone a major face lift.

A better understanding of trout behavior and pattern design has begun to reshape "attractor" thinking. True attractor patterns that do not specifically represent anything in nature have all but disappeared. Patterns like the Humpy and Royal Wulff, which have long been thought of as attractors, are beginning to be viewed as multi-imitators. Recent patterns like Turck's Tarantula and the Stimulator are very successful multi-imitators.

Many of today's patterns are more practical and more closely resemble the natural. Anglers who take advantage of these recent advancements are those who always seem to have leaping fish at the end of their leaders. A general understanding of hatches and on-stream observation results in huge dividends. Remember—fish less, observe more, catch more. . .and be prepared!

Fly patterns continue to change. While no single tying style or pattern will be the ultimate elixir, new ideas, techniques and materials will make many of today's favorites tomorrow's unknowns. Hatches and insect stages that go unnoticed today will be discovered tomorrow. I urge tyers to delve into such surface attractions as midge, caddisfly, stonefly and cranefly, where there is much work to be done. The frontier is still awaiting the next generation of tyers and anglers. Go for it! Maybe you will come up with the next Adams, Elk Hair Caddis or Royal Wulff.

Sofa Pillow and Improved Sofa Pillow, old and new stonefly imitations.

Stimulators, a further refinement of downwing style adult stonefly imitations.

Joe's Hopper and Dave's Hopper, old and new grasshopper imitations.

Turck's Tarantula and Trude, multi imitators.

Hatching PMD and Callibaetis Cripple imitate specific stages of mayflies.

Parachute Hopper and Henry's Fork Hopper—more recent hopper refinements.

Adams (still very popular) and more exact Extended Gray Drake.

Callibaetis Sparkle Dun and Thorax, perhaps previously imitated with Adams.

The Midge of yesterday and more specific Hatching Midge of today.

Chapter 3

Tools

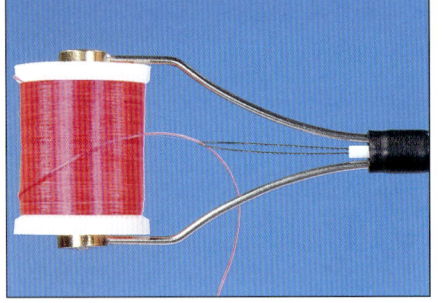

Ceramic bobbin.

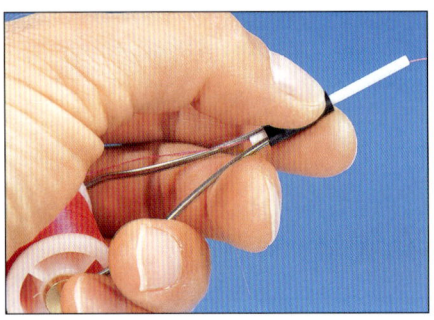

Rest the bobbin in the palm of your hand with your thumb and first finger on the plastic pad. Tighten your fourth and fifth fingers around the spool to apply tension.

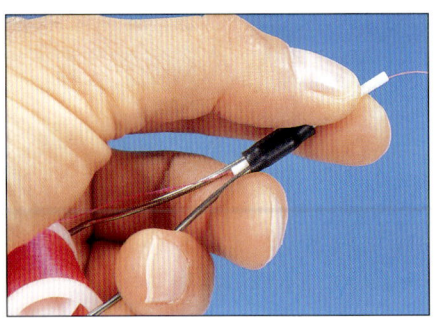

Incorrect method of holding the bobbin.

Good tools are the difference between frustration and fun. Do not skimp on the quality of your tools. If you buy the right tools to begin with, you will not have to buy them again.

Application Jar

This is an effective way to keep lacquer from evaporating and scenting the air. Attach the jar to the shaft of your vise with rubber bands or tape, and it will always be handy. When applying lacquer, pick up a small drop on the tip of the bodkin and spread it over the head. If lacquer does not soak into the thread head slowly, it is too thick and should be thinned. Lacquer can soak into the base of the hackles or legs but should not glue the individual fibers, wings, or guard hairs together.

Blender

This is useful for blending colors, textures, and sparkle together. Any texture or color is instantly available, such as the mix for tying the Kaufmann Stone. Note that natural dubbing materials (goat, muskrat, Haretron) blend much more easily than synthetics. Long strand synthetics should be cut into lengths of one inch or less before blending.

Bobbin

A good bobbin is like having a third hand at the vise. The Matarelli is the best stainless steel bobbin. Tiemco offers a superb ceramic bobbin that is nearly indestructible. Both are lightweight, durable, finely polished, and easily adjustable for tension simply by spreading out or squeezing together the arms. Tension is properly adjusted when you can quickly pull size 6/0 or 8/0 thread without breaking it. If tension is too loose, thread unspools as the bobbin hangs from the hook.

Rest the bobbin in the palm of your hand and grip the plastic pad with your thumb and first finger. Do not hold the round shaft because it will roll between your fingers and you will have less control. Do not hold the thread. If you squeeze the spool in your palm, the thread won't feed out. By easing off the tension and winding with more force, you cause the thread to feed out as you wrap it around the hook.

The top of the bobbin shaft should be close to the hook shank; that is, you should be wrapping a small (one-inch diameter) circle around the hook shank, not a large one. The small circle allows you to quickly place thread exactly where you want it. It is helpful to have a half-dozen bobbins so it is not necessary to re-thread one when you change thread colors. A short shaft works better for short shank hooks and smaller flies. A long shaft is better for tying on long shank hooks.

Bodkin

This is a needle point used for picking out dubbing, lacquering heads, freeing up hackle, and, if it has a hole in the end, for tying half hitches. Select one with a hexagonal shaft so it will not roll off the table.

Cements

Head lacquer should be fast drying and of relatively high gloss. There are many such products available. Vinyl cement (Flexament) is used for reinforcing or stiffening feather material such as turkey wing quills. Apply vinyl cement with a small brush or a bodkin. Crystal epoxy puts an impenetrable gloss on thread heads and wingcases, but it must be applied thinly. Zap-A-Gap secures eyes and wire.

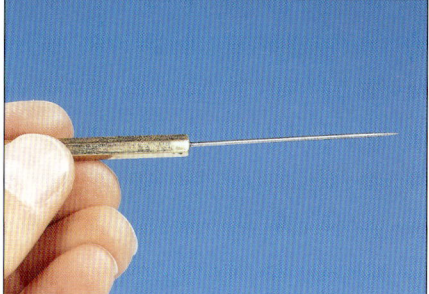

Bodkin.

Hackle Gauge

Compact and efficient, the Hook and Hackle Gauge attaches to the vise shaft and allows you to select size 4 to 24 hackles quickly and accurately. It also measures hook size.

Hackle Pliers

Hackle pliers are pinchers used to hold material securely while you wrap it around the hook. If they help, use them. Otherwise, they are simply another tool to look for, pick up, and set down. There are several styles. Some have metal-to-metal pinchers, others rubber or plastic-to-metal pinchers. The Tiemco spinning hackle pliers are unique and functional.

Plastic to metal hackle pliers.

Lamp

A concentrated beam of light allows you to see the fly clearly. If possible, get a light that burns clear, cool, and bright and that has an adjustable arm. Magnifiers are available for tyers who need additional aid. Jewelers often use a binocular magnifier which has a headband mount and hinged visor. They work well for fly tying.

Material Clip

There are two types: spring and the Thompson slot style, which is my pick. This sanity saver slips onto the vise collet and holds tinsels and other materials out of your way until you are ready for them.

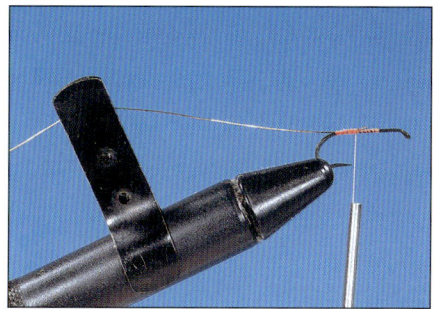

Slot style material clip.

Scissors

Scissors should have a fine point and finger holes large enough so you can carry them on your hand. When you carry the scissors on your hand, you always have them ready to cut without wasting time looking for them, picking them up, and putting them down. Scissors can be carried on your thumb and first finger or on your thumb and any other finger you feel comfortable with. You can also carry them on your thumb and in your palm, inserting a finger when you need to make a cut. All cuts should be made with the tip of your scissors. If possible, make only one exact cut. When making close cuts, steady the scissors against the hook or vise. Do not cut paper or wire with precision scissors.

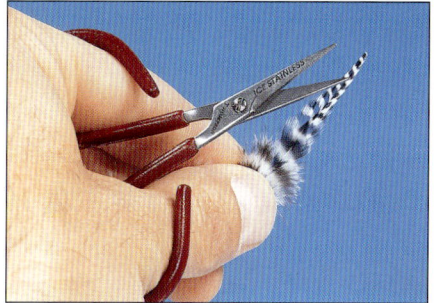

Adjustable finger hole scissors.

Smooth-Nosed Pliers

Smooth-nosed pliers with a fine point are used for smashing barbs before you tie the fly. They are also used to flatten lead bodies. Tiemco DeBarb pliers are the best.

Stacker

A stacker is indispensable for making the length of hair tails and wings even. Having both a large and small diameter stacker is nice, but,

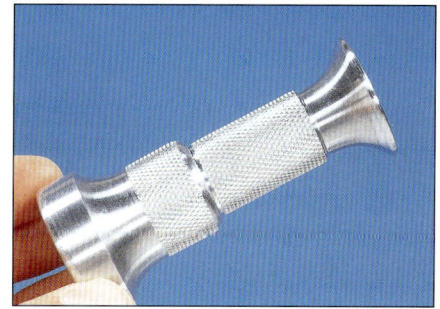

Stacker.

16   Tying Dry Flies

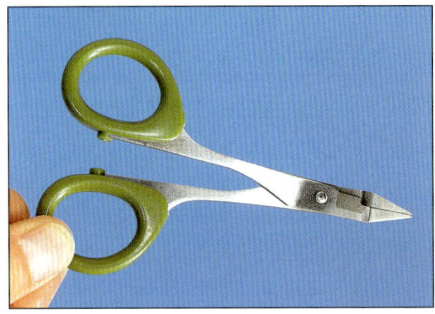
Debarbing pliers.

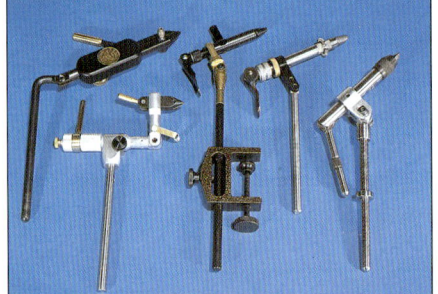
Regal, Renzetti, Thompson, and Dyna-King vises. C-Clamp or base available.

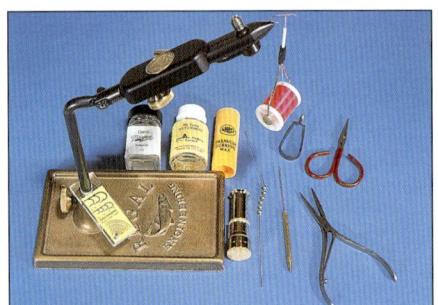
Setting up the tying bench.

A compact tying case is ready when you are. This is the JW Creekside.

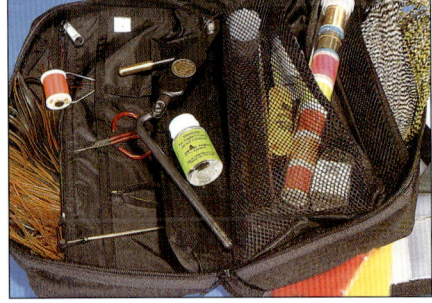
Larger tying cases carry enough material to tie most patterns. Pictured is the JW Pro.

if you are only purchasing one, get a large diameter. The material to be stacked is placed with the natural tips pointing down into the bottom of the stacker. Place one finger over the open end and tap it onto a hard surface. Hold the stacker level or *slightly* angled up at the bottom and slowly remove the end.

Threader-Cleaner

This is a simple tool used to unclog wax that builds up in the bobbin shaft and to pull thread through the shaft. Thread the bobbin by inserting the end of the threader-cleaner with the wire loop into the bobbin. Trim the end of the thread and insert it through the wire loop. Pull the wire loop and the thread through the bobbin shaft. The Matarelli threader-cleaner and the Tiemco threader are real mind and time savers.

Vise

A vise should hold a hook securely. The Regal, Dyna-King Professional, Renzetti Master, and many other top of the line vises hold a hook so tightly that you can break the hook before it slips from the jaws. The Regal holds the largest and smallest hooks without adjustment. The Dyna-King Professional requires minimal adjustment. I like base vises because you can set them up anywhere. The Regal bronze, Dyna-King Professional, and Renzetti have heavy bases that will not rock when you are tying. All are available with a C-clamp, which is more secure and offers greater height adjustment. The Thompson A is the old standby and the best inexpensive vise. I do not recommend foreign vises if for no other reason than you cannot always get parts. You should adjust the height of your vise so you have eight to 10 inches of clearance between the table's surface and the jaws.

Waste-Trol

This is a wire hoop basket that attaches to the vise. It acts as a waste container and catches dropped tools and materials and spilled lacquer.

Wax

Wax eases dubbing application and increases thread strength. Tyers should be using waxed thread, but sometimes additional wax makes it easier to dub coarse materials.

Setting Up The Tying Bench

Most tyers begin tying at the kitchen table or office desk. It usually does not take long to outgrow such quarters. A desk devoted solely to tying is ideal, but a card table can suffice. It is important to keep your vise set up permanently so you can take advantage of short periods of free time. You may find that a few minutes at the vise is a great stress reducer and a way to vicariously escape to your favorite trout waters. If you have to set up and tear down your tying area every time you want to tie flies, you may tie infrequently. If you just tie a fly or two here and there, you may be surprised how many you will have in a short time.

A light background allows you to see hooks, tools, and materials clearly. Light blue poster board is perfect. Be certain to keep all dangerous objects and materials away from children and pets.

Fly Tying Storage Cases

There are many wooden boxes and soft material cases available for storing and organizing supplies. Some are designed for travel, others for home use. Organization is a key factor. If you can view your inventory quickly, you have more fun tying.

Chapter 4

Hooks

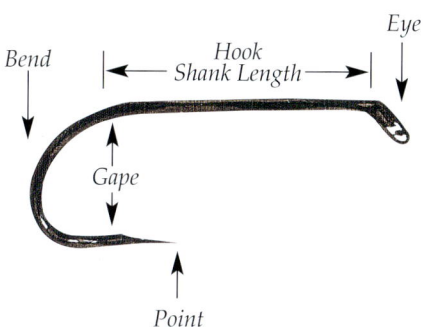

There are several premium hook manufacturers, including Partridge in England and Dai-Riki, Daiichi, and Tiemco in Japan. Premium hooks use the latest technology and hook designs and the strongest tempered steel. The hook points are sharp, the eyes are closed tightly without any rough edges, and the finish is blemish free. In relation to lower quality hooks and the overall value of flies, the cost of premium hooks is negligible. Fishing the best possible hook is another way to maximize your angling success. I prefer Tiemco hooks because Tiemco offers the largest selection of contemporary styles and sizes, and the hooks are easy to obtain. In addition, Tiemco has been responsive to the needs of tyers.

The following is a brief look at hook terminology.

Gape

The gape is the distance between the hook point and shank. For the most part, manufacturers adhere to a standard gape for each size of hook, making the gape the tyer's standard unit of measure. The smaller the number, the larger the gape. A size 8 is larger than a size 10. The hook length, wire diameter, bend, and eye design may vary, but the gape is mostly uniform for any given hook size. A standard hook gape is roughly half the length of the hook shank.

If a hook gape is too narrow, hooking fish may be difficult. Tyers should remember not to impede the hook gape with bulky materials, which can reduce hooking capability. If the gape is too wide and the hook rides inverted (hook point up), the hook point can penetrate a fish's eye or brain, causing serious injury or death.

Wire Diameter

Manufacturers have standardized wire gauges somewhat; a size 12 standard hook usually has the same diameter wire regardless of its manufacturer or configuration. An X system is used to denote wire diameter that is smaller or larger than standard gauge. Because hooks are manufactured in even and odd sizes (8, 9, 10, 11, 12, etc.), each X denotes one size. A 1X fine size 14 hook has the same diameter as a hook one time (1X) smaller, or a size 15. A 2X fine size 14 has the diameter of a standard size 16. A 2X heavy size 12 is the same diameter as a size 10. Dry flies may be tied on hooks that are lighter, heavier, or longer than standard.

Shank

The shank is measured from the eye to the beginning of the bend. There is also an X labeling system for hook shank length. A 2X long size

10 means the hook length is the standard length of a hook two sizes larger, a size 8. A 6X long size 10 denotes the shank length of a size 4 standard length hook. Depending on the actual length of the natural, dry flies may be tied on 1X, 2X, or 3X long hooks.

Eye

Eyes that are not completely closed or that have a rough closure can cut leaders and make tying a neat head difficult. Check hook eyes; they are important. The most common eye designs are turned down (TD), followed by turned up (TU) and straight. These may incorporate a tapered, loop, or ball design. Standard dry fly hooks usually have a turned-down tapered eye (TDTE). Turned-up and straight eyes are sometimes used by tyers who are concerned about a turned-down eye blocking the hook gape and, consequently, the hooking ability of the hook. This can be a concern with some manufacturer's hooks, especially size 18 and smaller. The shape of the eye, in conjunction with your leader knot, helps determine how the fly will ride on or in the water.

I prefer to attach turned-down and turned-up eye hooks with a Turle knot. The Turle knot allows for a straight pull and will not rotate or swing around the eye like a clinch knot will. When the leader is not extending straight out from the eye, parallel to the hook shank, the fly is cocked at an angle and is not fishing properly. The Turle knot keeps your leader from becoming wedged in the corner of an improperly designed or manufactured eye where it is easily broken. The Turle knot secures itself behind the hook eye so it does not create a knot in front of the fly. A clinch knot tied on a size 20 hook can enlarge the imitation by over 25 percent.

Point

The point is the most fragile part of a hook, and care should be taken to avoid damaging it, especially on back casts. During tying, hook points should not be buried in the vise jaws. Chemically sharpened hook points do not need sharpening before you fish them, but they should be checked often for broken or dulled points while you are fishing. A traditional method for determining if a hook point is sharp is to drag the point across your thumbnail. If the hook leaves a scratch, it is fairly sharp. If it stops dragging, it is very sharp. All premium hooks are very sharp. All dry fly patterns listed in this book have a recommended hook. Unless you are substituting another hook style or manufacturer, you need not be overly concerned with hook terminology.

Barbless Hooks

There are many positive reasons for fishing with barbless hooks. A barbless hook penetrates a fish's mouth more easily than a barbed hook, which means more fish are hooked. Fish hooked with a barbless hook are easy to release; simply back the hook out in the same direction it went in. This can usually be accomplished instantly and with one hand, which means fish experience less stress and have a better chance of survival. It also means you spend less time reviving fish and more time fishing. Barbless hooks are also easy to remove from yourself! Unfortunately, very few hook styles are manufactured barbless. Smash the barb, using a smooth-nosed pliers, before you tie the fly.

Recommended Hooks

My approach to hooks is the same as my approach to tying dry patterns: keep it simple. I don't need nine different standard dry fly hooks any more than I need nine different adult damselfly patterns. I tie my dry flies on the following Tiemco hooks, but you should feel free to use any other style or other manufacturer's hooks. All hooks pictured are actual size.

Tiemco 900BL, sizes 10-16, *extra light wire (1X), standard length,* black, barbless, perfect bend (half circle), turned-down tapered eye (TDTE). This is the dry fly hook of choice, and it is occasionally used for nymphs.

Tiemco 100 or *100BL,* sizes 8-24, *extra light wire (1X), standard length,* bronze, turned-down eye. My second choice. Tyers who have the 900BL will not need these.

Tiemco 101, sizes 20-26, *extra light wire (1X), standard length,* bronze, straight (ring) eye. Useful for small flies where the open ring eye allows a bit more hooking power in sizes 20-22 and smaller.

Tiemco 200R or *200RBL,* sizes 4-18, *standard wire, 3X long,* bronze, straight eye, semi-dropped point. My favorite adult stonefly hook; also useful for many nymphs.

Tiemco 5212, sizes 6-12, *extra fine wire (1X), 2X long,* bronze, down eye. First choice for hoppers and drake patterns.

Tiemco 5263 or *5263BL,* sizes 6-10, *standard wire, 3X long.* Useful for stonefly imitations.

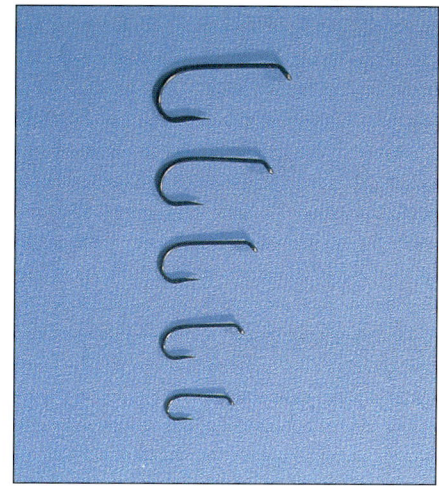

900BL, sizes 10-18.

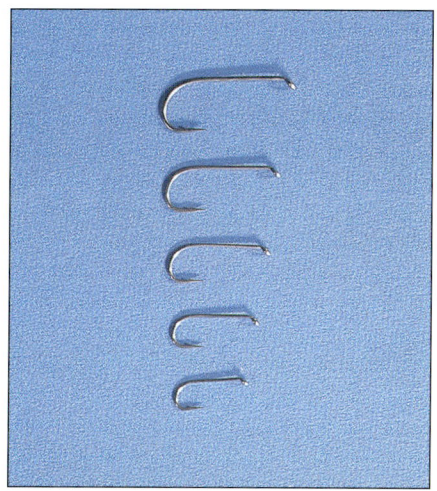

100, sizes 10-18.

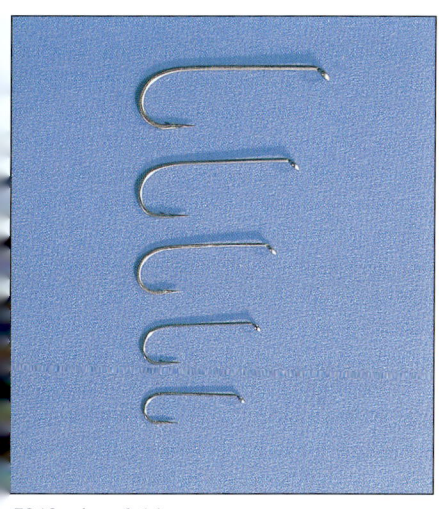

5212, sizes 6-14.

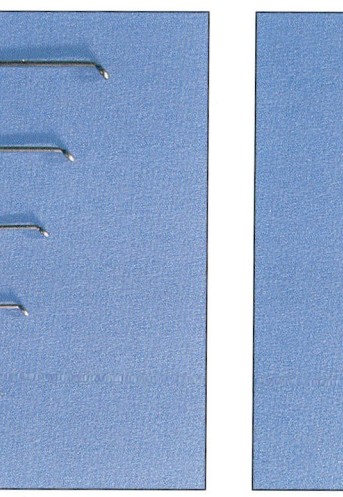

5263, sizes 6-14.

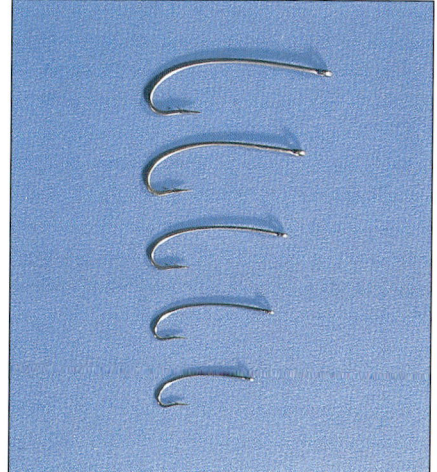

200R, sizes 8-16.

Tying Dry Flies

Chapter 5

Materials

Dubbing material.

Dubbing material after it has been "dubbed" onto thread.

Dubbed body. The dubbing strand above has been wrapped around the hook.

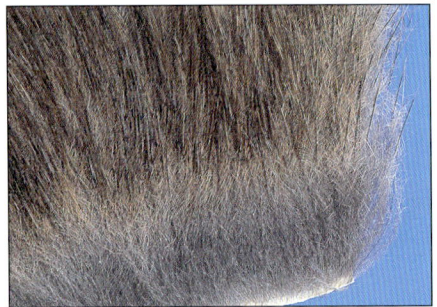
Muskrat is an excellent natural fur, and it dubs easily.

Antron fibers. Blend this with other dubbing for sparkly effect.

A dry fly will only be as good as the materials and workmanship that go into it. If you begin with a strong light-wire hook, water-repellent dubbing, and stiff hackle, you end up with a high quality dry fly, providing, of course, that your tying skill is polished. Using poor quality materials results in poor quality flies, regardless of your workmanship.

Select the best materials possible. They usually cost a little extra, but we are only talking pennies per fly. Hooks and hackle are of the utmost importance. Do not attempt to skimp and get by with whatever you have. Remember, this is your hobby, your escape to a fantasy world of wild things in wild places. There is little room for compromise.

Constructing a scraggly subsurface fly is often desirable, but surface flies are usually designed to represent delicate insects that fish often inspect up close. This is especially true of finicky trout in slow, clear water. Of course, not all dry flies must be flawless and perfectly presented, but the phrase "matching the hatch" is especially apropos in the art of tying and fishing the dry fly.

Today's anglers are more refined, but so, too, it seems, are the trout. Fish that would rush to grab a Humpy 15 years ago now often seem to approach a Sparkle Dun skeptically, slap it with their tail, and reject it. While fishing may demand more refinement, tying a more realistic imitation is not difficult.

This chapter explains the different materials and guides you in selecting what you need for tying purposes. The materials described here allow you to tie all of the 26 demonstration patterns and the other patterns described and pictured in this book. If you do not want to obtain it all at once, pick up enough supplies to tie a couple of patterns at a time. Eventually, as you begin to amass material, you will find that less is required to tie new patterns because you already have most of it. If you are like me, you will want to get most of the materials to start. That way you lessen the chances of finding you are missing a small item on Sunday afternoon or when on location attempting to match the hatch.

Dry fly tyers who purchase the best grade of hackle and Tiemco hooks will have about 40 cents invested in a fly, as opposed to $2.00 or more if they were to buy the finished fly. Don't overlook the fact that you receive a great deal of satisfaction and enjoyment from tying and that you can tie the exact size, style, and color of fly for where, when, and how you intend to fish. We have a great many clients who tie the easy nymphs and dries and buy the difficult ones. If you do not enjoy tying tiny winged dries, don't tie them. Buy the challenging patterns and tie the Elk Hairs, Griffith Gnats, Sparkle Duns, spent spinner, and thorax-style patterns. Remember, tying flies is fun—keep it that way.

Thread

Thread sizing is denoted by numbers in smaller sizes and letters in larger sizes. Size E (commonly used for rod building) is larger than A, followed by 1/0, 3/0, 6/0, 8/0, and, finally, the smallest available, 15/0. Dry flies require fine-diameter thread that does not build up bulk. Size 6/0 waxed Danville (Flymaster) is the accepted standard, but size 8/0 Uni-Midge is useful for flies size 18 and smaller.

Some hair flies require stronger thread. I recommend size 3/0 or single-strand floss for covering medium to large Humpy bodies, switching back to 6/0 for hackle and heads. Spun deer and caribou bodies can be tied with 6/0, but Kevlar thread allows you to apply extreme pressure and easily flare large amounts of hair. Again, switch to 6/0 for tails, wings, and hackle.

Danville size 6/0 flattens out and allows you to construct a small, neatly-tapered head, which is the hallmark of a professionally-constructed fly and is necessary if you are to secure your leader properly.

As a matter of aesthetics and tying ease, thread should match the dubbing color. When thread and dubbing colors match, dubbing a thin body is much easier because less dubbing is needed to cover a like-colored thread. Also, as you construct the fly you can wrap a matching color thread over dubbing; it will be unobtrusive and seldom visible.

Dubbing

The primary body ingredient in most dry flies is dubbing. Some is natural (rabbit or muskrat), and some is synthetic, mostly nylon. Natural dubbing is available either on the skin or blended. Synthetic dubbing is usually blended. Blended means the material has been chopped in a blender and is loosely matted.

The word *dubbing* has a dual meaning. Dubbing (the act) is applying any material directly onto a single strand of thread or between a loop of thread that is twisted to form a single strand that then is wrapped around the hook shank to help form the fly. Natural fur and blended synthetics are most commonly used, but any soft, smooth material that can be dubbed is referred to as dubbing (the material). There are many name brands, colors, and textures of dubbing. Besides color variations, olive dubbing is not all the same. Important qualities to consider include sparkle, diameter, and texture. Texture is an important consideration especially in regard to animation qualities and fly size.

Dry fly bodies should be constructed with a slight taper and should be free of long guard hairs because any protruding hairs can affect fly posture. Bodies should be dubbed relatively tightly, but, if dubbing is too tight, it inhibits floating qualities because not enough air pockets will be trapped in the dubbing. Unlike nymphs, dry fly bodies need to be more exact and delicate.

Selecting Dubbing Material

Tyers do not need every dubbing material, but a general selection of Superfine, Antron, and assorted smooth, coarse, reflective, and natural materials is of value. Many times, procuring additional dubbing is a matter of color. Dubbing is relatively inexpensive; a $1.75 packet of Antron will probably last years. Collect dubbing and colors in a systematic manner. It is frustrating to sit down to tie an *infrequens* (Pale

Antron dubbing is perhaps the most useful. Great sparkle and ties easily.

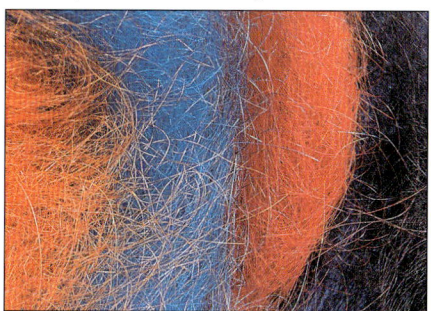
Goat is often used in blends. It is a mainstay for nymph tyers.

Hare-Tron is a mixture of rabbit and Antron fibers.

Kaufmann Stimulator blend—several colors of goat and a dominate color of Hare-Tron.

Synthetic dubbing—available in many colors and textures.

Superfine is a fine diameter synthetic and is easy to dub.

Mallard dyed woodduck color—referred to as "mallard woodduck."

Natural teal is used for wings.

Natural gray duck wing quills, left and right.

Natural light dun CDC. The best quality is on the left; it has lots of dense fibers.

Morning Dun) only to find that you do not have the right color or texture of dubbing.

Keep dubbing organized so you can see what you have at a glance and find it when you want it. Until recently I stored my dubbing in small plastic bags inside large plastic bags. I could never find what I knew I had and accumulated many duplicates. Dubbing organizer boxes are an excellent way to organize, label, and store small amounts of dubbing. These small, compact, 12-compartment plastic boxes allow most dubbing to feed out the holes in the bottom.

Antron Dubbing: Don't confuse this with Antron yarn. Antron dubbing is blended 100 percent Antron. It is smooth, sparkly, easy to work with, comes in an excellent selection of colors true to nature, and makes fantastic dry fly bodies. It is the all-purpose favorite.

Goat: Also called Angora. Indispensable for tying nymphs, goat is used for the Stimulator thorax and for some Stimulator body blends.

Hare-Tron: This is a blend of natural rabbit and sparkle Antron fibers, which offers translucence and ease of use. It is available in good colors and blends easily. This is a favorite all-purpose dubbing for nymphs and some dry flies. The many short, fuzzy hairs in Hare-Tron will accentuate and enhance dry fly bodies, but any long guard hairs should be removed.

Superfine: Developed by Wapsi, this is a smooth synthetic that is half the diameter of most other dubbing. It is the standard smooth-textured dubbing for medium to small dry flies, dubs easily, is waterproof, and is the current favorite.

Fine and Dry Dubbing: Is the standard smooth-textured ultra-fine-diameter dubbing for extra delicate work. It is readily available, and the color selection is excellent. It has superb floating qualities.

Waterfowl: Mallard, Teal, and Goose

Mallard: Mallard is the most commonly used duck feather. Mallard flank feathers, which are located along the sides of the bird, are incorporated into wings. The natural feathers are barred dark gray and white. The most common dyed color is woodduck (lemon yellow). It is used to tie Cahill and Quill Gordon wings. Duck wing quills are used for tying wings (Black Gnat, Henryville Special, Royal Coachman, Blue Dun).

Teal: Teal flank feathers have a more pronounced black and white barring. They are excellent for tying dry fly parachute wings.

CDC: These seemingly insignificant feathers are found in the immediate vicinity of the oil preen glands of ducks. Because of their location, they are well impregnated with a duck's water-repellent oils. There are only a handful of feathers per bird, and the best come from wild ducks.

Good CDC is easily recognized by the fact that the feathers have *dense* fibers. It almost looks like duck down. The barbules of most other feathers extend at a right angle from the fibers. This allows the fibers to "marry" or adhere to one another. CDC barbules are unique in that they *spiral around* the fiber stem. This prevents them from clinging together and creates space between the fibers. This, in turn, creates air pockets, CDC's floating qualities, and a unique "light pattern." In addition, all fibers react in an independent manner, creating a unique action. For this reason, CDC should not be treated with any floatants.

CDC offers an almost magical, animated, translucent light pattern and traps air bubbles—properties that are not otherwise obtainable. CDC is useful for representing legs, tails, shucks, wingcases, and even hackle. The key factor is obtaining prime CDC.

Miscellaneous Feathers

Peacock is popular for bodies. Turkey quills and turkey flats (shoulder feathers) are used for wings. Turkey biots make wonderful bodies. Partridge body feathers are useful for legs and wings. Ringneck pheasant tail fibers are used for bodies, and golden pheasant tippets are sometimes needed for tails.

Miscellaneous Synthetics

Round rubber is needed for legs. Fine wire is used for ribbing. Closed cell foam is used for overbodies on emerging midges and adult beetles. Micro Fibetts and Betts' Tailing Fibers are synthetic nylon fibers with a tapered point that replace hackle fibers for tails. Z-Lon is a sparkle nylon that is available in two textures. Crinkle Z-Lon is perfect for tails, spinner wings, and shucks, and the smooth variety is used to create sparkle in the wings of mayfly spinners. Braided macrame cord is needed for stonefly bodies. Shimazaki Fly Wing is used for wings. Antron yarn is a beautiful, soft, four-ply yarn interwoven with silver sparkle fibers. It is perfect for tying sizes 6-10 Wulff-style flies, a few adult stonefly imitations, and for tails, shucks, wings, and highlights.

Hair

Hair is used to tie wings, overbodies, and tails. It is often flared or spun, and then trimmed to form bodies and heads. Aside from color, texture and length are the critical considerations.

When constructing wings and tails, you can tell at a glance if the hair is long enough, but overbodies are more difficult to judge. Humpy-style overbodies require about four times the length of a standard tail. When selecting soft hair to flare, remember that the tips will be trimmed off and you will still need enough to hold onto.

Wings, overbodies, and tails should be tied with stiff elk, deer, or moose hair. Stiff hair is desirable because it will not flare, or spread apart. Trimmed bodies and heads require soft, hollow hair, which flares easily and has the best floating qualities. Caribou and deer are the softest hairs and make the best trimmed bodies. To check for fiber stiffness, pinch a few fibers between your thumb and forefinger or tie a small amount onto the hook. Soft hair will flare; stiff hair will not.

Elk: The most useful and popular variety of hair is elk. It is generally longer, larger in diameter, and stiffer than deer. Elk is more durable than deer and is usually easier to prepare, stack, and tie with. It is available in a wide range of natural and dyed colors. I prefer elk for most upright and divided hair wings (Wulff, Humpy), down hair wings (Stimulators, Elk Hair Caddis), and for tails and overbodies. As you select elk, moose, or deer hair, remember that long hair is needed to tie combination tails and overbodies on Humpies and wings on oversize stonefly imitations (Stimulators, Improved Sofa Pillows). Long hair is also necessary to tie extended and reverse style bodies (Paradrakes and Henry's Fork Hoppers).

Deer: Deer hair is available in all lengths, textures, and colors. In general, it is softer and shorter than elk. Soft deer is very good for clipped bodies and is the best choice for a single upright flared wing (Sparkle Dun, Comparadun). Stiff deer is also useful for tails, wings, and overbodies, but I usually prefer elk because it is more durable and stacks faster than deer.

Peacock eyed tail. The herl immediately below the eye is best.

Mottled brown or oak turkey wing quills, left and right.

White turkey primary wing quill dyed brown. The short side has biot quills.

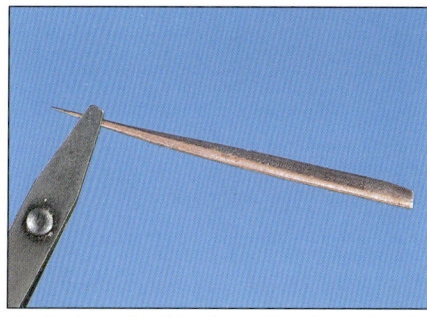
A single turkey biot is used to form dry fly bodies.

Turkey shoulder feathers are useful to make thorax-style wings.

24   *Tying Dry Flies*

Elk is used for tails and wings. Color pictured is medium dark.

Natural deer is available in many colors and textures. Coastal blacktail on right.

Elk dyed yellow (left) and white deer body dyed yellow (right).

Moose body is straight and stiff—perfect for tails and Humpy backs.

Caribou is the softest hair. It packs tightly and flares easily.

Moose: Moose body is very stiff and is either very dark chocolate brown or black. It is my first choice for a dark tail or Humpy overbody. It stacks quickly and is durable. You should have both short and long lengths of moose. Moose mane has little value for dry flies.

Caribou: Caribou is fine-textured, short, dense, and very soft. It is perfect for clipped bodies and heads. It ties, flares, and packs easily to form a dense, high-floating body.

Calf: Use of calftail and calf body hair is limited to dry fly wings and occasional tails (House and Lot Variant). White hair is used most often, and it is easy to see under most light conditions. I wonder why tyers have not incorporated dyed calf for wings?

Calf body hair is straight, fine-textured, and makes stacking and tying a dense dry fly wing relatively easy. I prefer calf body, but long enough hair for size 10 and larger flies is difficult to obtain. Calf body hair should be fairly dense, straight, and pure white.

Calftail is the standard calf used on dry flies, and many tyers prefer it over calf body. Calftail is kinkier and larger in diameter than body hair; it is more difficult to stack. Calftail may float a bit better than calf body, but I still like the looks of body hair. Many tyers use calf body for size 12 and smaller and calftail for size 10 and larger. When purchasing calftail, look for straight, dense, even hair with a fine diameter. Stay clear of especially kinky, glossy, cream-colored hair. The coarse and wavy hair toward the top of the tail should be avoided.

When stacking calf, a large-diameter stacker should be used because individual hairs can more easily spread out and fall to the bottom to even up. Compared to other hair, calf hair is kinkier and is the slowest to stack. Figure on about 40 strong taps to even up calf, two or three for moose.

Tanned Hair: Except for calf, always buy tanned hair. It is easy to work with, clean, odorless, and will not become buggy and infect your valuable tying materials. Inspect all hair, making certain the tips are unbroken and of uniform length. Look at the lighter band of color below the dark tips. If it is even across the tips, the hair is of uniform length. Hair should always be straight and free of any set or radical curvature. Large-diameter fibers should usually be avoided. Check the base of the hair. If it is relatively free of fuzzy underfur, it will be easier to prepare. Finally, check the length to make certain it is what you need.

Most Useful Hairs And What They Are Used For						
	Stiffness	*Length*	*Wings*	*Tails*	*Overbodies (Backs)*	*Clipped Bodies*
1st	Moose	Moose	Elk	Moose	Moose	Caribou
2nd	Elk	Elk	Calf	Elk	Elk	Deer
3rd	Deer	Deer	Deer	Deer	Deer	
4th	Calf	Calf	Moose			
5th	Caribou	Caribou				

Hackle

Hackles are bird and fowl feathers that can be utilized for many aspects of fly tying. The term hackle refers specifically to domestic rooster neck and saddle feathers that are used to make the hackle on dry flies. Hen chickens also have both neck and saddle hackles; these are commonly used for dry fly wings. Hackles are the most critical dry fly material and will be thoroughly explained in Chapter 11.

Recommended Material List

Threads, Tinsel, Wire, Floss
Thread: Black, brown, olive, gray, orange, tan, cream, white, yellow, fluorescent fire orange, fluorescent green
Floss: Yellow, black, tobacco brown, dark olive, bright olive, red, fire orange
Fine wire: Gold, copper
Tinsel: Fine; gold, silver

Dubbing:
Antron Fibers: Clear (white) for spinner wings and blending dubbing
Antron Dubbing: 30 colors
Antron Yarn: White, cream, pale yellow, black, rust, gray, gold, orange
Hare-Tron: All colors
Superfine: All colors
Fine and Dry Dubbing: Assorted colors
Goat: Black, amber, ginger, fiery brown (rust), hot orange, yellow, purple, claret, gold, brown
Muskrat
Red Fox
Hare's Ear/Mask

Hair:
Calf: White body and tail
Caribou
Moose Body
Deer: Natural light, natural dark, bleached light, dyed black, golden brown, yellow
Elk: Natural light, natural dark, bleached light, dyed brown, green, olive, orange, gray, red, black, gold

Feathers:
Turkey: Mottled turkey wing quills and turkey tail
Turkey flats (shoulder): White and medium blue dun
Turkey Biot: Natural gray and white, dyed olive, yellow olive, tan, rust
Partridge: Brown
Peacock: Eyed tail
Duck Quills: White, gray
CDC Duck: Natural white, dun, gray, dark blue dun, black
Mallard: Natural, dyed woodduck
Teal
Ringneck Tail
Golden Pheasant Tippets

Miscellaneous:
Z-Lon: Light, dark blue dun, dun, rusty brown, light olive, dark olive, tan, gold, amber, white, yellow
Darlon: Synthetic similar to Z-Lon. Good substitute; colors vary from Z-Lon.
Micro Fibetts or Betts' Tailing Fibers: White, light dun, dark dun
Round Rubber: White, yellow, black
Shimazaki Fly Wing: Various gray patterns and colors
Closed-Cell Foam: Black, yellow
Macrame Cord: Orange, gold, rust, yellow; size 1.5 to 3.5mm

Hackle:
Hen Saddle: Variegated brown
Hen Neck: Medium blue dun, grizzly
Saddle Hackle: Red Chinese strung (tails)
Hackle: Grizzly (barred black and white), brown, medium blue dun to start; then get black, ginger, and dyed grizzly in brown and olive
India Saddle Hackle: If you do not have dyed Hoffman saddles or small enough Metz saddles, India saddles are usually obtainable in brown, furnace, cream, dyed black, blue dun

Calftail is crinkly but long. Use it for large dry fly wings.

Calf body is straight but short. Use it for smaller dry fly wings.

Z-Lon is useful for tails, shucks, wings, and highlights.

Betts Tailing Fibers and Micro Fibetts make perfect tails.

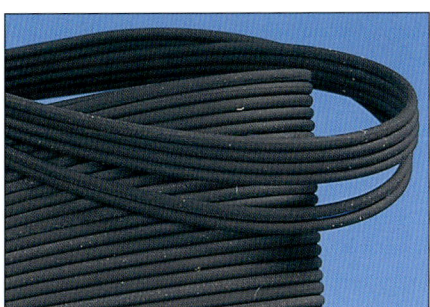
Round rubber makes great legs and is easy to work with.

Macrame yarn is useful for extended body stoneflies—see page 118.

Shimazaki Fly Wing is available in many patterns and colors. Trim to shape.

Antron yarn is useful for tails, shucks, wings, and bodies.

Hackle is the most critical dry fly material. See Chapter 11, beginning on page 50.

Tying Dry Flies

Renegade

Sparkle Dun

CDC Baetis Spent Spinner

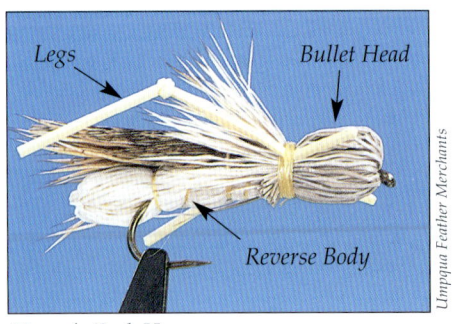
Blue Dun

Henry's Fork Hopper

Chapter 6

Parts Of A Dry Fly

Once you have a complete understanding of dry fly parts and how to construct them, you will be able to visualize what the finished fly will look like and to physically construct it. Throughout this text, fly pattern dressings are listed in the order they are *secured onto the hook*. This order is not necessarily the order in which materials are *wrapped around the hook*. As you progress through the instructional photos, the tying sequences will become clear.

Tag

A tag is simply a couple of turns of tinsel on the hook shank behind where the body would normally begin. The only dry fly with a tag described here is the Renegade.

Shuck

Hatching or emerging midge and mayfly imitations can have a shuck, which is usually imitated by a "tail." The actual shuck is the nymphal case from which the adult midge and mayfly usually hatch on the water's surface. A certain percentage of hatching insects become trapped in their nymphal case and, for whatever reasons, are unable to completely escape, becoming stillborn or cripples, which are easy prey for fish. Shucks are easily represented with a standard tail of Z-Lon or CDC duck feathers, or a combination of both. Examples include the Hatching Midge and Sparkle Dun.

Antennae

Adult caddis and midge imitations are about the only dry flies that might require antennae. Hackle stems and soft feathers are usually used. The best examples are the Goddard Caddis and Hatching Midge.

Tail

Adult caddisflies, damselflies, dragonflies, craneflies, midges, and terrestrials do not have tails. Stoneflies have a split tail, but it is relatively unimportant when compared to the overpowering physical aspects of the body, wings, and legs. As a result, most corresponding imitations do not have tails. When they do, the tail should usually be considered an extension of the body and tied accordingly. Most tailed dry flies represent adult mayflies, whose tails are an important physical aspect of the insect's appearance.

There are several styles and variations of tails. The standard-style bunch tail is mostly used for hair flies—Humpies, Wulffs, Catskill-style flies (Adams, Light Cahill, etc.). Standard-style tails help float the fly, but are not the most accurate imitation of mayfly tails. Single and multi-fiber split, or V, tails are much more accurate but do not provide the buoyancy needed for rough water. Therefore, anglers who are designing their own imitations or deviating from standard patterns must make a judgment call. Consider the water to be fished, overall buoyancy of the fly, and the degree of accuracy required.

Standard tails should be mounted directly on *top* of the hook and extended straight back, as if an extension of the hook shank. A tail that is cocked off at an angle or tied onto one side of the fly may cause it to float or to ride on the water improperly. Flared tails are standard-style tails that have been spread wide for visual effect or for added buoyancy and stability. Split, or V, tails are mounted along each side of the hook and are usually sparse. Sometimes a half dozen or, on smaller, more delicate flies, only a single fiber is tied along each side of the hook. The most common tail materials include hackle fibers, moose, elk, and Micro Fibbetts or Betts' Tailing Fibers.

Hackle Tails: Hackle-fiber tails are adequate for slow- to medium-speed waters. Hackle fibers used for tailing must be stiff and completely free of web. The best place to select tailing material on a neck is midway along the side of the neck where fibers are longest and stiffest. While the hackles and hackle fibers are also long at the bottom of the neck, they are webby and soft. A neck with long, stiff tail material is difficult to find; for this reason many tyers use hair on larger flies. Depending on the size of the fly, hackle fibers for a standard-style tail should number between 15 and 40. A size 14 requires 20 to 30 fibers.

Hair Tails: Select straight, stiff hair and be certain it has been cleaned of all under fur and stacked so the ends (tips) are of uniform length. Hair tails are usually best for larger flies and when fishing fast water. A tight wrap of thread at the base of the tail flares the hair slightly. Loose wraps at the base help keep hair from flaring. If tails are too bushy or heavy, fish sometimes unintentionally push them away and are unable to seize the fly. Use 10 to 25 hair fibers on a standard-style tail.

Rib

Rib is any material other than hackle that is wrapped around the body. Ribbing should be evenly spaced and *tightly* wrapped. When checking the durability of a fly, I always attempt to pull or slide the rib off the back of the fly. It should be tight.

While ribbing can be used to set off and add a slight amount of flash to a fly and to depict segmentation, its main purpose on a dry fly is to secure and reinforce palmered hackle or fragile peacock bodies. Rib can be wrapped in the opposite direction from hackle and peacock. This is referred to as reverse wrap rib. Fine wire or thread are the most useful ribbing materials.

Body

Technically, the body of an adult insect is divided into two parts: the abdomen and the thorax. Both are casually referred to by fly tyers as the body, but some patterns call for both a body (abdomen) and a thorax. The thorax area is the forward section of the body. When tying patterns that specify both thorax and body, the body should occupy roughly 60 to 75 percent of the hook shank.

Bodies should be constructed with a *slight* taper, which should continue into the thorax. Remember that most adult insects have delicate,

Red Tail Mosquito

Adams

Fluorescent Green Royal Humpy

Callibaetis *Spent Spinner*

Brown Paradrake

Green Drake

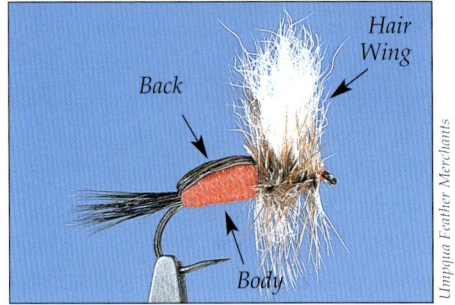
Red Royal Humpy

Hatching Midge

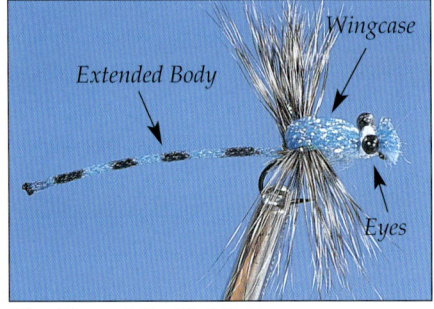
Blue Damsel, Braided Butt

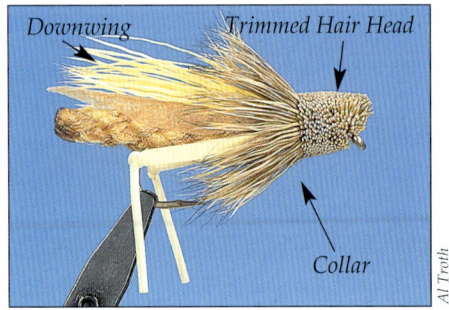
MacHopper

fine-diameter, almost transparent bodies. Forming a slight taper is very difficult unless you begin with the smallest possible diameter body at the rear of the hook.

Flies that include a thorax are two-part ant bodies and the Hatching Midge. Many patterns refer to the thorax area regarding the placement of hackle, legs, wings, etc., but do not actually have a specific thorax.

Most dry fly bodies are tied with dubbing; examples include the Adams and Light Cahill. Some mayfly, stonefly, and terrestrial imitations have a body that extends beyond the hook shank. The Green Drake Paradrake incorporates elk for the extension; the MacSalmon uses macrame cord. The Henry's Fork Hopper has an extended reverse-style hair body. Other popular bodies include spun and trimmed deer and caribou bodies (Irresistible) and quill bodies (Quill Gordon, CDC *Callibaetis* Spent Spinner, and Rusty Spent Spinner).

Overbody

The overbody, or "back," is any material that is tied in at the tail area and pulled forward over the top of any part of the body. Elk, moose, deer, and closed-cell foam are all popular materials. Fly examples include the Humpy, Black Flying Ant, and Foam Beetle patterns.

Wingcase

The wingcase is usually associated with nymphs, but some surface emerger-hatching-style adult patterns (Hatching Midge) require a wingcase. A wingcase is any material that is tied in at the back of the thorax and pulled over the top of the thorax and tied down, or, as is the case with some nymphs, any material that is tied in front of the thorax and extends over the top of the thorax.

Legs

Legs are used mostly on terrestrial patterns (beetles, hoppers) and are tied with rubber, hair, hackle fibers, or trimmed hackle stems. Legs are also specifically represented on caddisflies and mayflies with hackle fibers, but more often, standard-style hackle is intended to represent legs.

Eyes

The only adult imitation with eyes that is described in this text is the Braided Butt Damsel. Tyers imitating adult damsels and dragons should remember that the eyes on these insects are very pronounced. Burned monofilament makes the best eyes. Pre-burned eyes can be purchased, or you can burn your own. Hold a section of monofilament in a smooth nose pliers and touch it to a flame, or tie a short section of monofilament in place and then burn it. I use a small, fine-tip cauterizing instrument that melts the monofilament without damaging nearby feathers. The larger the diameter of the monofilament, the larger the eyes. Amnesia is available in smaller diameters and is colored.

Head

This term refers to the area immediately behind the thread head and is more common in nymphs than dry flies. The head is easily confused with the thorax. Dry fly heads are usually constructed with hair and tied bullet-head-style (Henry's Fork Hopper) or trimmed hair (MacSalmon).

Collar

A collar may represent legs. It is usually a bunch of hair tied in front of and encompassing the thorax and body area 360 degrees and extending half to three-quarters the body length. Examples include the Henry's Fork Hopper and MacSalmon.

Hackle

Hackle is an important aspect of most dry flies and is explained in detail in Chapter 11. There are four styles of hackle—standard, thorax, palmer, and parachute.

Standard: Standard hackle is the most common and it is usually placed in front of the body. It is wrapped both behind and in front of the wings and is densely packed. Demonstration patterns include the California Mosquito, Adams, Light Cahill, Blue Dun, and Royal Wulff. Variations of standard style hackle include placing it at the back of the body, as seen on the Renegade, or in the center of the body, as seen on the Black Flying Ant, Chapter 15. Standard-style hackle can also be evenly spaced through the thorax—see the Stimulator, Chapter 29.

Thorax: Thorax-style hackle is reserved for flies with a thorax-style wing. It is evenly spaced both behind and in front of the wing and usually clipped short on the underside of the fly. See the Blue-Winged Olive Thorax, Chapter 22.

Palmered: Palmered hackle is evenly spaced through or over the body. Demonstration patterns include the Griffith Gnat, Elk Hair Caddis, Stimulator, and Dave's Hopper.

Parachute: This is a unique style of hackle. It is wrapped horizontally around the wing over the top of the fly, much like a helicopter blade. Demonstration patterns include the Parachute Adams, PMD Parachute, Parachute Caddis, Green Drake Paradrake, E/C Caddis, and Braided Butt Damsel.

Wings

Wings are the single most overpowering visual aspect of adult insects to both fish and fishermen, and they are often the primary acceptance trigger for fish. Anglers also rise to a nicely tied winged fly.

Wings and hackle are the two major components that differentiate dry flies from nymphs. Of the two, wings are the most important. Many dry flies do not have hackle, but they all have wings. Unlike hackle, there are *many* different wing styles and associated tying techniques.

Some dry fly wings are intended specifically to imitate those of a natural insect, while others are intended to be impressionistic or are meant to create or to represent movement (fluttering wing). Each material creates a different effect, and tyers should consider various properties of individual materials. When selecting wing material, consider floatability, silhouette, density, mass, color, and light-reflective properties.

Wing proportions and positioning are crucial and must be exact if the desired effect is to be achieved. A slight error may cause the fly to tilt, land, or float in an unnatural and unwanted manner, presenting the wrong visuals to a fish. Tyers should have a thorough understanding of wing styles and how best to construct them.

Except when tying clipped hair body flies (Irresistible), all wing styles except downwings should be *tied in first.* If a problem occurs, you have not wasted time and materials on the rest of the fly. More impor-

Royal Lime Trude

Elk Hair Caddis

Yellow Stimulator

Pale Morning Dun Thorax

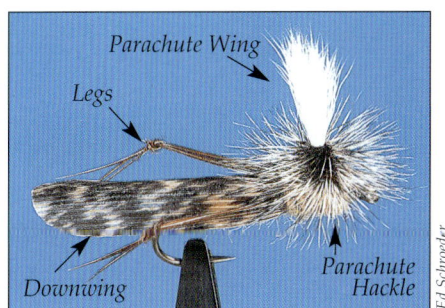
Parachute Hopper

Tent downwing (feather) and single upright (hair)—double downwing.

Downwing (hackle tip).

Single upright, parachute (hair).

Tent downwing (feather).

Single downwing (hair).

Double downwing (hair).

Double downwing (feather).

tant, tying the wing first allows a good perspective of proportions (especially the head and body area) and helps you to form a tapered underbody. All tie-ins are easily covered with the body. Wings are easier to secure in position before other materials have crowded and covered the tying area. Wings that are tied down across the top of the body are usually constructed after the body is in place.

As you progress through the tying instructions, pay close attention to tie-in technique, proportions, and positioning and you will easily master wings. As a primer to wing construction, let's look at the various styles of wings, the materials generally used, and specific fly examples. If you are unsure of a particular wing type, refer to this chapter.

Downwing: Downwings are tied flat, or down, across the top or back of the fly. They are usually mounted behind or before the hackle but not always. They extend to or slightly beyond the hook bend. Many downwings realistically represent caddisfly, stonefly, and terrestrial wings at rest and in motion, as well as adult mayfly and midge wings.

Downwings are tied with deer, elk, hackle tips, CDC, duck quill, turkey, hen saddles, and many other materials. They can be all shapes and sizes, including double wings (underwing and overwing). Nearly all styles of downwings are covered in the tying section demonstration patterns, including these downwings:

Hair: Elk Hair Caddis, Stimulator (some have a double downwing).

Hackle Tip: California Mosquito, Black Flying Ant (actually a delta wing, which is a downwing tied flat instead of on edge).

Feather: Henry's Fork Hopper (has double downwing).

Tent Wing: The tent wing is another type of downwing that is useful for imitating caddisfly wings. They are usually tied with turkey or other wing quills that have been treated with Flexament and trimmed to a V shape. See Parachute Caddis, Chapter 25. They can also be constructed with two hen saddle feathers positioned like a tent as seen on the Slow Water Caddis. See the pattern directory.

Spent Wing: Spent wings are the standard style for imitating spent mayfly spinners, which lie on the water with their wings spent, or splayed out, from their body at 90 degrees. Wings are tied at about the 80-percent mark and are usually as long as the hook shank. Hen hackle tips, Antron, poly, CDC, partridge, and turkey flats are all used to represent spent wings. The CDC *Callibaetis* Spent Spinner details the technique.

Single Upright: As the name implies, this is a single post or clump of material tied upright and is often referred to as a parachute, clump, or thorax-style wing. When tied with white or fluorescent material, this wing offers excellent visibility, making it a favorite with anglers. Tyers like this wing because it is easy to tie and it lends itself to many effective

Single upright, parachute (hair).

Single upright (feather thorax style).

Single upright, flared (hair).

Upright and divided (hair).

patterns. Single upright wings are usually mounted at the 75- to 80-percent mark on the hook, except thorax-style flies, where wings are placed at the 50- to 65-percent mark. Wings are usually as tall as the body is long, or twice the hook gape. Common materials include calftail, calf body, turkey flats, deer, elk, poly, and CDC feathers. Demonstration patterns depicting these wings include the Adams Parachute, PMD Parachute, Blue-Winged Olive Thorax, and Green Drake Paradrake.

Single Upright, Flared: Referred to as a comparadun wing or no-hackle hairwing, these are similar to the single upright, but they are flared in a half circle (180 degrees) across the top of the fly. This creates an unobstructed view (for the fish) of the wing and body and helps to balance the fly. The hair floats well, and its sparse appearance creates a different light pattern on the water's surface than standard hackle does. Tyers like them because they are fast to tie. Wings should be tied with *hollow* deer or standard elk and mounted at the 80-percent mark. They usually should be about as tall as the hook is long, or twice the hook gape. Demonstration patterns include the Sparkle Dun and CDC Comparadun.

Upright and divided (feather).

Upright and Divided: This is the standard or traditional style of dry fly wing; it causes many tyers endless (but needless) frustration. The right materials and tying techniques simplify matters, making upright and divided wings fun, quick, and satisfying to tie. Except on a clipped hair body, these wings are always tied in first. Hairwings are generally heavily hackled and are tied at the 65- to 70-percent mark; others are tied at the 75- to 80-percent mark. They are constructed with duck quill, duck body, hackle tips, calf, deer, elk, and almost any other material you can think of and are usually twice as tall as the hook gape is wide. The following demonstration patterns explain the tying details.

Hair: Humpy, Royal Wulff, Irresistible
Hackle Tips: Adams
Feather: Light Cahill (sometimes called a rolled or woodduck wing)
Duck Quill: Blue Dun, Royal Coachman, Black Gnat, No Hackle

Upright and divided (quill).

Spent or delta (hackle tip).

Spent (feather).

Upright and divided (hackle tip).

Chapter 7

Basic Tying Techniques

This chapter explains the basic tying techniques needed to begin fly construction. They should be fully understood and practiced before beginning Part II. It should be noted that all directions are given for tying right handed. Left-handed tyers should turn the vise around and reverse all instructional directions.

Inserting The Hook

Inspect the hook carefully before you begin tying. Check the point, eye, shank, and hook temper. Smash the barb. Hooks should be mounted in the vise with the shank parallel to the table. I like to insert only the lower bend of the hook in the forward topmost part of the jaws. This allows you to tie materials onto the hook more easily. The point and barb should be exposed because vise jaws can weaken a hook point. This is especially true of small light wire hooks. Be careful not to catch your thread on the hook point. To avoid the point, tilt the thread-wrapping circle so the thread is closer to the eye at the bottom of the wrap.

Securing The Thread

The function of thread is to secure material onto the hook, which is referred to as the tie in and tie off. Thread is always positioned at the exact location where material is to be secured. Whenever a material is secured onto the hook, it is referred to as the tie in or tie on. If that same material is wrapped around the hook, it will be tied off. Tie down is synonymous with tie in and tie off. Thread should always be wrapped in the same direction and as tightly as possible. The number of wraps should be limited to those that are absolutely necessary.

You will break the thread. This could be the result of exerting too much tension on the thread, chafing the thread on the hook point, or encountering a rough burr on wire, tinsel, etc. When the thread does break, hold on to the broken end with your fingers or hackle pliers and, if possible or necessary, half-hitch the broken end to keep it from unravelling. Rethread the bobbin, tie on the thread, and continue.

Thread is secured to the hook by doubling back, or wrapping, the thread over the top of itself. Hold the end of the thread in your left hand and place it at a right angle against the hook. Keep tension on the thread and, with the bobbin in your right hand, wrap the thread forward in a clockwise direction around the hook, then backward over the short end.

Thread and materials should always be wrapped clockwise. Any time thread or materials are wrapped around the hook, constant tension must be applied. The only exception is when using the up-between-the-fingers, or cinch, tie-in technique. The idea is not to allow previously placed wraps of thread or material to unwind or loosen.

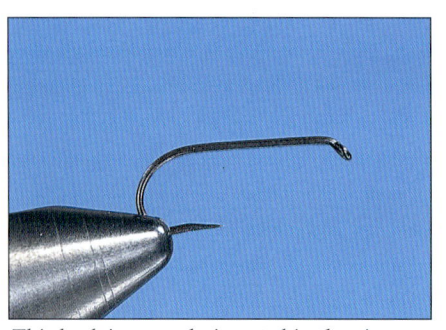
This hook is properly inserted in the vise.

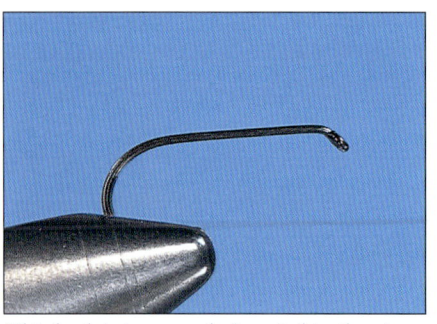
This hook is improperly inserted in the vise.

Hook shanks are round, smooth, and slippery. If a foundation of thread is not wrapped over the hook before materials are secured, the finished fly may spin around the hook shank. When you begin a fly, secure thread onto the hook shank and wrap it to the place where the first material will be tied in, or onto, the hook.

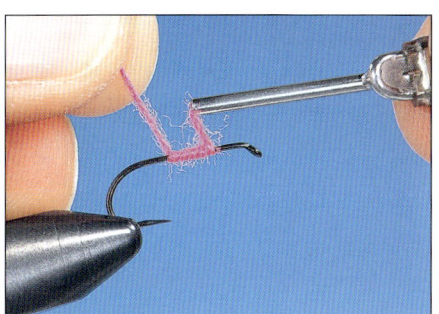 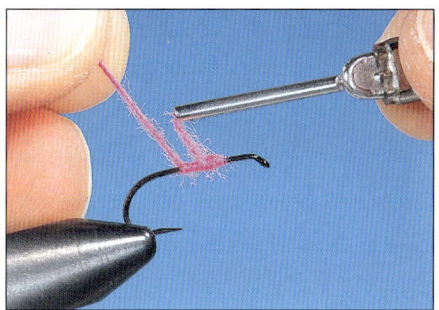 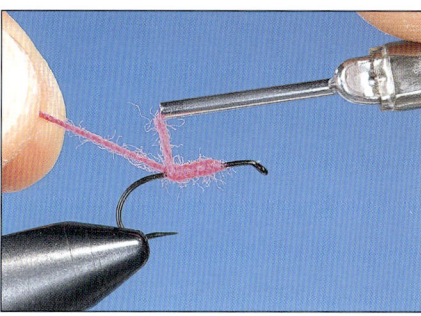

1. Securing the thread is easy. Floss is being used for visibility. Position the thread at a 90-degree angle against the side of the hook. Hold it taut and wrap forward in a clockwise direction, always keeping tension on the thread.

2. Remember to hold the bobbin on the finger pad (not the shaft) and wrap in a small-diameter circle. Reverse direction and wrap back over the preceding turns of thread. If you like, omit wrapping the thread forward and simply wrap it back over the top of itself.

3. About six turns of thread have been wrapped over the short end, which will secure it. Trim off the short end and position the thread where the first material tie in will be.

Thread Heads

The thread head is where the fly is finished off with a knot just behind the hook eye, after which a drop of lacquer is applied. To make an indestructible, smooth, and beautifully finished head, cover it with a *thin* coat of five-minute epoxy and allow it to dry for 24 hours in a warm place.

Heads should be *small* in diameter, neat and *smooth* in appearance, and *slightly tapered.* This is the hallmark of a finely-crafted fly. Beginning tyers tend to crowd the head and not leave enough room to finish off the fly. A crowded head makes a sloppy fly, often precludes threading your leader through the hook eye, and makes it difficult to tie a Turle knot properly. *Leave a small space immediately behind the hook eye completely bare* until you are ready to finish the head. This ensures enough room. Finish the head with about *10 wraps* of thread.

The thread head is the last step in completing a fly. Practice constructing it first so you can see how simple the process is. When the illustrated instructions are followed, a perfect head is assured every time.

Perfect thread heads are easy—anyone can make one. Try it.

If you can make one on a bare hook, you can make one after the fly is complete if you leave enough space. Don't forget!

If your heads look like this, they need refinement.

Tying Dry Flies

Half Hitch

When properly executed, the half hitch is a quick, simple, neat, and effective knot for tying off the thread at the head of the fly. The half hitch is simply a thread loop around the hook. I like to place two half hitches at the rear of the thread head area. (One half hitch will not hold, and three will not cinch up tightly.) Proper placement will ensure a neat head. Before cutting the thread, cinch the two half hitches by pulling the thread counterclockwise around the hook (over the top from the back side). You will feel the two half hitches cinch together. Back off slightly on the tension and cut the thread close to the head so no loose end protrudes from the thread head. Lacquer the entire head.

A half hitch tool is helpful to some tyers, but try to execute the half hitch without one. If you have trouble, use the tool.

The whip finish is very popular with many tyers. If done properly, the half hitch is just as durable and has the advantage of being quicker, easier, and neater. Those who purchase whip finish tools receive explicit directions.

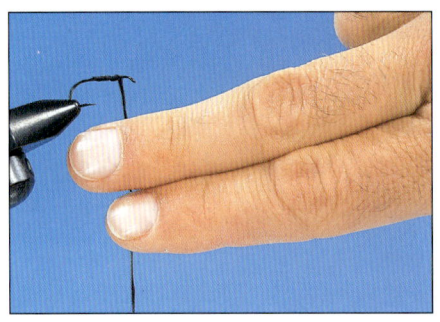

1. Using your right hand, place your first two fingers on the thread. Thread should be across the tip of your first finger. Your palm faces away. Your second finger keeps downward tension on the thread, and your left hand supplies tension on the bobbin as needed.

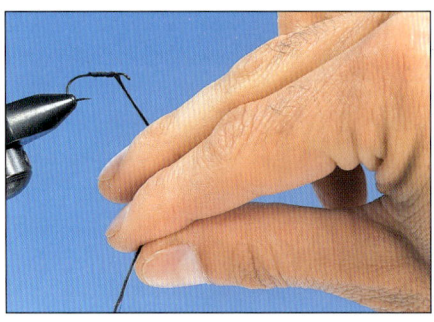

2. Bring your thumb up to your first finger, pinching the thread. Rotate your hand clockwise 180 degrees, forming a loop. The palm of your hand should be facing you. It is important that the thread is positioned on the tip of your first finger.

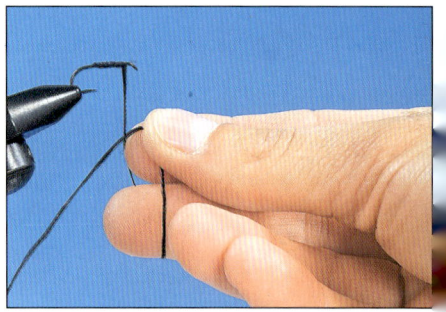

3. The loop is formed and is ready to be placed around the hook.

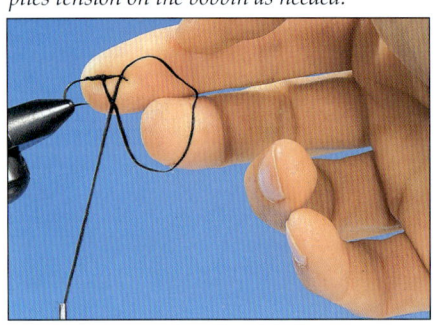

4. Place the loop around the hook, holding it in place on the far side of the hook with your first finger. Note the position of the thread across the tip of the first finger.

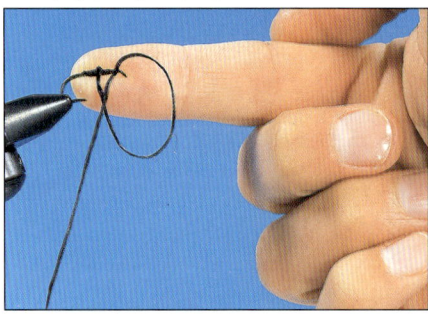

5. Remove your second finger from the loop. Keep your thumb in position as you draw the loop closed, which keeps the thread in front and away from the front of the fly. (See photo 4.) The thumb was removed for visibility in this photo.

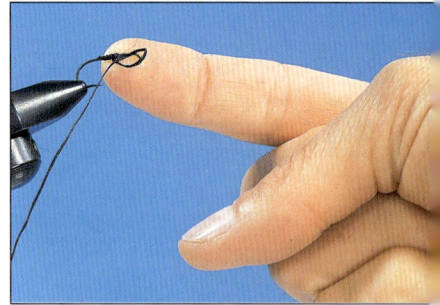

6. Remove thumb when the loop is nearly closed. The first finger stays on the loop until it is completely closed, ensuring proper placement. Place two half hitches, cinch them tightly counter-clockwise, back off slightly on the tension, trim the thread, and lacquer.

Securing Materials With The Up-Between-The-Fingers Technique

The up-between-the-fingers (pinch) technique is the best method to *quickly* accomplish a tie in or tie on at the *exact* position desired. This method prevents you from chasing material around the hook with the thread and eventually catching and tying it at an unintended location in a haphazard manner. Materials should be tied evenly along the hook shank, not *around* it.

Some parts of a fly, such as most tails and wings, are simply *secured in place* and are not wrapped around the hook. Materials that form a body (abdomen) and hackle must be wrapped *around* the hook.

Tie a length of Antron yarn onto the hook to form a tail. Antron would only occasionally be used for a dry fly tail, but it serves to demonstrate the tie-in technique.

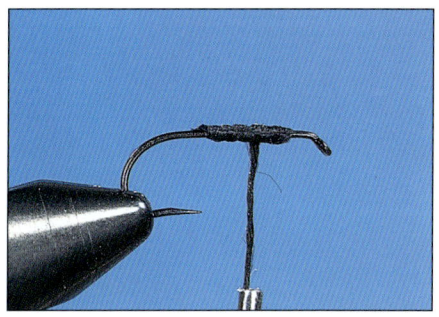

1. Secure the thread onto the hook. The thread is positioned at this position to tie in a tail because it will ensure a level or properly tapered underbody. Floss is used for visibility.

2. Cut a two-inch section of yarn and position it on top of the hook. Attempt to tie the yarn onto the top of the hook.

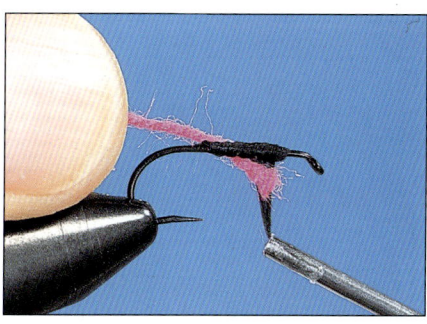

3. The thread pushes or chases the yarn around the hook.

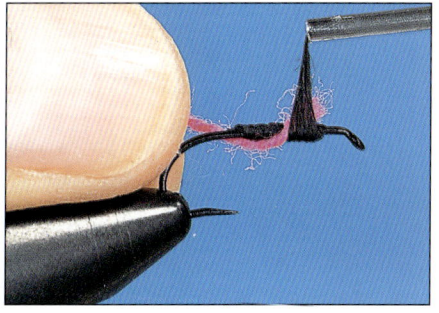

4. It may eventually be caught, but not at the position you want.

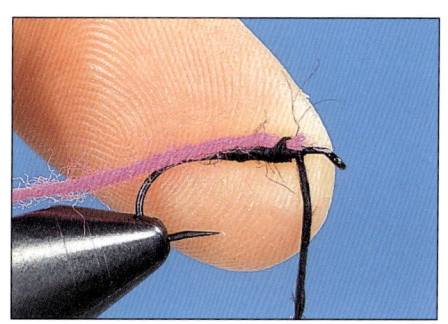

5. Position the yarn end and your first finger on top of the hook shank at the tie-in position (where the thread is). You can either position one finger at a time or simply pinch the yarn and hook with your thumb and first finger.

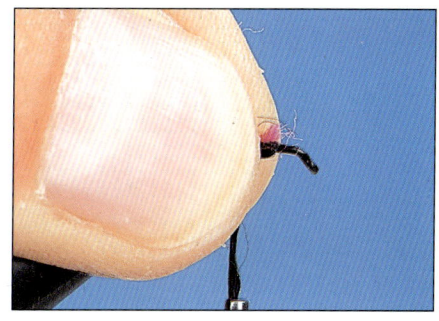

6. Thumb and first finger have pinched the yarn and thread and the hook.

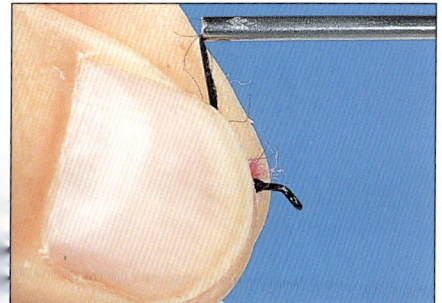

7. Bring the thread up between your fingers. Do not open your fingers to accomplish this. If necessary, bring the thread in front of your fingers and slide it between them.

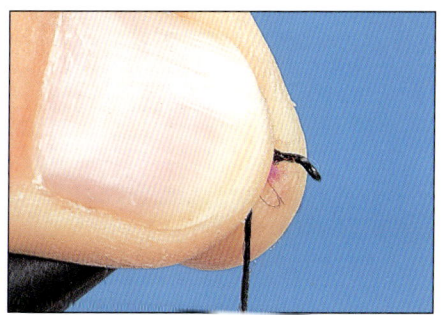

*8. Once in position, bring the thread down over the opposite side of the hook, placing a turn of thread around the yarn. If the yarn is not positioned where you want it, reposition it and **hold** it where you do want it.*

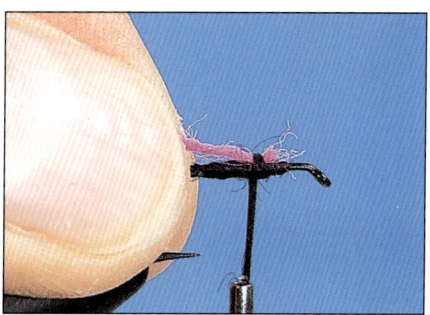

9. Yarn is properly positioned on top of hook with one turn of thread. From this position, we would secure the yarn down along the top of the hook, but, first, let's look at another tie-in technique.

36 Tying Dry Flies

Securing Materials With The Loose-Wrap-And-Cinch Technique

Often it is more expedient to take a loose (tensionless) wrap over the end of a material you want to tie in. Your first finger or thumb keeps the material in position while a loose, or tensionless, wrap of thread is taken over the material. When the loose wrap of thread is in place, it is cinched tight, locking the material in place. It's easy.

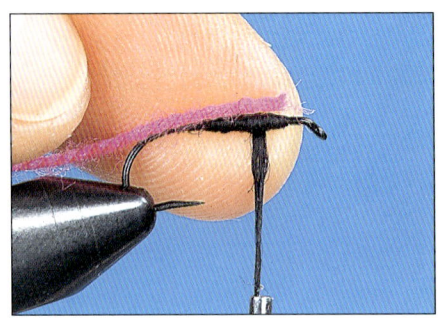

1. Position your first finger and the very end of the material to be tied in as shown.

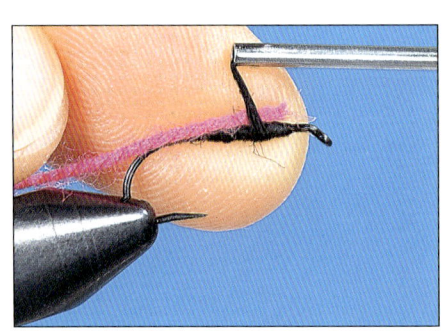

2. Your first finger keeps the material and previous turns of thread in place while a tensionless turn of thread is brought to the top of the hook.

3. As you bring the thread down the opposite side of the hook, slide the thread between your finger and the yarn. Your first finger keeps the yarn in place. Pull the thread tight at the bottom of the 360-degree circle around the hook.

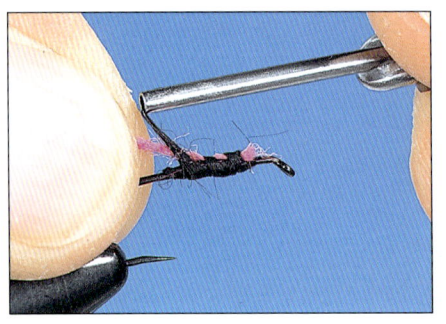

4. Pinch the yarn as shown, and, holding it at an angle above the hook shank, wrap the thread toward the back of the hook. Yarn (or any other material) usually should be secured straight along the top of the shank.

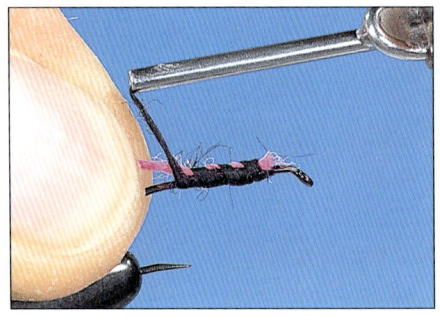

5. By doing this, a level or slightly tapered underbody is formed, ensuring a perfectly tapered finished fly. Secure the material back to just short of where the hook shank begins to curve downward.

6. Tail is secured at the standard position. Note that the thread hangs over the hook barb position (barb has been smashed flat). Other materials would be tied in at this position, such as ribbing or a back. The abdomen, or body, would begin here.

Wrapping Materials With The Over-The-Top-and-Hold-It Technique

Tie in another length of yarn, which will become the abdomen (body). This will be wrapped around the hook with the over-the-top-and-hold-it technique. When materials are to be wrapped around the hook, the thread must be repositioned to the tie-off area after the material is tied in. The tie-off area is usually at the front of the part you are constructing, in this case the body (abdomen). Materials are usually wrapped in a forward direction. The left hand does *all the wrapping*. The right hand only holds the material at the bottom position until the left hand comes back over the top of the hook and begins another wrap around the hook. The right hand also acts as a bobbin rest, keeping the bobbin out of the way when material is being wrapped.

Basic Tying Techniques

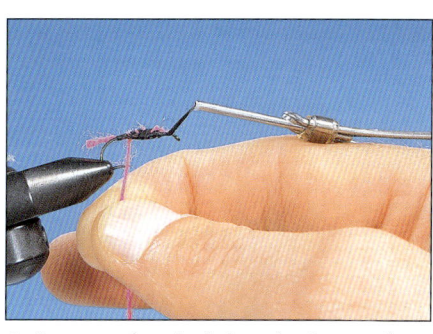

1. Secure a four-inch length of yarn along the top of the hook back to the tail area. Rest the bobbin over the top of your right hand. Using your right hand, grasp the yarn with your thumb and first finger and hold it under the hook. This is the **hold-it** position.

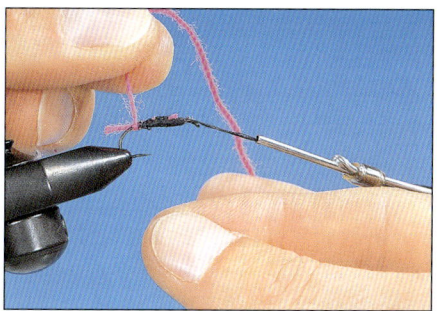

2. Your right hand always stays in this position—under the hook. Your left hand does all the wrapping. Grasp the yarn with your left hand and make a 360-degree turn around the hook. This is the **over-the-top** movement.

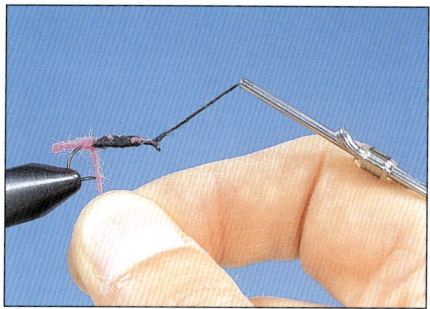

3. After a 360-degree turn has been accomplished, your right hand holds the yarn as shown until you bring your left hand counter-clockwise back over the hook, ready to make another turn. This is the left hand over-the-top, right hand hold-it technique. Materials are almost always best wrapped with this method.

Tying Materials Off

Once the material has been wrapped in place, it must be tied off, or secured onto the hook. Take a couple of turns of thread over the material where you want it to end on the fly, tying it off. All material that is wrapped around the hook will be tied off in this manner.

1. Hold the yarn (or any other material) in your right hand at the underside of the hook.

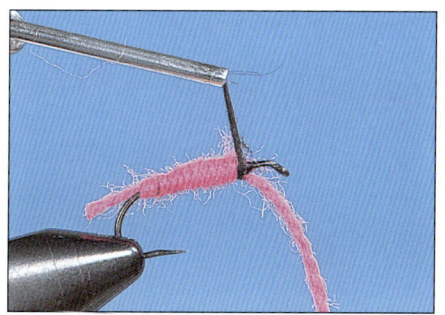

2. With your left hand, take a turn or two of thread around the hook at the tie-off position. The left hand brings the thread (bobbin) over the top and releases it, curving back over the hook to pick it up again.

3. Hold onto the material end while these one or two turns of thread are being placed.

4. Release your right hand from the material. Pick up the bobbin with your right hand and make additional turns as needed to secure material (tie off). Remember to make tight wraps with the thread.

5. Once secure, trim off the excess. To make a clean cut, hold the bobbin (thread) out of the trim area. Gather up **all** material to be cut and hold the ends taut. Place the tip of the scissors against the shank and make one clean cut.

6. If done correctly, there will be no materials or wild fibers protruding.

Dubbing

There are two methods to form a strand of dubbing. Material can be applied directly to a single strand of thread (direct dubbing) or it can be inserted into a loop of thread and twisted tightly (dubbing loop). The dubbing loop method is used mostly to form shaggy or segmented nymph bodies (see my book, *Tying Nymphs*). It is not discussed here.

Smooth dubbing, such as rabbit, muskrat, Antron, and Superfine, is very easy to dub directly and tightly onto a single strand of thread. This is the quickest and easiest method for constructing a dubbed dry fly body. Practice dubbing the least amount of material—simply change the thread texture! The coarser the dubbing material, the more difficult it is to dub tightly. When dubbing a coarse material like goat, do a little at a time and do not concern yourself with the fact that it is not tight. When you wrap it onto the hook, overlapping wraps will secure enough fibers, and any excess can be pulled out.

1. Sparse application of dubbing, which would be about right for size 16 and smaller dry flies.

2. Same application of dubbing, but black thread was used instead of orange. This is a compelling reason to match thread color to the dubbing color.

3. Standard application of dubbing for dry flies. Note taper. Most dry flies should be relatively sparsely dressed and look "delicate."

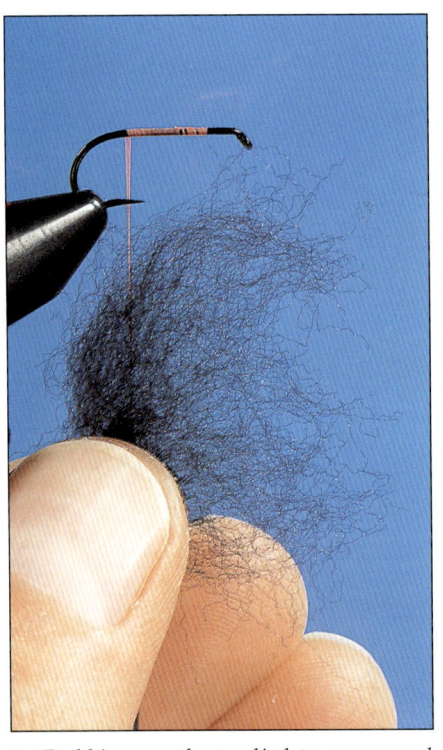

1. Dubbing can be applied to pre-waxed thread without additional wax, but a little additional wax makes dubbing easier for beginners and when dubbing coarse materials. Hold what you think you need between your thumb and first finger. Ten percent of this is plenty!

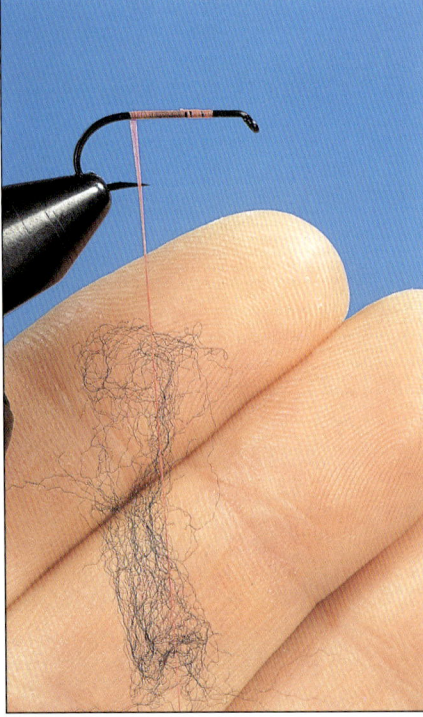

2. For most dry flies, dubbing should only be considered coloring and sparkle, not bulk. The thread is usually bulky enough! Orange thread is used for demonstration contrast. Always match thread to dubbing! Apply dubbing to no more than two or three inches of thread. Wrap into place and dub more as needed!

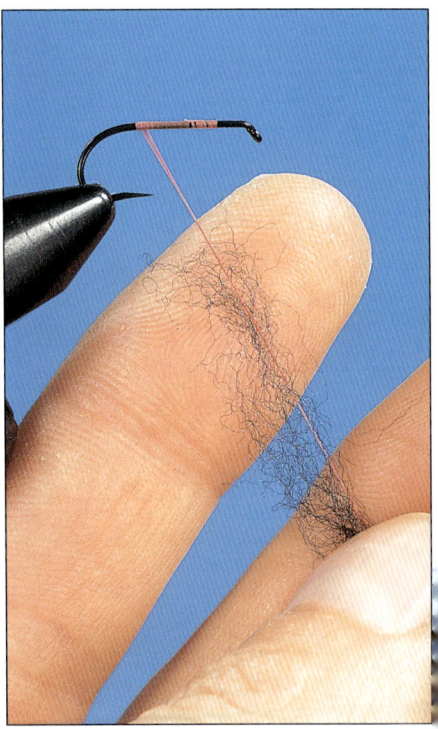

3. Spread dubbing fibers evenly and sparsely along the thread. Spread your fingers as seen in the photo. Start the dubbing three-fourths of an inch below the hook point, and dub the top-most fibers into place. Dubbing is best applied to the thread by starting at the top-most fiber position and working down the strand of thread.

Basic Tying Techniques 39

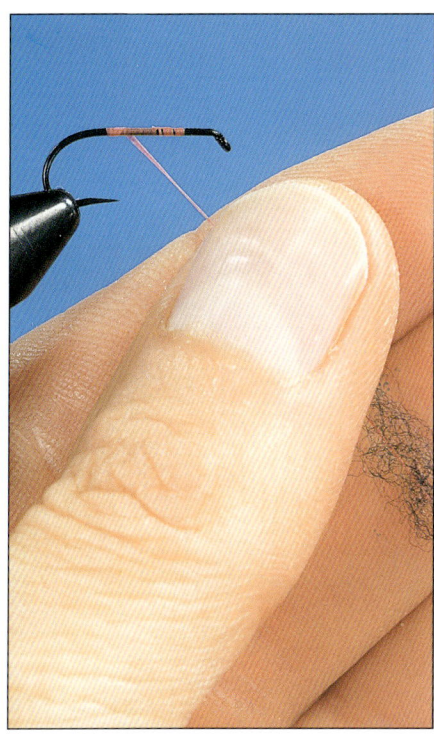

4. This allows the dubbing material to be applied tightly because the excess materials and space are squeezed out below your fingers as you work down the strand of thread. Press your thumb tightly against your fingers and roll your thumb over your fingertips tightly, rolling the thread in the process. Keep tension on the thread with your other hand.

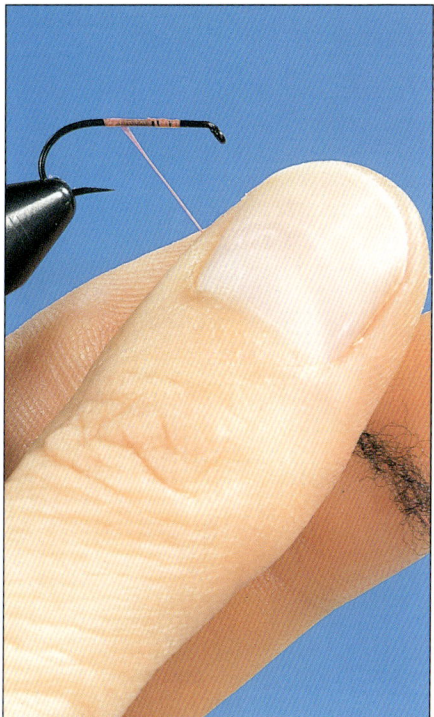

5. One roll (two or three at most) secures the material to the thread. The actual "roll" usually begins with the thread between your thumb and the first and second joints of your first and second fingers. It ends with your thumb at the tips of your fingers.

6. Top half of the dubbing is properly installed. Notice that there are no undubbed or wild fibers extending from the top-most area of dubbing.

7. This shows an improper strand of dubbing. The top-most undubbed fibers should have been rolled onto the thread. It has been started too close to the hook shank. Dubbing is too heavy and uneven, and it spirals around the thread. If your dubbing looks like this, try again.

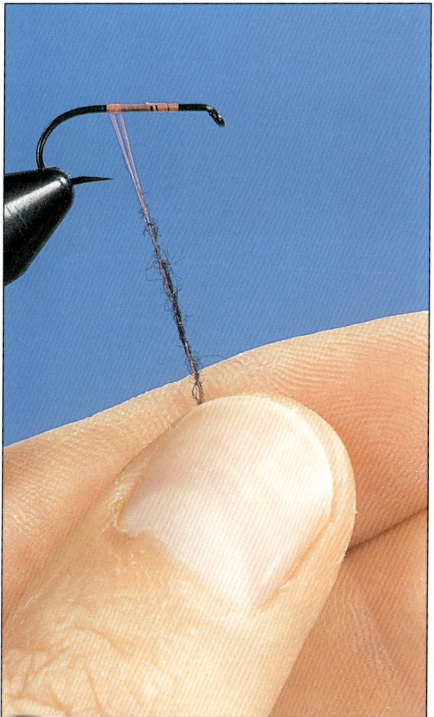

8. Continue working down the thread until all the dubbing is rolled in place. Always roll your fingers in one direction. Do not roll them back and forth.

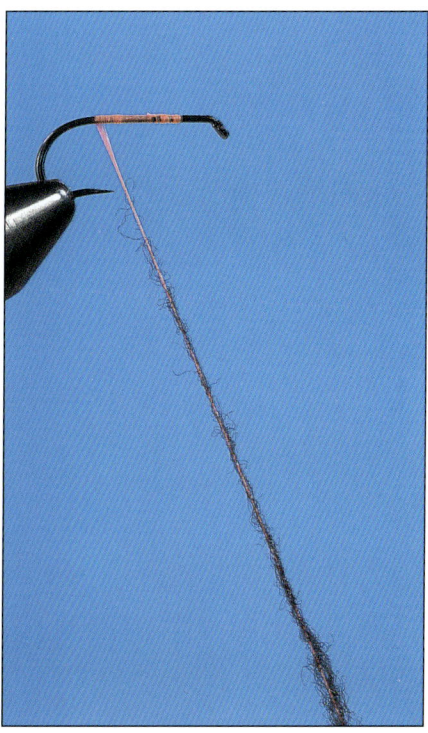

9. Perfect application of dubbing. Note built-in taper in dubbing. Top-most fibers are rolled onto thread and begin about at the hook point. **All** other fibers are rolled tightly onto thread in a smooth, even manner. Wrap dubbing around hook—begin at back and work forward, creating a slight taper. That's it!

Searching for sea-run browns on the Rio Grande in Patagonia, Argentina, February, 2000.

Trout inhabit some of the world's most beautiful landscapes. Those who seek their haunts are rewarded with much more than the tug on their fly line. Mary Erickson, High Sierra, California, June, 2000.

Part II

Tying Instructions

Lake bred brown near Turangi, New Zealand.

Part II illustrates in explicit detail the many and varied techniques required to construct dry flies. The 26 demonstration patterns have been selected for their tying techniques, fishing versatility, and angler interest. They encompass most major food sources of trout, including mayflies, caddisflies, midges, stoneflies, damselflies, beetles, ants, and hoppers. Both tying history and associated angling techniques are discussed.

Patterns and tying techniques follow a logical sequence; you should progress from start to finish without deviation. The photos and illustrations are exact. If you pay careful attention, your tying skills and enjoyment level will increase dramatically. Once you have studied and tied all the flies in Part II, you should be able to "read" virtually any dry fly pattern dressing and to visualize the finished fly or to tell at a glance how a particular dry fly is constructed.

Chapter 8

Foam Beetle

Riverborn Flies

Foam Beetle
- Hook: 900BL, sizes 6-18
- Thread: Black
- Overbody: Black closed-cell foam
- Abdomen: Black thread, peacock, or any color dubbing to suit
- Legs: Black CDC, deer, Krystal Flash, or rubber, extending at right angles to body, trimmed to desired length
- Indicator: Glo-Bug yarn, color to suit

Beetles come in all shapes, sizes, and colors.

During a visit to Idaho's Silver Creek, my guide opened a small cardboard box containing several size 8 black hair beetles. Smiling, he carefully selected two and said, "These are like candy." I tucked them into my vest and chuckled to myself, "Yeah. Right. These ultra selective, spooky fish are going to eat these oversize monstrosities? Ha!"

By mid-afternoon I was frustrated enough to give one a try. I switched to a 4X tippet and cast the bulky beast onto the opposite grass bank. I pulled it off the bank with an audible splat just upstream from a pair of nice rainbow that had ridiculed my earlier match-the-hatch efforts. The beetle boldly advertised its presence with a considerable dent in the surface film, sending out widening water shock waves from its landing. I helped the advertising campaign with a healthy twitch just before it entered the fishes' window. Both rainbow immediately became alert and seemed to be squabbling over who would retrieve the prize. Naturally, the smaller fish won, and I dropped my rod tip in near disbelief.

The remainder of the afternoon gave me a different perspective about western spring creek fishing, beetle imitations, and what is known as hatch breaking. Only a few flies have the power to break the feeding concentration of selective fish, and the beetle is one of them.

Water beetles of the order Coleoptera comprise the largest group of insects in the world. There are over 30,000 species in North America alone! Both fish and fishermen have long capitalized on this bonanza. English writer Alfred Ronalds, in *The Fly-Fisher's Entomology* published in 1836, describes beetle imitations. However, it was Vincent Marinaro's 1950 publication of *A Modern Dry Fly Code* that brought beetles to the attention of American anglers. Gerald Almy wrote *Tying And Fishing Terrestrials* in 1978; to my knowledge, it contains the best tying, fishing, historical, and natural history information about beetles in print.

Anglers visiting New Zealand and Tasmania quickly learn the value of beetle imitations. The Manuka is the best-known beetle in New Zealand. It is often available to trout by the tens of thousands, and fish gorge on them non-stop, *almost* until they float belly-up.

Tasmania has more species of beetles than anyone has been able to classify. I was fishing the remote Highland Lakes area when a trio of huge beetle bombers zoomed past my head at hyper speed and crash-dived onto the water, creating a commotion. Before they could regain their composure and get airborne, only one was left. The other two became victims of *Salmo trutta*. This looked like good action to me, but, unfortunately, I didn't have the required ammunition. I will next time!

Anglers visiting down under will want to have a broad selection of beetles sizes 6 to 16 plus some magnum beetles, just in case.

Fish readily accept beetles because they are often available in huge numbers and offer fish a sure target. Beetles are also high in caloric value, and capturing just one big beetle could be equal to a hundred or more caddisflies.

Beetles float flat and low in the surface film, and tyers should concentrate on size, shape, and color. Most common colors include black, iridescent green, yellow, chartreuse, red, and brown. Legs can be important if the beetle is making a commotion in an attempt to swim or to take flight, and they also help balance and stabilize the fly. Anglers interested in exact imitation should note that beetles have six legs.

The best beetle months are June through September, but early spring also can be very good, especially in the eastern and southern states. Lake anglers should look for beetles along brushy shorelines, foam lines, at the base of cliffs, and along windward shores. Stream anglers can happen upon beetles anytime. Even if not noticeably present, they're often worth a cast.

The beetle pattern that follows is a good warmup and demonstrates a dubbed body, hair legs, and the construction of an overbody, or "back." Traditionally, beetle backs have been tied with deer hair, but closed-cell foam is more durable, easier to work with and floats better. Tyers who wish to substitute deer hair should twist the hair before pulling it over the back, which makes it easier to handle and tie down. A peg of fluorescent green, orange, or red yarn may be added on top of the head area for better visibility. Tyers looking for an action-packed beetle can tie the legs with round rubber.

Umpqua Feather Merchants

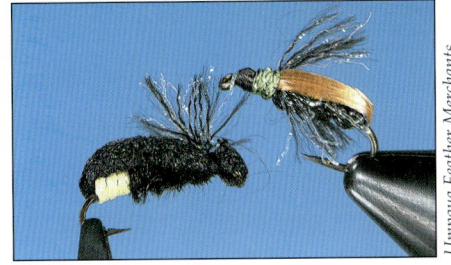

Firefly and Jumping Beetle, both by Harrison R. Steeves, II.

Umpqua Feather Merchants

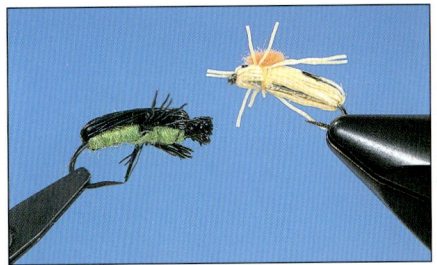

Fluorescent Green Deer Hair and Whitlock Japanese beetles.

Umpqua Feather Merchants

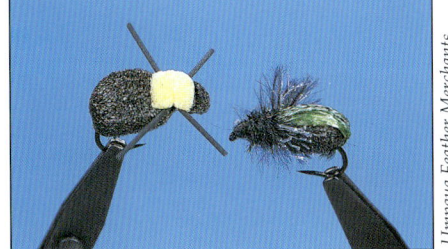

Foam beetle and Kiwi Fleetle.

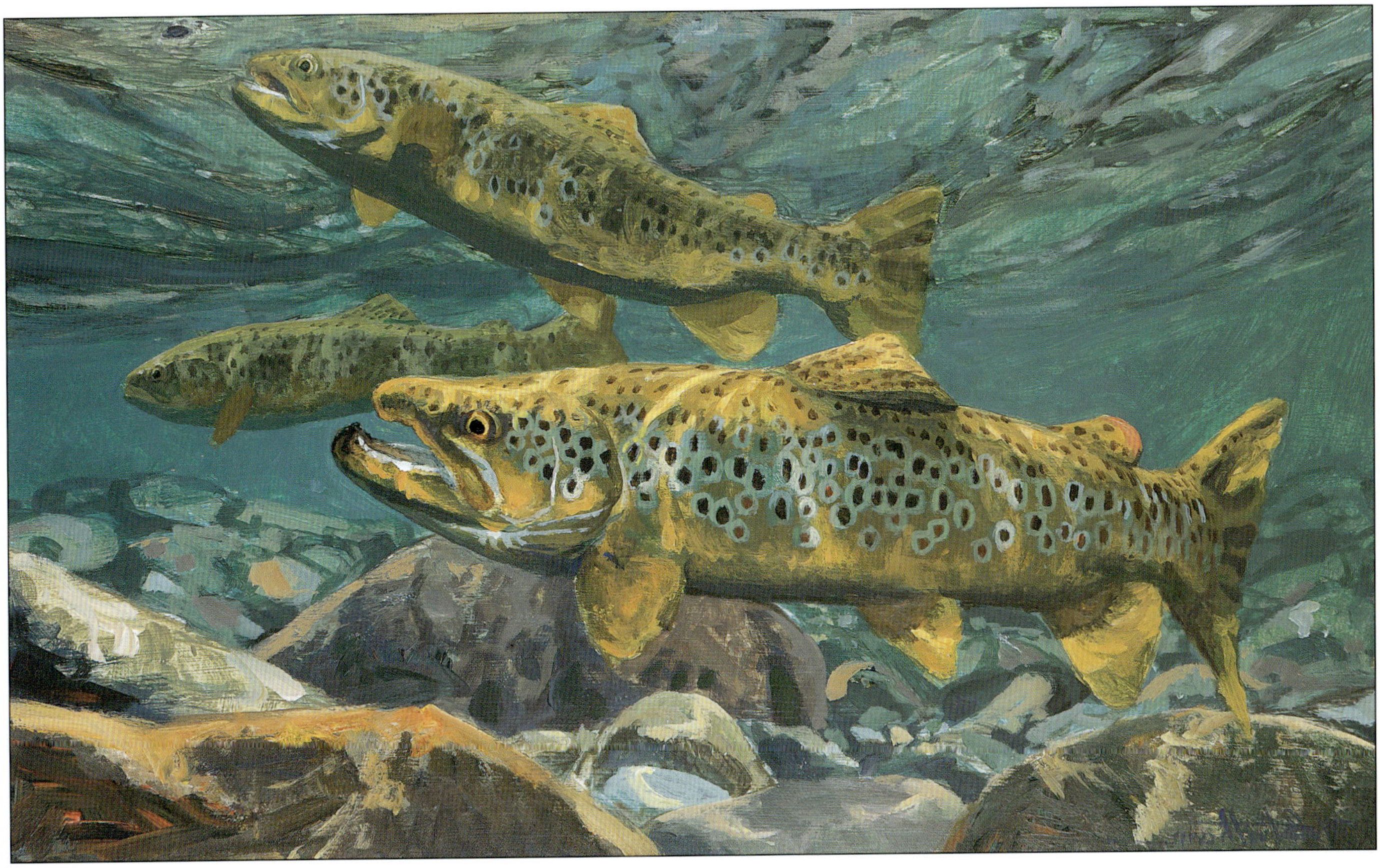

Brown trout sipping beetles.

44 Tying Dry Flies

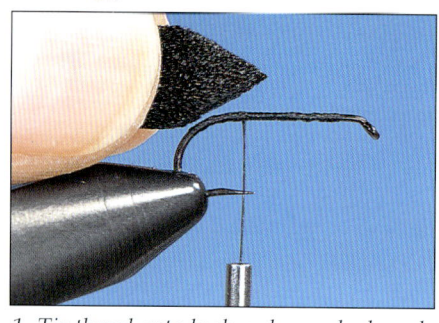

1. Tie thread onto hook and wrap backwards to standard tail tie-in position, shown here. Cut a strip of closed-cell foam about as wide as hook gape. Trim end to a point. This makes it easier to secure foam and lessens bulk.

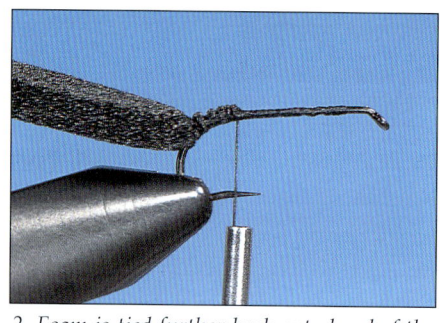

2. Foam is tied further back onto bend of the hook than usual, which forms a more pronounced curve or beetle appearance of the overbody. Using the up-between-the-fingers technique, tie foam flat on top of hook.

3. Apply dubbing to the thread and form the body to the 65-percent mark.

4. Trim a small bunch of deer hair about 1-1/4 inch long. Pull out the short fibers.

5. Hold the fibers against the top of the hook. Using the up-between-the-fingers technique, secure them onto the top of the hook.

6. The fibers flare.

7. Pull all fibers back between your fingers and wrap thread tightly against base of fibers. This keeps them from getting in the way when forming body and positions them to be arranged at a right angle to the hook.

8. Apply more dubbing and finish the body to the 90-percent mark.

9. Pull the foam over the top of the body with your right hand, forming the overbody. It should be wider than the width of the body. Hold the foam in place with your right hand and secure it.

10. Tie in a short section of Glo-Bug yarn at overbody tie-down. Trim overbody even with hook eye. Trim excess legs. Legs should number three to six and extend at right angles. Trim Glo-Bug yarn flush with overbody.

11. Finished Foam Beetle.

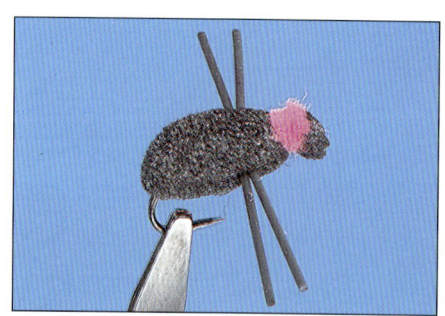

12. Rubber can be threaded through a needle and the needle pulled through the foam as shown, or tie in an X along the side of the body. Any color strike indicator can be incorporated.

Chapter 9

Proportions

A concise understanding of dry fly proportions is a key factor in successfully tying dry flies. Like the pieces in a finished jig saw puzzle, all pieces or parts of the fly combine to project the desired visuals to fish and to react properly on or in the water. A tail that is too short may cause the fly to sink. A crooked tail may cause the fly to ride on its side. If a wing is too tall or heavy it may cause the fly to fall forward on the water. Wings and hackle that are not properly proportioned may distort the visuals or completely change the fly's character. Perfection is the name of the game.

The proportions presented here are explicit guidelines for standard upwing mayfly construction, but tyers may occasionally wish to modify them for specific reasons. Proportions for downwing imitations (caddisflies, stoneflies, damselflies, midge, and terrestrials) vary greatly and it is not practical to provide explicit guidelines for each. Proportions for these imitations are discussed throughout the Tying Instruction and Pattern Directory sections. The flies pictured in color are tied to exacting specifications and are also an excellent guide for proportions.

Proportions for upwing dry flies are determined by the width of the hook gape, which is the distance between the hook shank and the hook point. Besides the *distance* that all materials extend from the hook, the *location* that materials are positioned onto the hook is equally important.

Throughout this text, specific locations along the hook shank will be referred to as a percentage of the overall length of the hook. The illustration explains how these numbers relate to the hook shank.

Wings: Standard upright wings should extend out from the hook 1-1/2 to 2 times the width of the hook gape. Wings are usually mounted between the 70 and 85 percent mark.

Hackle: Standard-style hackle should extend out from the hook 1-1/2 times the width of the gape. It can occupy as little as 20 or as much as 50 percent of the hook shank.

Tail: A standard tail should extend beyond the hook 2 to 2-1/2 times the width of the gape. Tail length is also commonly judged in relation to the hook shank. A standard dry fly hook shank is about twice as long as the gape is wide. Measuring the tail against the shank before securing it in place is a good guide. The hook shank begins at the eye and extends to where it *begins* to drop off toward the bend of the hook, where the tail is secured.

Body: A standard dry fly body begins at the tail. Its overall length is determined by fly design and how much space the hackle will occupy. The body commonly occupies 50 to 80 percent of the hook shank.

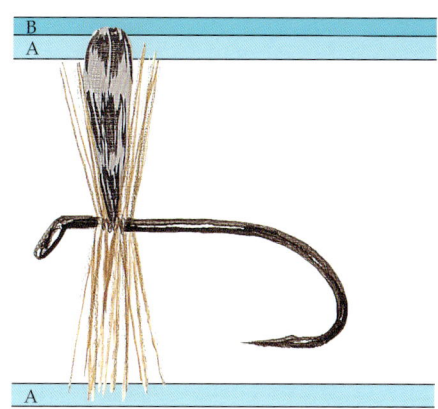

Hackle should extend to area A. Wing should extend to area B.

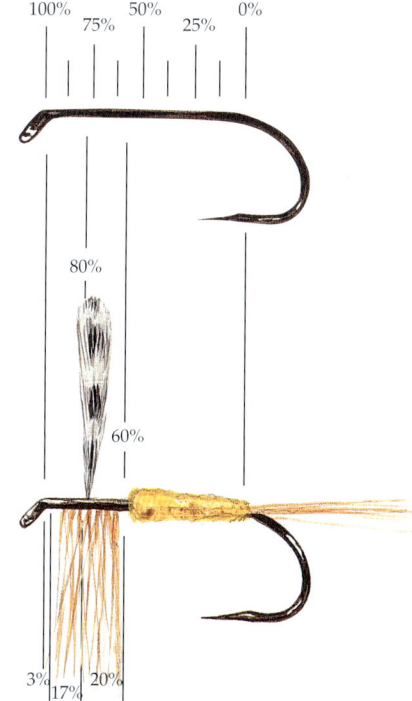

Chapter 10

Sparkle Dun, Comparadun, and CDC Comparadun

Craig Mathews

Sparkle Dun, PMD (Craig Mathews and John Juracek)
- Hook: 900BL, 16-20
- Thread: Yellow
- Wing: Hollow dyed gray deer, single upright and flared
- Tail: Olive brown Z-Lon
- Body: PMD Superfine

Craig Mathews

Sparkle Dun, Small Green Drake (Craig Mathews and John Juracek, 1980)
- Hook: 900BL, Sizes 14-16
- Thread: Olive
- Wing: Dyed gray hollow deer hair, single, upright and flared
- Tail: Olive-brown Z-Lon
- Body: Dark olive Superfine
- Note: Represents the mini Green Drakes, *Drunella flavilinea* and *Drunella coloradenis*, which hatch June through August.

Comparadun (Al Caucci and Bob Nastasi)
- Hook: 900BL, 10-20
- Thread: Color to match body
- Wing: Hollow mottled brown deer or color to suit, single upright and flared
- Tail: Blue dun hackle fibers split wide
- Body: Antron or Superfine, color to suit

In a few short years, Sparkle Duns have become standard equipment in the fly boxes of western anglers. Craig Mathews and John Juracek, who own and operate Blue Ribbon Flies in West Yellowstone, Montana, developed this pattern in 1985. In their book, *Fly Patterns of Yellowstone*, they explain that, while they were at the crossover fence to the Harriman Ranch on the Henry's Fork, they noted a great many stillborn Pale Morning Duns drifting on the slick current. Most were attached to their nymphal shuck, which sparkled and shimmered in the light. They thought this sparkling-shimmering feature was an important trigger that attracted trout. They duplicated the sparkling shuck with a piece of Z-Lon, which seems to be the key to the fly's effectiveness.

The Comparadun was first tied by Al Caucci in the mid 1960s. Al adapted the basic concept from an old-time pattern called the Haystack. Al Caucci and Bob Nastasi introduced the Comparadun in their first book, *Comparahatch*, published in 1972. Over the years, the fly has been redesigned and modified into a highly effective and imitative mayfly dun pattern. Tyers and anglers interested in learning more about Comparaduns should read *Hatches II*, in which Al and Bob detail North American mayfly hatches and where, when, and how to fish them.

Shane Stalcup, an innovative professional tyer from Denver, Colorado, has designed and promoted a very effective and beautiful CDC Comparadun. Shane incorporates CDC into the wing, and the result is a delicate, lifelike imitation of an adult mayfly. Shane adds a "face" of natural mallard to break up the color scheme and to add visual realism. CDC is further explained in the Hatching Midge chapter, page 62.

The Sparkle Dun, Comparadun, and CDC Comparadun are all similar in design and are the simplest dry flies. All are *very* effective and lend themselves to various water types and angling situations. They have only three parts: a tail, body, and wing. Fish accept these flies for adult, hatching, or stillborn mayfly duns and, perhaps, spent spinners. They are easy, fast, inexpensive, and fun to construct. They are also versatile and durable.

This is our first real winged dry fly pattern, and it has a single upright, flared hairwing. The wings portray a bold silhouette, and the fibers that touch the water on either side act as balancing outriggers. The wing is durable, and the effect is one of realism. The hairwing is spread out in the shape of a fan, 180 degrees across the top of the fly. The lack of hackle allows the fly to sit on and in the surface film. This wing introduces you to the stacker, which is a very useful and functional tool for evening the length of hair fibers. Practice stacking various hairs and refer to the following photo sequence when you tie the Green Drake Paradrake and Humpy.

Deer hair that is hollow well up into the tips is required for tying the Sparkle and Comparadun patterns. Hollow hair flares nicely, and tying thread sinks into it, allowing for a neater tie-down and a more realistic silhouette. To judge whether deer hair is hollow, press your thumbnail into it or tie a small amount onto the hook. If it flares easily, it is hollow. Try this with several types and textures of deer hair. The differences are amazing.

These patterns demonstrate a split tail (Comparadun) and trailing shuck (Sparkle Dun). Tyers can experiment by adding Z-Lon and CDC to wings and, perhaps, incorporate CDC into tails.

CDC Mahogany Comparadun (Shane Stalcup, 1992)
- Hook: 900BL, sizes 16-20
- Thread: Brown
- Wing: Natural dun CDC and natural mallard or teal flank
- Tail: Dun Bett's Tailing Fibers
- Abdomen: Mahogany turkey biot
- Thorax: Mahogany Superfine

CDC Callibaetis Comparadun (Shane Stalcup)
- Hook: 900BL, sizes 12-16
- Thread: Tan
- Wing: Natural dun CDC and natural mallard or teal flank
- Tail: Dun Bett's Tailing Fibers
- Abdomen: Tan turkey biot
- Thorax: Tan Superfine

CDC PMD Comparadun (Shane Stalcup)
- Hook: 900BL, sizes 16-20
- Thread: Yellow
- Wing: Natural dun CDC and natural mallard or teal flank
- Tail: Dun Bett's Tailing Fibers
- Abdomen: Yellow turkey biot
- Thorax: PMD Superfine

Yellowstone Cutthroat are noted for their surface feeding antics, but they can be, and often are, selective.

48 Tying Dry Flies

1. Dry fly tails and wings need to have even ends, or tips. When hair is trimmed from the hide, it is uneven with fuzzy underfur. Even the hair with a stacker. Pictured is a clump of deer hair. Notice the uneven tips.

2. Hold *tips* in your right hand and pull out all the underfur and short fibers. Repeat separation process until all unwanted fibers are cleaned out. This can also be done with a fine-toothed comb.

3. All short fibers have been removed, and the original clump has been reduced by 70 percent.

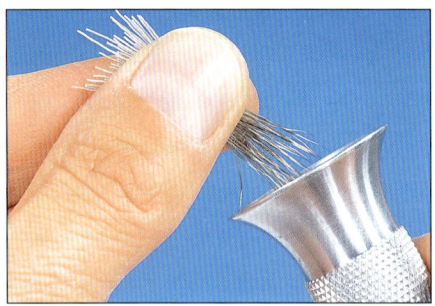

4. Place tips pointing down into stacker. Be certain there is enough space inside stacker for hair to spread apart and fall freely. Use a small-diameter stacker for small bunches of hair and a large-diameter stacker for large bunches.

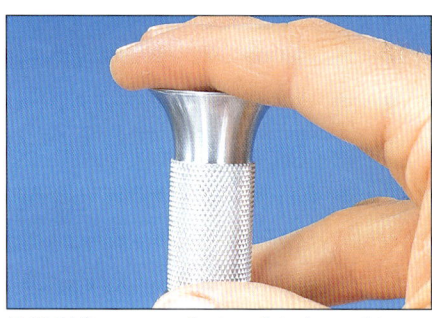

5. Hold fingers over the top of stacker and tap on a hard surface. Straight, large-diameter hair will stack quickly. Kinky, fine-diameter hair requires more pounding. Deer should stack with 10 to 15 strong taps, depending on texture and amount.

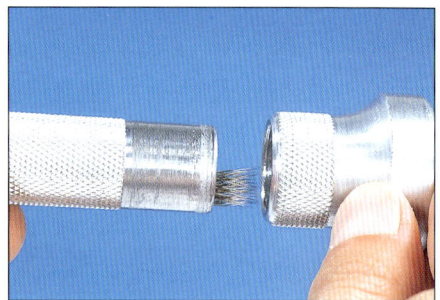

6. Hold stacker in a near-horizontal position and **slowly** remove bottom end. The tips should be even and protruding from the larger section of the stacker.

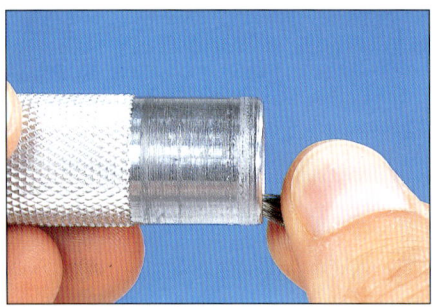

7. Grasp tips with your right hand and remove from stacker. Remove any maverick fibers from the evened tips.

8. If you are tying an overbody or extended-style body where a long length of hair is needed (Green Drake Paradrake, Humpy, Henry's Fork Hopper), the remaining short hairs must be removed. The butts are very uneven.

9. Grasp trimmed butt ends with your left hand beyond the short butt fibers. Notice that the natural tips are nicely stacked. Pull the short fibers out of the clump.

10. The clump would not normally be held in this position, but you can see that all the short fibers have been removed and all are nearly the same length. This is the proper hair preparation for overbodies and extended bodies.

11. Measure length (height) of wing against length of hook shank. The hair protruding in front of tie-in area should be equal to length of hook shank. Measure it. Using the up-between-the-fingers technique, secure in place.

12. After two to three turns of thread are in place, back your fingers off slightly, still holding the wing tie-in area in position. Wrap the thread backward to position shown.

Sparkle Dun, Comparadun, and CDC Comparadun

13. Grasp all butt ends as shown and trim at an angle, making certain there are no loose ends protruding.

14. Notice that the wing fibers are all the same length and that they are the same length as the hook shank. Wrap down hair butts with thread, forming a smooth, tapered underbody. If your wing does not look like this, try again.

15. Secure Z-Lon where thread was positioned in previous photo. Hold Z-Lon up above hook as shown and wrap thread back to end of body area, keeping Z-Lon on top of the hook.

16. Trim butt end of Z-Lon at an angle so it fits neatly against angle cut of the wing. It is best to hold butt ends with your fingers when you make the cut.

17. Wrap thread over ends and position thread at tail area. Underbody should be nicely tapered and free of wild fibers or uneven areas, making it easy to tie a perfectly-tapered body using a very thin strand of dubbing.

18. Dub body and wrap in a forward direction. Notice taper of the body and how thinly the dubbing is applied.

19. Dubbing should stop one turn short of wing. If wing is crowded with dubbing, it will not lie back at the desired angle. If there are a few dubbing fibers left on thread, remove them before proceeding.

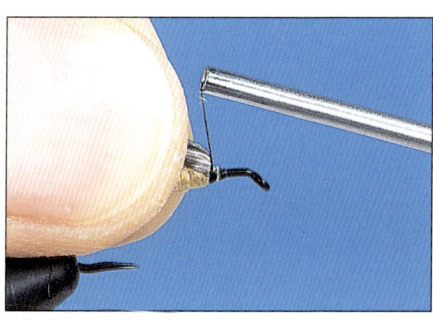

20. Using the three-finger triangle, sweep fibers back from hook eye, encompassing wing. Make certain you have every fiber under control. Wrap thread against wing, which will help it stand up.

21. Wing should be positioned as shown, angled slightly backwards. Place thread wraps immediately in front of wing without crowding head area. Thread has been slightly tapered to allow for easy placement of dubbing.

22. Dub on a little Antron, form a head, and then tie off a small thread head. Notice that dubbing has been placed up against front of wing, helping to angle it backwards and keep it in place.

23. Using your fingers, spread wing fibers down along sides of body so they form a 180-degree fan shape. The wing should not angle forward but should stand straight up or angle slightly backward. Flare the tail with your fingers.

24. A front view showing 180 degree half-circle wing and fan tail. It is important that fibers protrude straight from body, because these balance the fly and create the desired light pattern or surface impression.

50   *Tying Dry Flies*

Plymouth Rock (grizzly color) rooster. Saddle hackles hang along side of bird.

Rooster (bottom) and hen necks. Roosters have stiffer and longer feathers.

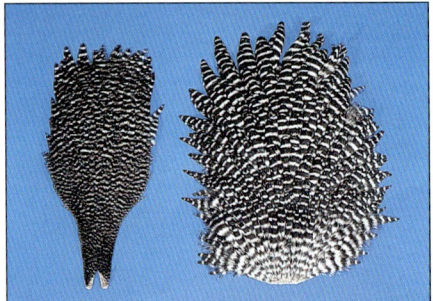

Hen neck (left) and hen saddle. Hen neck is excellent for hackle tip wings.

Rooster neck (bottom) and saddle. Saddle hackle is two to 10 times longer.

Quality necks have an abundance of all hackle sizes. This is a Metz.

Chapter 11

Hackle

Technically, hackle is any soft-stemmed feather with non-adhering barbules (fibers) other than those supporting direct flight functions. For our purposes the term *hackle* denotes domestic rooster (male) or hen (female) chicken feathers, either those from the neck (neck hackle) or those from the back (saddle hackle).

Hackle from a rooster's neck is commonly referred to as *hackle*, or neck hackle, gamecock neck, and rooster neck. Hackle from the back is referred to as saddle or saddle hackle. Prime (Grade 1) rooster hackle is long, narrow, resilient, and stiff and is used for hackling standard-style dry flies. It is also used for nymphs, but softer hackle (Grades 2 and 3) is preferred. Individual hackle fibers are used for tails and legs.

Hen hackle is short, wide, and soft. Because of its soft, water retentive properties, it is unsuitable for hackling dry flies. It is used for wings, legs, and tails. It is **specifically** referred to as *hen* hackle, either neck or saddle.

Hackling is the art of tying, or winding, hackle around a hook in the construction of a fly. *Hackle* is intended to represent legs, tails, wings, and gills. Hackle also plays an important role in creating animation, silhouette, and special effects.

Selecting, preparing, and winding hackle can cause tyers fits, but, once a proper hackle has been selected and prepared, the actual tying is fairly straightforward. If you can construct a body, you can wind a hackle. Most problems occur because of improper winding and tie-off technique and *not leaving enough space* to accommodate hackle. If you pay close attention to the following text, illustrations, and photo tying sequence, you should wrap a nearly perfect hackle on the first try.

What To Look For In Selecting Hackle

Look for skins that are fully hackled and have a complete range of hackle sizes. All necks have large, or wide, feathers, but not all have narrow feathers size 14 and smaller. If you desire to tie size 18 flies, be certain the neck has size 18 hackles. Saddle skins do not have the wide range of sizes that necks do, so be certain you buy what you need. Neck hackle should *always* be purchased on the skin. The same is true for saddle hackle, except for specific imported saddle hackle that should be strung. There are several genetic hackle producers that offer good quality. Of these, Metz and Whiting are the largest producers and easiest to obtain.

Necks And Saddles

Saddle hackle is preferred to neck hackle for tying dry flies and should be used whenever possible. Saddle hackle is longer, easier to work with, and has a narrower stem, which allows it to be wound or packed densely. This creates far superior floating qualities. Saddle hackle is not as narrow as neck hackle and can only be used on medium and large flies. Metz saddle hackle is readily available down to size 10. Whiting saddles are the narrowest available and can be found in size 16, but sizes 10 and 12 are more common. A size 12 or 14 fly is usually the dividing size between neck or saddle hackle. If you have saddle hackle, use it. If you do not, use neck hackle. The most popular dry flies are size 14 and 16, followed by 12 and 18, so there is no way to avoid purchasing both saddles and necks.

Good hackle is expensive, but it is not possible to tie a top quality conventional dry fly without quality dry fly hackle. Good hackle means more pleasure at the tying bench and flies that fish like dry flies should. The best advice I can offer is *buy the best regardless of price.*

Personally, I have a selection of both Metz and Whiting necks and saddles in a dozen colors each. I have collected them over the years, and I suggest you do the same. When I sit down at the tying bench I can tie almost any imitation I desire, which certainly increases my pleasure and angling success. It may be necessary to put your name on a waiting list for uncommon, hard-to-find colors. Grizzly dyed shades of olive, brown, and blue dun create a wonderful effect and are highly prized and in short supply. Strung Indian saddles usually run size 6 to 12 with lots of junk, but once sorted can yield some nice feathers and can be a temporary inexpensive solution for some colors.

Hackle Stiffness

Hackle fibers must be stiff. To check for fiber resilience, hold the skin in one hand, grasp the feather tip with the other hand, and bend the feather. Look at the fibers where they meet the stem. Stiff fibers separate from each other. If they cling together, you are looking at soft or webby fibers, which are weak and retain water. Notice the shadow area of the web becomes progressively wider toward the base of the feather.

All hackles have a tapered area of web that gradually disappears toward the hackle tip. A little web in the first couple of turns of hackle is acceptable, but the longer the web-free portion, the better. Hackle that contains less than 20 percent web is considered good. Premium dry fly hackle does not have any web in that portion of the feather you intend to use.

Fiber stiffness can also be checked by pressing against the fibers with your finger tips. If they feel stiff and bounce back immediately, they are stiff. Traditionally, anglers have pressed hackle against their lips. Individual fibers should also be relatively large in diameter. Fine diameter fibers are too weak; while they may be free of web, they are not strong enough to support a fly. Eventually you will be able to tell at a glance whether a hackle skin is worth buying or not.

Hackle Stems

Hackle should have a thin, soft, and pliable center stem (quill). Hackle with a thick stem is difficult to maneuver, takes up too much space, is often brittle, and is impossible to pack tightly. Stems graduate in thickness, becoming thicker toward the base of the feather. This thick section is trimmed off and the top section used for hackling. If the entire stem is unusually thick, flat, or brittle, do not use it. Check for flat stems by flexing the feather, tip to butt. If the fibers stand straight out from the

Left to right, the good, bad, and the ugly: Metz, Indian (dyed), and Chinese rooster necks.

India saddle hackle strung on string for ease of use.

Soft and wide hackle vs. stiff and narrow dry fly hackle.

Same feathers as above. Note how dry fly feather fibers separate and stand alone.

Note the diameter of the stem on the top feather. It is unusable for a dry fly

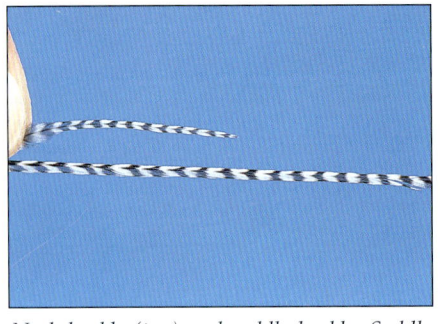
Neck hackle (top) and saddle hackle. Saddle hackles offer length and ease in tying.

Hackle width is the distance fibers extend from the center stem.

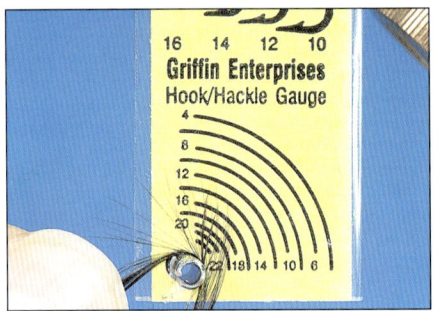
A hackle gauge is a consistent means by which to judge hackle width.

Hackle on left is properly sized to hook, extending 1-1/2 times gape. Other is too wide.

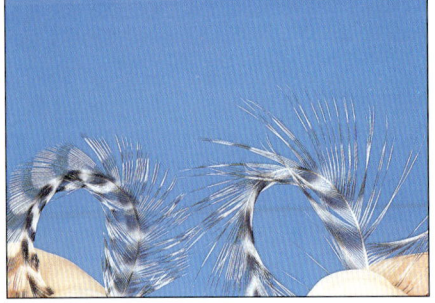
Note difference in fiber density between feathers. Which would make the best dry fly?

stem they are all right. If they flop to one side, avoid them. Old barnyard birds almost always have a thick stem. The older the bird, the thicker the stem. Hackle stems double or triple in thickness throughout their length, so tyers need to pay close attention to this matter.

Hackle Length

The usable length of individual feathers should be long enough to take at least five turns of hackle around the hook with enough left over to hold onto with either your fingers or a hackle pliers. Larger and western-style flies can require up to 12 turns of hackle (two hackles, six turns each, or one long saddle). Smaller and eastern-style flies may have a total of four to six turns of hackle. A hairwing-style fly such as a Humpy will require more hackle than a Light Cahill or parachute-style fly.

The longer the usable portion of hackle the better. If you do not need all the length, it is easier to hold onto and you can select only the premium portion. Avoid short hackles because they usually have wide fibers.

Hackle Width

Dry fly proportions are critical, and hackle width must be matched closely to hook size. Usually, hackle fibers should extend from the hook about one-and-a-half times the width of the hook gape. Therefore, the *fiber width* (hackle width) determines what size fly a particular feather is suited for.

To judge the width of hackle, select a feather from a neck and bend it. (Do not pull it out but hold the neck in one hand and grasp a hackle by its tip with your other hand.) You will get a good idea of its width, but remember that fibers always appear one hook size smaller than they actually are because they are not fully extended as they will be when wound around the hook. If you have a Hook and Hackle hackle gauge at your tying bench, simply bend the feather around the post or bend it around a hook. Do not judge feathers by stroking the fibers at a right angle from the stem. Once altered, fibers never resume their original strength, and they will not wrap as easily. Eventually you will be able to bend a feather and quickly determine its size.

Feathers should be uniform in width for most of their length. In other words, you want all hackle fibers to extend the same distance on your fly. At first glance it may look like the fibers become much more narrow toward the tip, tapering with the taper of the feather. To a degree this is true, but it is also an illusion, because the fibers tend to lie at a flatter angle closer to the tip of the feather. The fibers only taper off at the *very* tip, which is where you or your hackle pliers hold onto the feather.

Hackle Density

Hackle density is one of the most important considerations. The more individual fibers that are crowded along an inch of stem, the better. Hackle fiber density of 40 per inch *per side* is poor, 60 per inch is good, 80 is excellent, and 100 is premium. You can get a good idea of fiber density by simply eye-balling a section of hackle.

As a rule, if the hackle feathers are dense on the skin, so are individual fibers on the stem. Turn the skin over and look at the rows of bumps where feathers are imbedded in the skin. These bumps radiate out from the center much like veins on a leaf. If the bumps are close together, the skin is heavily hackled and the fibers are probably dense. Note that the dye process sometimes shrinks the skin, making feathers seem denser than they actually are.

A compromise of the preceding considerations (hackle width, length, stem diameter, stiffness, and fiber density) dictates the quality of the hackle. This selection process can be simplified by buying a silver or gold grade Whiting. You might look at stem diameter, but otherwise the hackle will be of good quality.

Selecting Saddle Hackles

At first glance saddles usually look beautiful, but they can have more irregularities than neck hackle. Individual fibers can be too thick, but are more likely to be too thin or too weak to support a fly. Check to be sure fiber length is the same along each side of the hackle stem and that the fibers extend straight out from each side of the stem. Be certain fibers are not excessively curved and check for fiber density.

Saddle hackle should be long. The extra length of saddle hackle often allows the use of only one feather where two would otherwise be required. Saddle hackle is often required to tie a palmered-style hackle through a body, especially when tying on longer-shank hooks in larger sizes. I like to hold the skin up so the hackles hang toward the ground. This gives a good measure of the quantity and length of the feathers. Saddle skins usually offer two or three sizes of hackles, so pay close attention to feather width. A saddle skin that offers sizes 8, 10 and 12 (or 10, 12 and 14) hackles is an excellent find. If you find size 14 and 16 hackles, buy them! The ideal saddle hackle inventory contains sizes 8 to 12 and, perhaps, a few size 14 and 16 hackles. Start collecting your stash.

Preparing Hackle

Once you have selected the right hackle, it must be properly prepared. Feel or look at the hackle stem. Notice where it slims down an inch or so from the butt. Notice where the web tapers down and the fibers narrow to their median width, also about an inch or so up from the butt. Cut the hackle stem in this area. Trim the soft, thick, wide section off the hackle. What remains is the select dry fly portion of the feather.

Before the feather is tied onto the hook, strip the fibers off the butt of the stem for about 1/16 inch, so that individual fibers will not be tied down onto the hook. When you *first* begin to wrap the stem around the hook, it should be void of all fibers. This ensures that all fibers will radiate *straight* out from the hook and will not be misaligned during the all-important first wrap of hackle.

This feather is too soft (webby) and short for dry fly work.

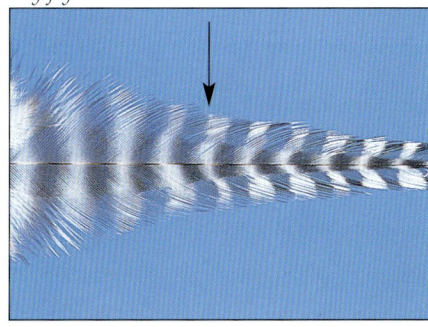

Both web and fiber width taper down at arrow. "Good" hackle from here to tip.

Web is non-existent from arrow to tip, denoting "premium" hackle.

Feather has been trimmed halfway between arrows and "excellent" hackle remains.

Light blue dun, dark blue dun, ginger variant, and ginger Metz necks.

Grizzly dyed olive, natural furnace, and grizzly dyed brown saddle patches.

Fibers at butt end of feather have been pulled off. Hackle is ready to use.

Two feathers—a grizzly and a brown. Note feather curvature: shiny, or top, side faces up.

Hackle has a shiny and a dull side. To tell the difference, look at the curvature of the feather. Bird feathers curve toward the ground, and the shiny side always faces out, or up. Just like the entire feather, individual fibers also have a curvature; depending on the direction they face when wrapped on edge onto the hook, they either curve forward or backward. Standard-style hackle should always be tied with the curve facing forward (dull side forward) because fibers curving this direction best support a fly. Palmered-style hackle is reversed.

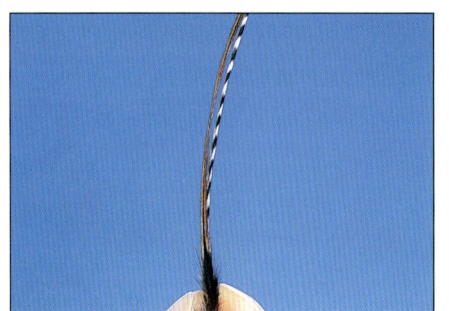

Note that fibers curve to right. The shiny side is on the left; dull side to the right.

Hackles have been wrapped in place, dull side forward. Note fiber curvature toward hook eye. Standard-style hackle is almost always tied in this manner.

Hackle is reversed, subsurface style, dull side to back. (This is a soft, wide hackle selected to exaggerate the subject.) Hackle on subsurface flies (nymphs, wets, and streamer-style) is almost always tied in this manner.

Palmered Hackle

Palmered hackle is very common in dry fly construction. In this text palmered hackle refers to the winding of hackle through or over the entire body area. Hackle is spaced at *even* intervals, much like rib, and should not be wrapped closely.

There are several methods for tying palmered hackle. We are going to learn the *front-to-back* technique. This is the easiest method and produces the nicest result. Front-to-back palmer makes it possible to use only the choice section of hackle, and the desired hackle sizing is easily determined and achieved. A perfect front-to-back taper occurs naturally.

Palmered hackle should be tied and wrapped with the *dull side facing backwards*. *This is contrary to standard dry fly hackling procedure*, but the slight amount of hackle support that is lost is more than overshadowed by the ease in tying and the improved visuals of the fly.

Practice installing hackle on a hook. Select a hackle that is no wider than one-and-a-half times the hook gape, prepare it as previously described, and give it a try.

Properly installed palmered hackle. Note extra turns at front and clean tie-down rib.

Palmered Hackle

1. Red floss and oversized wire have been used for better visibility. Insert the hook in the vise. Secure the wire rib at the back of the hook and wrap the thread to the front of the hook. Strip the fibers from the base of the hackle as shown.

2. Using the up-between-the-fingers technique, secure hackle at the front of the hook on its edge. The dull side of the feather should be facing you. Notice that the hackle stem is void of fibers for a short distance behind the thread tie-in.

3. Using the over-the-top-and-hold-it technique, begin wrapping the hackle around the hook toward the back of the hook, dull side facing back. Take two to three turns close together at the beginning, then spread the wraps apart.

4. Continue wrapping the hackle back to the end of the body area. Hold the hackle in your left hand and bring the wire over the hackle stem, securing it in place. Two initial wraps of wire should be taken, then space the wraps apart and wrap to the front of the hackle.

5. The wire is being wrapped through the palmered hackle using the over-the-top-and-hold-it technique. Be careful not to tie down any hackle fibers. The wire can be wrapped counter-clockwise (reverse wrap), which forms an X between the hackle stem and wire rib. This is the only time material should be wrapped in an opposite direction.

6. The wire rib is installed, securing the hackle. Take an extra turn in front of the hackle and tie it down with the thread. Notice that the palmered hackle appears as it did before the wire was wrapped through it. No fibers have been tied down.

7. Trim or break off the wire by working it back and forth. When wire is cut, a sharp end is often left that can cut the thread when it is wrapped over the wire end. If you do cut the wire, trim it close and press the end down with your thumb. Trim the hackle tip at the rear of the fly.

8. Finished palmered hackle. Notice the hackle width and taper. Palmered hackle is often undersized.

9. Improper palmered hackle. If your hackle looks like this, try again.

Standard-style hackle installed on a Humpy. Hair, or flies designed to float in rough water, usually require more and stiffer hackle than those designed for slow water. Fast water flies are best tied with saddle hackle, often a double saddle.

Standard-Style Hackle

Standard-style dry flies should have hackle standing straight out 360 degrees from the hook. When viewed up close, *no space* should show between wraps of hackle. To accomplish this, hackle should always be wrapped back to front, 90 degrees on edge, with each succeeding turn placed immediately next to the last. *Constant* tension must be applied. All fibers should be unencumbered or affected by previous or succeeding wraps or turns of hackle.

Fifty to 60 percent of a standard hackle is placed behind the wing and 40 to 50 percent in front of the wing. Hackle is packed *tightly against* the back and front of the wing. Five to 12 turns of hackle are usually required. Most wings can be positioned to slant forward or backward with hackle placement. Do not wrap hackle in between the wings.

Remember that the dull side of the hackle will face forward toward the eye of the hook. As a result, individual fibers curve forward. As hackle is wrapped forward (back to front), some of these individual fibers might occasionally get wrapped down. Careful winding, combined with occasional stroking back of previously wound hackles, eliminates this minor inconvenience. Trim or pull off any errant fibers that protrude from the head or rear area of the hackle, but be certain to trim them *closely,* because loose or protruding ends of hackle ruin the appearance of a fly.

A single neck hackle has been wrapped on a size 10 hook. It is sparse and soft. It is difficult to find size 10, or even 12, premium neck hackle. Use saddle hackle whenever you can.

This is a single saddle hackle. Saddle is inherently denser and stiffer and has a narrower stem than neck hackle. Neck hackle cannot be packed as tightly as saddle hackle. In other words, more turns of saddle hackle can be placed in the same space.

Single Hackle

The decision whether to use one or two hackles is determined by the length and quality of the feather, size of hook, water to be fished, and the overall visual effect desired. It also depends on the color scheme. To mix colors, use two hackles. A single hackle should be ample for delicate imitations, especially size 16 and smaller. Unless you have an exceptional neck hackle or a saddle, a double hackle is usually needed for size 14, and certainly for a size 12 or larger.

Hackles can be wrapped with your fingers or with the aid of hackle pliers. If you can wrap a hackle without pliers, do it. If your fingers provide a sure grip, you will find that you have more control over the hackle and it is more efficient. When using pliers you have to locate them, pick them up, secure them, test them, often realign them, and set them back down. You also have to be extra careful not to break the feather or pull the pliers off the feather. It is difficult to wrap two hackles simultaneously with pliers. Let's practice winding a single standard-style hackle in place without the aid of pliers.

Single Hackle

Hackle 57

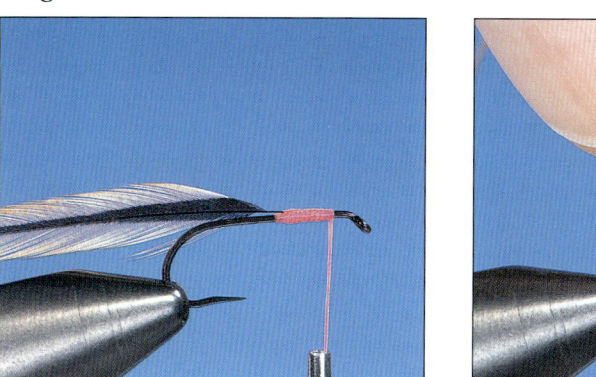
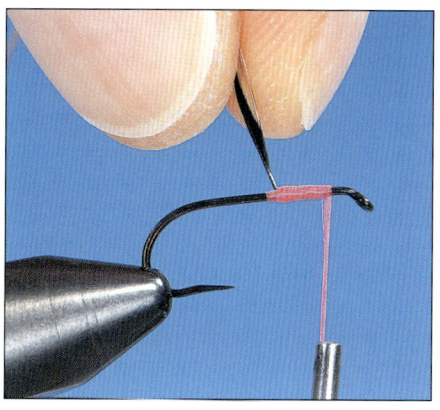
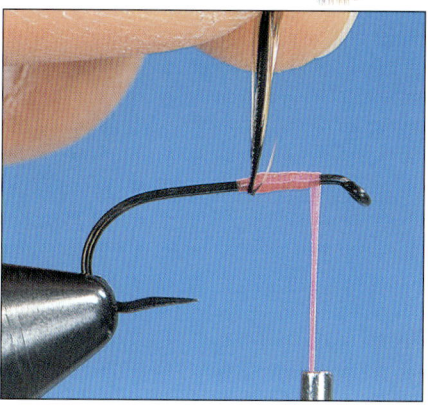

1. These photos demonstrate tying a single hackle over the front 30 percent of the hook shank. Prepare the hackle as previously described and tie it in on edge with the shiny side facing you. Note the tie-in position and that the individual fibers have been stripped off the stem a short distance behind the tie-in.

2. Keeping the shiny side facing back and the hackle on edge, angle the feather away from you. The hackle will be wound in place using the over-the-top-and-hold-it technique. It will be wound from this point forward to the location of the thread, where it will be tied off. Constant tension must be applied.

3. The first wrap of hackle is in place. Notice that there are no fibers extending behind the initial wrap. Continue wrapping the hackle. Each succeeding turn must be positioned immediately adjacent to the last. If necessary, stroke the fibers back gently after each wrap, but do not break the hackle resilience.

4. Half the hackle has been wrapped in place. Notice that it is densely packed and about 1-1/2 times the hook gape. Standard-style dry flies have a wing, which is positioned at about this point on the hook. The hackle is wrapped tightly against the back of the wing and tightly against the front of the wing. Continue the hackle to the front tie-off area.

5. All of the hackle has been wrapped in place. It is densely packed. Hold the hackle with your right hand and take two to three turns of thread over the hackle stem as shown here. Do not tie down existing hackle fibers. The thread is placed only over the stem.

6. Grasp the leftover hackle tip and all associated fibers as close to the hook shank as possible. You should be able to clearly identify the cut area. Using only the point, or tip, of your scissors, make one clean cut immediately against the hook shank. There should be no errant fibers or butt ends of the stem showing.

7. Notice how all the individual fibers extend straight out from the hook and form a near-perfect rectangle, top to bottom and front to back. There should not be any fibers sticking out from the thread head. Do not proceed until you have mastered the single hackle, either with or without the aid of hackle pliers.

8. This hackle is not of dry fly quality. Notice all the web extending out from the center stem. It has also not been tied onto the hook properly. Notice the errant fibers that have been tied down by the thread. When this hackle is wound around the hook, many more fibers will fall back along the hook shank. See the next photo.

9. This is an unacceptable hackle. Besides being webby and tied onto the hook improperly as described above, it has not been wrapped properly. Hackle wraps are spaced apart, and the head area is crowded.

Tying Dry Flies

The extreme tip of the hackle is the most fragile. Unless you intend to use the entire length of the feather, grip the pliers a short distance from the tip. There is less chance that the stem will break. Test the grip. The first wrap of hackle is the most critical. Be certain the hackle is tight and that it comes around on edge with the shiny side facing back. If necessary, use your fingers to get the feather positioned and started on the first wrap.

Using Hackle Pliers

Using hackle pliers has advantages. They allow tyers who otherwise could not to hackle flies. All tyers find them useful when tying the tiny flies that require short hackles. Pliers also allow you to use a longer section of hackle because only a *short* section needs to be held with the pliers, thereby freeing much more hackle to be wrapped onto the fly. Many tyers are able to wrap long hackles with their fingers but use pliers for short hackles.

The idea is to make tying fun and easy, so suit yourself. If you need or like pliers, use them. Practice wrapping a single hackle with pliers and then without pliers. See what you think.

Hackle pliers are designed to be operated with your first finger. Insert your first finger into the pliers and begin wrapping the hackle. With hackle pliers, all winding is done with your right hand. When the hackle comes around to the bottom position, move the bobbin around your right hand with your left hand and continue winding the hackle.

This method of winding a hackle is very efficient. Remember to keep constant tension on the hackle. When you reach the tie-off area, simply let the pliers hang and tie off the hackle as usual. Note that when wrapping a double hackle with pliers, you need to take all of the slack out of the feathers before attaching the pliers.

Double Hackles

Double hackles allow tyers to create a dense, heavy hackle, which helps to float flies in fast, broken water, especially larger flies. I often use three or four hackles. Double hackles also make it possible to mix colors. Adams hackle is a mix of grizzly and brown.

Polly Rosborough used another two-hackle variation that tyers might find useful. To imitate colored joints on insect legs or wing colorings, Polly incorporated an undersize hackle (perhaps yellow size 14) to represent these markings and a standard size hackle (perhaps blue dun size 10) to represent the balance of the legs.

Double hackles must act as one. If possible, they should be selected from the exact same location on the skin or the same side of the saddle, ensuring that they have like characteristics and will mesh together. When prepared, both feathers must be *exactly* the same length tip-to-butt and, except for special effect, *exactly* the same width. They should be tied in side by side with *no space between the stems*.

Double hackles can be wrapped one at a time or both together. When wrapping one at a time, the first hackle is wrapped with just enough space between wraps to accommodate the second hackle. At no time should the second hackle stem be wrapped over the first. Regardless of how carefully you weave the second hackle back and forth, an occasional hackle fiber will be tied down.

Wrapping double hackles simultaneously results in a denser hackle with the best possible alignment. It is also faster. Wrapping hackles simultaneously is best accomplished with your fingers, and long hackles make the task much easier. Wrapping two hackles together using hackle pliers is difficult because the hackles tend to spread apart.

Double Hackle

1. *Double hackles must be perfectly matched.* Hackle stems must be the same thickness, and fibers must have a similar curvature. The feathers, tip to butt, must be exactly the same length. These two feathers obviously do not match and would not make a double hackle.

2. These feathers have like characteristics but have not been prepared properly. They must both be facing the same direction, i.e., the shiny side should be facing you. The stripped stems at the tie in should be of equal length. The same two feathers have been realigned and properly tied in place in the following photo.

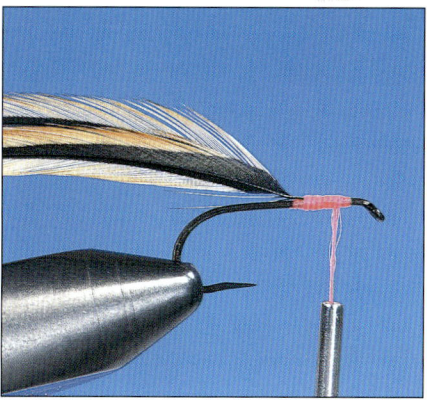

3. A double hackle must look and act as a single hackle. Hackles are kept together by tying them in side by side with no space between the stems. To keep them together, hold the hackles close to their base, or the hook shank, as you wind them.

4. Using the over-the-top-and-hold-it technique, hold the hackle with your left hand and wrap it over the top of the hook as shown here. As you finish the turn on the opposite side of the hook, slide your fingers toward the tip of the feathers so your right hand can hold them in place until your left hand can pick them up and continue winding them.

5. Half the hackle has been wound in place. Notice that the bobbin is resting over the top of the right hand. This allows both hands to work freely without interference. The hackles are positioned at the bottom pick-up point where your left hand will grasp them and continue winding them forward toward the tie-off area.

6. The left hand is winding the hackles, and the right hand is waiting at the bottom of the photo to temporarily hold them while the left hand comes back counter-clockwise to pick them up. Some double hackles will stay adjacent to each other, and there is no need to hold them close to their base as you wrap them.

7. The hackles are at the tie-off location and are being tied off at the thread head area.

8. Note the method of holding the hackle stem and its associated fibers for the tie-off. Also note the position of the scissors. They are being steadied against the hook shank, and the cut is being made with the very tip of the scissors, which makes the closest cut. All fibers are trimmed with one cut.

9. A finished double hackle. It is much denser than a single hackle and may occupy up to 50 percent of the hook shank, making it perfect for a fast water hair fly. Practice a few double hackles. They are easier than you think. Do not proceed until you completely understand hackle preparation and installation.

Chapter 12

Griffith Gnat and Cluster Midge

Griffith Gnat (George Griffith)
- Hook: 900BL, 12-22
- Thread: Black or to match body
- Rib: Thread or fine gold wire
- Body: Peacock or other to suit
- Hackle: Grizzly or other to suit, palmered

Cluster Midge (Renè Harrop)
- Hook: 900BL, 12-22
- Thread: Black or to match body
- Wing: White CDC, single upright
- Rib: Thread or fine gold wire
- Body: Peacock or other to suit
- Hackle: Grizzly or other to suit, palmered

Most waters offer explosive midge populations; anglers should be prepared. A swarm of midges gather along shoreline vegetation at Lake Taupo, New Zealand.

The Griffith Gnat, one of the simplest dry flies, is a good general imitation of insects belonging to the order Diptera, which includes all two-winged insects: mosquitoes, gnats, black flies, craneflies, and a multitude of midges (chironomids). It is also a good bet for tiny caddisflies and mayflies when you are caught without a more exact imitation. Most anglers, however, use the Griffith Gnat to represent midges.

In the mornings, midges wash up on windward shores and can pile up many inches deep. When such hatches are in progress, finding a square yard of lake surface that does not have a feeding trout patrolling it is difficult. Frenzied feeding conditions are the rule.

Lake anglers should not cast their fly at random and expect fish to rise to it exclusively. When food is constantly available, fish settle into a comfortable feeding rhythm, feeding at their leisure, knowing food will be available when they are ready. Anglers should time their presentation so it is at the exact position *where* and *when* the fish is expected to feed next.

The Griffith Gnat and Cluster Midge will allow you to practice installing a peacock body, thread rib, palmered hackle, and, if you tie the Cluster Midge, a single wing. This style of wing is an anomaly and is only seen on the Cluster Midge.

This style of fly can be tied in color combinations other than grizzly-peacock. Try grizzly-red, blue dun-peacock, furnace-peacock, light variant, or grizzly-tan or cream combinations.

I have always liked peacock on my flies because it offers a natural, animated iridescence unlike any other material. It acts, looks, and feels alive. Peacock should be purchased by the complete tail, and only the choice herl should be considered. Examine the herl along the complete tail. The thick, wide herl begins immediately below the eye and extends down the stem for about four inches. Peacock herl is present only along one edge of the flat quill, or stem. To construct a juicy-looking body, it is imperative that the smooth, herl-less side of the quill precede the herl side as you wrap it around the hook. If not, succeeding wraps of bare quill will over wrap, or cover, the preceding turns of herl. Two or more herls may be required to provide the desired hook coverage, and they must all be properly aligned. Inspect the top and bottom of the quill, as one side offers longer herl. Peacock herl is extremely fragile and should always be overwrapped with thread or fine wire.

Griffith Gnat and Cluster Midge

1. Select one or two matching CDC feathers and even the tips. To achieve a secure tie-in and construct a small thread head, tie wing "reverse," extending in front of eye. It will later be tied upright, creating a very secure and neat tie-in.

2. Hold them in your left hand up against the hook shank to measure the proper length. Reposition your grasp on the feathers so they protrude from your fingers as far as the hook shank is long. Secure in place with the up-between-the-fingers technique.

3. Tie in the rib (fine wire or black thread). Trim wing butts at an angle. There are no loose fibers. Position thread as shown.

4. Select one to three choice peacock herls. Tie in with bare side of stem forward and tall side of herl facing up. Tie down like the Z-Lon shuck on Sparkle Dun, and position thread at tie-off area behind wing as shown.

5. Peacock has been tied off. It looks like it is crowding the eye, but it is not. Trim peacock. This is a perfect example of where a close scissors cut is necessary. If a close cut is not made, peacock ends will crowd head area.

6. Prepare and tie in a **palmered** hackle (shiny side facing forward). Secure hackle (dull side facing you) with five turns of thread in the space in front of peacock body. It is okay to wrap a couple turns of thread back into peacock body.

7. Using the over-the-top-and-hold-it technique, wind the hackle back toward the tail palmer style to the position shown.

8. Hold hackle tip with your left hand (or hackle pliers), and grasp rib with your right hand. Secure hackle at the rear with two turns of wire and rib body with wire.

9. If you have space, wrap a complete turn of wire in front of hackle area. Hold rib with your right hand and, working bobbin with your left hand, tie it off and trim.

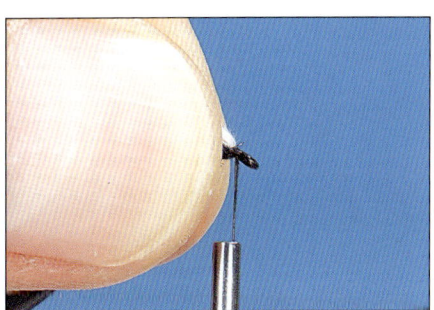

10. Using your fingers, pull the wing back as shown and finish a thread head. Wrap the thread slightly over the top of the wing, standing it up at a slight angle toward the back. Only a few turns of thread are necessary.

11. Finished Cluster Midge. Note the proportions of the wing, body, and hackle. Tie more, until you are comfortable working with the peacock, hackle, and rib. If you had trouble with the wing, tie the fly without the wing (see photo 12).

12. A finished Griffith Gnat without a wing. Omit steps 1, 2, 3, and 4. Concentrate on a thick peacock herl body and evenly-spaced palmered hackle, as shown here.

Chapter 13

Hatching Midge

Hatching Midge (Randall Kaufmann)
- Hook: 900BL, sizes 12-18
- Thread: Black
- Shuck: Gray or black CDC with a few strands of matching Z-Lon over top
- Rib: White thread
- Abdomen: Black Superfine or thread; very thin
- Wingcase: Gray or black CDC pulled loosely over top of thorax
- Hackle: Grizzly, three to four turns standard style, evenly spaced throughout thorax; hackle slightly undersized
- Thorax: Peacock
- Antennae: Gray or black CDC protruding slightly out over eye

By their sheer numbers, midges, or chironomids, are considered the most important food source of trout, especially in lakes. Midges inhabit just about every damp spot on earth, and they hatch nearly every day that water is ice-free. Midges come in all sizes and colors, but black, olive, and gray in sizes 16-22 are the most prevalent. Northwest lakes such as Dry Falls, Lenore, Nunnally, and many of the fabled lakes in the area around Kamloops, British Columbia, offer sizes 8 and 10 magnum midge fishing.

I have spent many hours drifting in a float tube observing midges emerge, hatch, and take flight. Feeding activity is usually centered on emerging pupa just subsurface, but the surface "hatching" stage is also preyed upon, especially when winds are calm and humidity is high. Damp conditions delay flight, and fish often gulp the waiting hatchlings at the surface.

The Hatching Midge represents a pre-adult midge halfway out of its nymphal shuck. It is also an excellent representation of a stillborn midge—those that, for one reason or another, become entangled or are otherwise unable to complete their emergence or transformation into adults. Anglers should fish these dead drift, perhaps with a slight twitch, on lake waters. Long 10- to 15-foot 5X to 7X leaders are sometimes necessary. Anglers interested in learning more about midge fishing lakes should read *Lake Fishing With A Fly*.

This style of fly also lends itself nicely to emerging or hatching mayflies. Vary the size and color to suit your needs. Tyers who have a basic understanding of tying nymphs will tie the Hatching Midge with ease. I have selected it because it is an excellent review of basic technique and nymph-dry fly parts, including a shuck, wingcase, antennae, thorax, and hackle.

Hatching Mayfly, PMD (Randall Kaufmann)
- Hook: 900BL, sizes 16-20
- Thread: Yellow
- Shuck: Gray CDC with a few strands of Z-Lon over top
- Rib: Yellow thread
- Abdomen: Yellow goose or turkey biot
- Wingcase: Gray CDC pulled loosely over top of thorax
- Hackle: Grizzly, three to four turns standard style, evenly spaced throughout thorax; hackle slightly undersized
- Thorax: Peacock
- Antennae: Gray CDC protruding slightly out over eye

Midges crawl from their nymphal shucks on the water's surface. Once free, they extend and dry their wings and take flight.

Hatching Midge 63

1. Cover hook shank with thread. Select a CDC feather with even tips. Shuck should be length of hook shank or slightly shorter and tied flat. Tie material in at the 60-percent mark. Wrap back to tail tie-in, creating level underbody.

2. Tie in rib at tail area. Dub Superfine onto thread sparsely and wrap body as shown. Note position where CDC butt ends were tied down and trimmed. This is where abdomen will end.

3. Individual strands of thread (ribbing) have an annoying habit of separating. Twisting thread keeps it together, but do not soil section which will be used on the fly. Rib must be tight. Check with your fingernail. Tie off and trim excess.

4. Select a CDC feather for wingcase. When pulled over top, tips (natural ends) will become antennae, which is a short tuft. If you judge length properly, you will not need to trim it. CDC can be trimmed with your fingers (looks natural) or your scissors.

5. Change hands. Tie in with up-between-the-fingers technique and wrap forward, creating a smooth foundation tapering slightly toward hook eye.

6. Trim butt ends. Proper wingcase tie in. Note that the area where the thread head will eventually be placed has not been infringed upon and that the wingcase is secured directly on top of the hook. Position thread as shown.

7. Select and prepare a hackle, which will be wrapped standard style, except that it will be evenly spaced (three to four turns) through thorax area. Tie in peacock herl.

8. Photo shows proper method for making a close, clean cut. Your right hand acts as a bobbin rest, keeping thread out of cut area. Hold peacock taut with your right hand. Rest scissors against hook shank and trim with scissors points.

9. Wrap hackle, shiny side facing back, forward through thorax and tie it off at same position at which peacock was tied off. Make one clean scissors cut. There should be no wild hackle fibers protruding from tie-off area.

10. Fold hackle away from top of thorax or trim it. Pull wingcase forward loosely over top of thorax. There should be plenty of air space between thorax and wingcase. Pinch your thumb and forefinger around hook eye and secure wingcase in place at back of thread head.

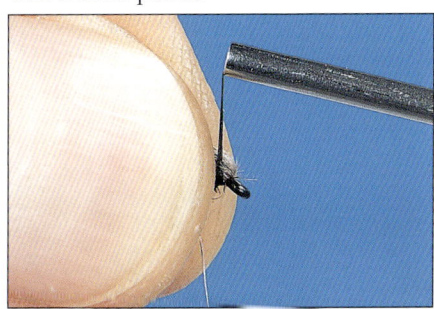

11. Using your fingers, encompass all fibers. Now it is easy to wrap a few turns of thread forward to hook eye and back to rear of thread head and finish it off. Ten turns of thread are enough.

12. Finished Hatching Midge.

Tying Dry Flies

Chapter 14

California Mosquito

California Mosquito
- Hook: 900BL, sizes 12-18
- Thread: Black
- Tail: Grizzly hackle fibers (red is another possibility)
- Rib: White silk thread
- Abdomen: Black floss (consider thin black dubbing)
- Wing: Grizzly hackle tips tied down-wing style
- Hackle: Grizzly

The discovery of a "hot" pool demands a break, a skinny dip, lunch, and a little fishing.

Orange sneezewwwd, Dugaldia hoopesii, *along Piute Creek slow the most jaded mountain traveler.*

Fish accept mosquito imitations for what they are intended to represent, but I believe they usually accept them for hatching or adult midges, which figure more prominently in a fish's diet. Like the midges, mosquitoes belong to the order Diptera, which literally means flies with two wings (one pair). When at rest, their wings lie down across the top of their body. For this reason, I like mosquito patterns with a down wing. Adult mosquitoes are easily distinguished from midges by the mosquitoes' habit of sitting with their hind legs in the air, while midges raise their forelegs. . .and do not bite.

The California Mosquito is a productive fly for crappie, bluegill, small bass, grayling, and trout. It is especially popular with western alpine anglers, not because it is the best possible pattern, but because visitors encounter so many mosquitoes and assume trout like to eat them. I always have a few California Mosquitoes in my fly box.

During late June 1994 Sam Glasser, James Foster, Chris Peaslee and I visited the waters of Evolution Valley in California's King's Canyon National Park. To reach this remote valley, considered one of the prettiest in the High Sierra, requires about a 20-mile trek. Once there, anglers find plenty of side canyons and benches to explore above the valley.

During early summer, the streams, cascades, and waterfalls flow full force, and flowers are in their prime. People have yet to arrive because mosquitoes are in charge of crowd control. During our trip, mosquitoes did their job and forced us to camp below McClure Meadow, where conditions were drier and a breeze kept the bugs at a tolerable level.

Evolution Creek is seductive and both tranquilizes and heightens the spirit. Dancing riffles, slick chutes, smooth granite glides, enticing pools, and splashy pocket water shelter plenty of seven-inch golden trout. In the spring, the creek is a crescendo of water forms and sounds—peaceful and subdued one moment, raging and out of control the next. Its

Lakes in the Sierra are crystalline. Chris Peaslee handles this prize rainbow carefully.

James contemplates the vista above Sapphire Lake, King's Canyon National Park.

Rare California golden trout. A more exquisitely colored trout is difficult to imagine.

waters are a contemplation in sublimity and a window into some of nature's most powerful magic.

After arranging camp, I submerged myself in its chilly, therapeutic waters behind a boulder around which grew yellow cinquefoil and orange leopard lily. A golden trout darted away as I entered, and John Muir's favorite bird, the water ouzel, fished for insects nearby. Soon the golden trout rejoined me and suspended itself a few inches below the water's surface. We swam together, our destinies bound by pure water and nature's good grace.

Rushing water splashed off the nearby boulder and separated into tiny droplets. These soared into the air, forming miniature rainbows which burst in my face. I closed my eyes, faced the sun, and my psyche drifted with the current, swirled into a back eddy, then raced on. I opened my eyes and noticed an adult stonefly drift into the pool. The golden rushed to the surface, exposed its brilliant yellow and fluorescent fire orange colorings, and inhaled the stonefly only inches from my face. It was over in a second, but the spectacle will be long remembered.

Sam and I walked upstream, and he flicked his barbless dry fly to other, less sacred trout. He allowed all to escape, enjoying their sensational coloring and frantic dash to freedom. Other waters in the area offer larger brookies and rainbows, but these pools hold a magical fascination over all who visit. Reluctantly, we hoisted our packs and left; the day promised adventure and another remote campsite surrounded by 13,000-foot peaks, perpetual snowbanks, delicate flowers, and rising trout. It would be just another day in mountain paradise.

The California Mosquito pattern demonstrates how to tie down-wing-style hackle-tip wings. This wing style is often used when tying midge and terrestrial patterns such as ants. This is the first pattern to incorporate dense standard-style hackle. If you have trouble, refer to Chapter 11 (hackle). If you intend to fish this pattern in fast choppy water, take an extra turn or two of hackle. For use in very slow or still water, take a turn or two less. The best method of preparing and installing a hackle fiber tail is also demonstrated.

James and Chris stop for a breather and survey their tortuous, ever upward route.

Golden trout are one of the rewards after a rough day on the trail in King's Canyon.

Evolution Creek casts its magical spell on all who visit. Chris casts for goldens.

Golden trout are the payoff for many western high country anglers.

66 *Tying Dry Flies*

1. Select a wide hackle with stiff fibers. Select tail fibers from beyond the shadowed area. The average feather yields one tail per side, two tails per hackle.

2. Hold tip of feather in your right hand. Using your left hand (thumb and first finger), grasp a large number of fibers and align them at a right angle to stem. This evens tips between your fingers before you remove fibers from stem.

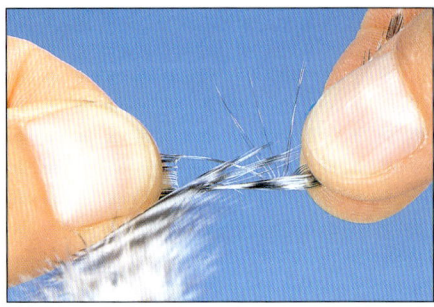

3. With your right hand, pull the hackle tip and the stem away from your left hand, leaving the butt end of the fibers extending from your left hand.

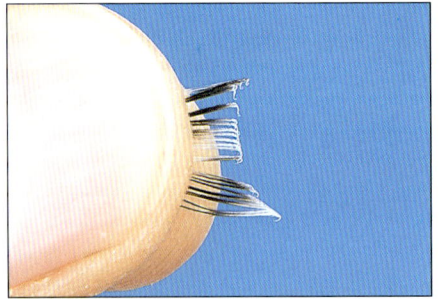

4. You are holding fibers in your left hand. If butts are mostly the same length, tips will also be even. If you do not pull them off stem correctly, it is very difficult to even them individually. Practice until you can do it easily.

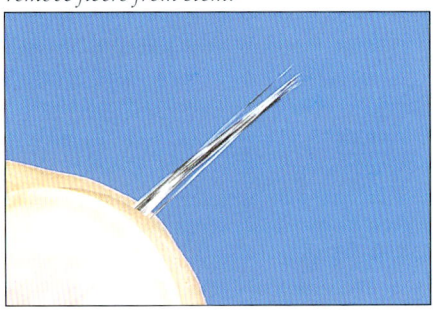

5. Grasp the hackle butts with your right hand, making certain you do not alter their alignment.

6. Measure them against hook shank. Tail should be about as long as hook shank. Hold fibers in your left hand and secure them onto hook at the 70-percent mark.

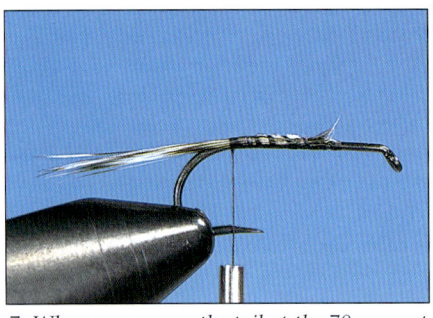

7. When you secure the tail at the 70-percent mark, hold onto it with your left hand. Hold the tail above and along the top of the hook as you wrap the thread back to the end of the tail area, forming a level underbody.

8. Wrap thread back to 70-percent mark and tie in rib with three to four thread wraps. At same tie-in location, tie in black floss. Rib and floss are being held above and along top of hook shank as they are secured in place.

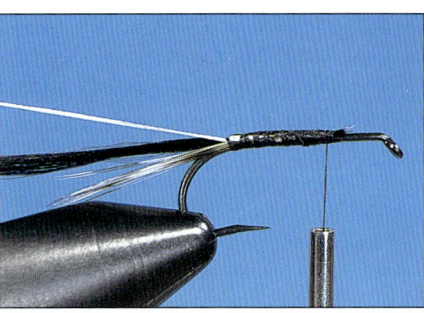

9. All tie-downs should be along and on top of hook, not alternating from side to side. Material has been properly secured, forming level underbody, and thread has been positioned at tie-off area for abdomen and rib. Abdomen is ready to wrap, then rib.

10. It may be necessary to twist floss slightly as you wrap abdomen. Keep floss abdomen tight and level. First turn of rib must be tight and not too wide, or it will fall off back of body. This rib is wide to demonstrate maximum angle for first wrap.

11. Select two matching grizzly hackle tips (hen, or wide saddle from the base of the skin). You are looking at the shiny sides.

12. Face shiny sides together so they flare apart in a V. Even tips so they are exactly the same length. Trim off butt ends so feather is easier to handle. Hackle tips must be placed perfectly on end.

California Mosquito 67

13. Position tips in your right hand to measure their length, as shown. Wings should be about the length of the body and are tied in at the 70-percent mark.

14. Grasp wings with your left hand and hold them tightly in place and down against hook shank.

15. Secure in place with two to three turns of thread. Back fingers off slightly and take two to four more wraps backwards. Secure.

16. Wings should look like this, on edge, flaring away from each other and extending slightly beyond hook bend. Pull on the wings; they should be secure.

17. Note steep drop-off at end of wing tie-down where bare hook shank begins. If this is too abrupt, hackle will slide forward or fall off this drop. After tying in hackle, smooth it out with a few wraps of thread.

18. This is the first standard-style hackle we will tie. Hackle will cover space shown. Thread is positioned at hackle tie-off area. Space in front of thread becomes thread head. If you have trouble with hackle, review hackle chapter.

19. The first wrap of hackle should look like this. All fibers come straight out from the fly, and first wrap is almost on top of wing. Succeeding wraps are adjacent to one another, covering thread base.

20. Finished California Mosquito. Put a drop of lacquer at the back of the body for added durability.

21. Red Tail Mosquito.

Expansive fields of lupine greet the alpine angler in the John Muir Wilderness, High Sierra, California, July 20, 2000.

Chapter 15

Black Flying Ant

Black and Brown Flying Ant
- Hook: 900BL, sizes 12-20
- Thread: Black
- Back: Black deer
- Abdomen: Black or brown Antron
- Wing: Dark blue dun hackle tips, delta-wing style
- Hackle: Brown, furnace, or black, tied in center of hook
- Thorax: Same as abdomen

Black and Cinnamon Fur Ants.

Foam Ant (Gary LaFontaine) and Cinnamon Flying Ant.

Dark Flying Ant and Hardshell Ant. Hardshell sinks and represents a drowned ant.

Ants are true terrestrials and belong to the order Hymenoptera and family *Formicidae*, so named because they inject formic acid in their bites. They are much more important in the diet of trout than most anglers realize. Ants undergo four stages: egg, larva, pupa, and adult. Queen and male ants are usually winged; the commonly-observed worker ants are wingless. An unexplained mating signal brings all winged ants into an aerial swarm. This signal also can trigger several distant colonies simultaneously, and the resulting swarm can number in the tens of millions. After mating, the chance fall of spent males over water triggers a rise of frenzied trout unlike any you have imagined, literally creating a windfall for trout and anglers alike.

Ants are vulnerable to wind currents, especially thermal up and down drafts. Warmer air rises, carrying ants with it. When it cools over higher elevations and bodies of water, the ants are forced down. Updrafts along our major north-south mountain ranges send many ant swarms on unscheduled flights. Never underestimate the importance of upslope blow-in!

Other than the mating ritual, ants are ground dwellers and commonly live adjacent to waterways where they climb over rocks and vegetation and continually fall or are blown onto the water. This small but consistent supply of ants usually goes unnoticed by anglers, but trout eagerly await them.

Adult ants have a head, thorax, and abdomen, but usually the head and thorax are the only features tyers need to represent. This is referred to as the two-hump strategy with emphasis on a tiny waist. Legs are prominent on medium and large specimens, and the pale-veined wings on flying ants are of paramount importance. Ant wings can be laid back much like a resting caddis, flared up at a 45-degree angle, or spent like a mayfly. As you construct your imitations, keep these thoughts in mind.

I recommend at least two styles of flying ants: down delta wing (sizes 8-18) and a wingless fur ant (sizes 14-18). Black, rust, and brown are the most useful colors. In addition, I like a fast-sinking hard-shell pattern that I fish drowned. To construct it, fashion a two-part body with acetate floss. With a good length of thread hanging from the center waist point, drop the fly into acetate for about 60 seconds. Remove without touching the body, replace in vise, hackle carefully, and let dry.

The Black Flying Ant pattern demonstrates a delta wing and how various techniques can be incorporated into another style or pattern. The overbody, dubbed body, and standard-style hackle have all been demonstrated previously.

Black Flying Ant

1. Position thread at the 30-percent mark and tie in a small clump of about 20 black deer hair fibers (stacked and cleaned of all underfur). Tie down onto bend of hook.

2. Trim butt ends as shown.

3. Apply black dubbing onto thread and form a rounded mound as shown. Note that all demonstration patterns are tied on a size 10 hook; smaller amounts of material will be used on smaller hooks.

4. Grasp deer hair fibers with your right hand and pull them tightly over top of the dubbing (body), forming back. Rest your fingers on hook shank and, with your left hand, bring bobbin over top and secure hair in place.

5. Trim off butt ends. There should not be any errant fibers or dubbing. Tie off should be neat.

6. Delta hackle tip wings are tied same as hackle-tip downwings (Mosquito), except that these are not on edge, but are flat. Holding them in your right hand, move them into position to desired length, extending one-quarter to one-half length of shank.

7. Hold wings in place with your left hand and secure with up-between-the-fingers technique. If necessary, tie them in one at a time. They should look like this. If they are not perfectly flat, you can usually manipulate them into place with your fingers.

8. Trim off wing butt ends. Notice amount of space left on hook shank. Hackle will be tied standard style at center of hook shank. Prepare and tie in hackle as shown and position thread at hackle tie-off location.

9. Wind hackle in place and tie off. This is plenty of hackle.

10. Apply black dubbing to thread and form a small mound (thorax). Thread head is very small, almost unnoticeable.

11. Finished Black Flying Ant.

12. Brown Flying Ant, sparsely dressed.

Chapter 16

Adams

Adams (Len Halladay)
- Hook: 900BL, sizes 10-20
- Thread: Gray
- Wing: Grizzly hen hackle tips, upright and divided
- Tail: Grizzly, or grizzly and brown hackle fibers, or moose
- Body: Muskrat or gray Antron
- Hackle: Grizzly and brown mix

Female Adams
- Hook: 900BL, sizes 10-20
- Thread: Gray
- Wing: Grizzly hen hackle tips, upright and divided
- Tail: Grizzly, or grizzly and brown hackle fibers, or moose
- Butt: Yellow Antron or Superfine
- Body: Muskrat or gray Antron
- Hackle: Grizzly and brown mix

The Adams fishes well in all waters. Pictured is a colorful New Zealand stream and the amazing rainbow trout it shelters. These are fragile fisheries. If you get there you don't need to hook them all.

The Adams was designed by Len Halladay in 1922 and was first fished by Charles Adams on the Boardman River. It has been one of America's favorite flies ever since and is known throughout the angling world. Over the years it has been said to imitate deer flies, mayflies, caddis in flight, and, in smaller sizes, gnats and mosquitoes. Jim Quick, in his classic book *Trout Fishing And Trout Flies*, classifies the Adams as an impressionistic natural, aligning it with mayfly duns. Today, most anglers rely on the Adams to represent a multitude of grayish and brownish mayflies. It has a well-deserved reputation as a "when all else fails, cast and chance" pattern.

Montana angler-author Gary LaFontaine, whom I call the investigative fly reporter, believes the Adams is consistent because it is *never wrong*. It does not trigger curiosity or caution, and fish are likely to accept it for a mixture of drift items.

The Adams is probably at its best when enlisted for the western hatch of *Callibaetis* in sizes 12-16. Northwest anglers fish it for black drakes *(Siphlonurus)* in sizes 10-12. When the occasion presents itself, a size 10-12 works well for *Siphlonurus occidentalis*, or gray drakes. When fish are feeding somewhat indiscriminately on *Baetis*, a size 16-20 Adams can be useful. I like to tie the Adams with a moose tail and heavy hackle for fast water and with a grizzly hackle fiber tail and sparse hackle for calm water.

The name Adams also denotes a "color combination." The brown and grizzly hackle combination is commonly referred to as an *Adams hackle*. Other grayish-brown imitations of the Adams include Adams Irresistible, Adams Wulff, Adams Loop Wing, Adams Hairwing Dun, Adams Humpy, and the famous Adams Parachute.

New techniques to master here are the placement and construction of upright and divided hackle-tip wings and the proper placement of hackle behind and in front of the upright wings. This is the standard style of hackling upright and divided-wing dry flies and should be fully mastered before you continue. If you have trouble, carefully review Chapter 11 (hackle) and practice winding hackle on a bare hook.

Tyers should note that the tying technique for the Adams is identical to that of the Blue-Winged Olive, which is a very effective and popular *Baetis* imitation. See the pattern directory.

Adams

1. Position thread at the 75-percent mark. Select two matching grizzly hackle tips. Face shiny sides together. Hold in position with your right hand. By measuring before you secure wing, there is no miscalculation.

2. Thread is between the fingers and is positioned to begin the tie-in. Wing butts are a bit long and will prove to be unwieldy; trim them down to an inch or less. Wrap thread away from first cinch-down wrap (toward hook eye).

3. Wings have been tied in much like a downwing (see Mosquito). Trim butts closely. Be certain to trim every fiber. Notice wing position in relation to bare hook shank toward eye, which will become thread head.

4. Lift wing with your right hand and allow fibers at base of wing to fall free. Place one wrap of thread **immediately** against wing stems, tying down fibers and standing the wing upright. If wings are not angled properly, push forward at their base.

5. Tie down hackle fibers. Position thread as shown. Tie in tail at this position. Wrap thread back over tail, keeping tail along the **top** of hook shank.

6. Tail is tied in place, and butt ends have been trimmed. Thread is hanging halfway between hook point and where barb would normally be. This is the standard rear position of thread when securing a tail and where body will begin.

7. Dub and wrap body forward, reversing a turn or two to fill in any low spots. It is okay to wrap hackle over dubbing.

8. Prepare two hackles (one brown, one grizzly) and tie in behind wing. Hackle butts should not protrude in front of wing. Tie in hackle on edge on top of dubbing and position thread at hackle tie-off area. Note bare hook behind eye.

9. One turn of hackle is in place. Thread has slipped forward and almost fallen off hook. When this happens, you have lost a turn of thread. If too many turns slip off, last material tied in place will fall off. A half-hitch alleviates this problem.

10. Hackle has been wrapped **tightly** against back of wing, which keeps wing from angling back. Sweep wing back and place a wrap of hackle **immediately** in front of and against wing. This keeps wing from falling forward.

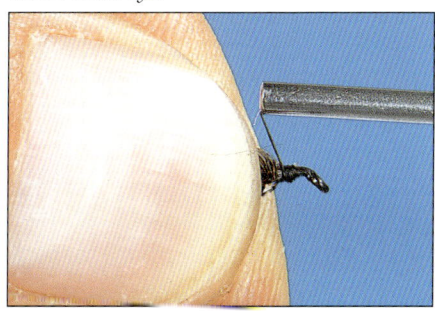

11. Tie off hackle. Sweep all fibers back out of the way, and you can clearly see thread head area. You will also be able to complete the thread head easily without tying down any hackle fibers. Stroke or handle wing and hackle gently.

12. Finished Adams.

Chapter 17

Light Cahill and Quill Gordon

Light Cahill (Dan Cahill)
- Hook: 900BL, sizes 12-20
- Thread: Pale yellow
- Wing: Mallard flank dyed woodduck, upright and divided (woodduck flank was originally used)
- Tail: Light ginger or cream hackle fibers
- Body: Light ginger or cream Superfine
- Hackle: Light ginger or cream

Quill Gordon (Theodore Gordon)
- Hook: 900BL, sizes 12-18
- Thread: Gray
- Wing: Mallard dyed woodduck, upright and divided
- Tail: Blue dun hackle fibers
- Body: Stripped peacock quill
- Hackle: Blue dun

Hendrickson (Roy Steenrod, 1916)
- Hook: 900BL, sizes 12-16
- Thread: Gray or black
- Wing: Mallard flank dyed woodduck
- Tail: Dark blue dun hackle fibers
- Body: Dark gray, tan, or pinkish-tan dubbing
- Hackle: Dark blue dun
- Note: Old-time standard-style adult imitation of *Ephemerella subvaria,* a major early-season hatch east of the Mississippi. Duns hatch in the afternoon, and spinners fall in the evening. This pattern is often referred to as a Dark Hendrickson.

It is believed that Dan Cahill first tied the Cahill around 1880 and that Theodore Gordon tied a variation of the Cahill and called it the Light Cahill around 1890. The pale cream dressing popular today is credited to William Chandler, who first fished it on the Neversink River in New York. The Light Cahill has been praised as "one of the best dry flies ever devised." The Light Cahill is the preferred imitation during light-colored mayfly hatches, especially for *Stenonema canadense,* for which it was originally devised.

Theodore Gordon is believed to have first tied the Quill Gordon around 1890-1895. It was possibly designed to fish the *Iron fraudator* hatch, which is very closely related to *Epeorus pleuralis*. The Hendrickson, a similar pattern, comes to us from Roy Steenrod, circa 1916. It was first fished on the Beaverkill River in New York to imitate the female *Ephemerella subvaria*.

The Light Cahill, Quill Gordon, and Hendrickson embody the Catskill fly tying and angling tradition and have been praised as the "perfect flies." Edward Hewitt, Herman Christian, Roy Steenrod, and Theodore Gordon are considered the founding fathers of the Catskill tradition. Anglers interested in learning more about Catskill fly tyers should read *Catskill Fly Tyer* by Harry Darbee with Mac Francis.

Many flies have been patterned after these early imitations, and, if you can tie the Light Cahill and Quill Gordon, you can tie many others. The only difference between the two is the construction of the body. The Light Cahill has a dubbed body, and the Quill Gordon has a stripped peacock quill body.

Tying a perfect stripped peacock quill body is difficult. There are several methods for eliminating the herl, including soaking peacock eyed tails in wax and then peeling them off, soaking them in a bleach solution, and using an eraser. All work, but, unless you have a lot of free time, buy them pre-stripped. If you are tying only a few I suggest scratching the herl off between your thumb and forefinger. This method insures that the quill is soft, easy to tie with, and of the best quality.

The eyed section of the tail offers the best barring, but the widest and easiest quills to use are found immediately below the eye. For larger flies, use two or three quills. Always tie them in toward the tips, but not too close to the ends because they are fragile and break easily as you wind them. Tying in toward the tips creates narrower segments toward the tail—just like the natural. Be certain you have a smooth, tapered

Light Cahill and Quill Gordon

underbody. I often wrap additional thread or dub a *slight* amount of fur to smooth out the underbody.

Properly constructed quill bodies are smooth and slender. They appear much like a delicate mayfly body. When the fly is complete, treat the quill body with Flexament.

Tying instructions for the Light Cahill explain how to secure upright and divided feather wings. Pay close attention to proportion, which is critical for a well-balanced dry fly. Unlike most western-style dry flies, Catskill-style patterns are tied sparse and delicate. In addition, wings are usually a bit longer than normal and are cocked slightly forward.

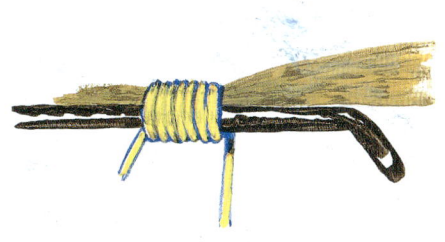

Thread is wrapped backwards and then forward.

Incorrect wing and tail tie in. Note uneven body area.

Incorrectly dubbed body. Dubbing is too fat and loose.

Three to six turns of thread will hold the wings upright.

Correct wing and tail tie in. Body area is smooth and level.

Correctly dubbed body: smooth, slightly tapered, and tight.

Divide wing with your finger. Place thread through wings into butts of tie down.

Thread hooks into butts of wing tie down.

One oblong X of thread separates wing.

74 Tying Dry Flies

1. The Light Cahill has an upright and divided feather wing. Select a mallard feather with even tips.

2. Cut out the center stem below height of wings. (You do not want stem in the wings.)

3. Stroke fibers together and, holding them in your right hand, measure them against the hook shank, ensuring that they are the proper length. They should be as tall as the hook shank is long.

4. Change hands and position feathers at the 80-percent mark. Using the up-between-the-fingers technique, secure them in place. Note that feather tips are of equal length.

5. Feather has been tied in place on top of hook shank.

6. Trim butts off at an angle, but not too close to thread tie down. There must be enough to catch the thread when dividing the wings (see step 9).

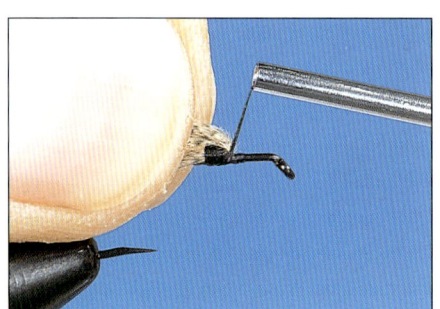
7. Wrap thread against front of wing. Five wraps, properly placed, should do it. This thread has split. Twist the bobbin to tighten thread.

8. Wing has been positioned upright. Notice that there are very few wraps of thread in front of wing—every wrap should be effective.

9. Divide wing in half with your fingers. We are going to X thread between wings, catching back of the X in the butts. This will separate fibers into equal halves.

10. You will want to hold half the wing between your fingers as the "X" is placed. Wings can be slanted at any angle. After they have been tied in place, you can change the angle with your fingers or hackle placement.

11. Front view of finished wings. A 30-degree spread is about right. Catskill style wings are slanted slightly forward and are about 20 percent longer than hackle. Notice that wings have been tied in place with a minimum amount of thread wraps.

12. Top view.

Light Cahill and Quill Gordon

13. Select a bunch of hackle fibers and secure tail behind wing. Tail technique is identical to that of the Mosquito. Tail fibers fit snugly and evenly against wing tie in, creating a level underbody.

14. Dubbed body should be sparse and wrapped just short of wings. Remember that this is a size 10 hook. A size 14 would have a much smaller body diameter and sparser tail. Cream thread would normally be used and would not be visible through dubbing.

15. Prepare hackle and tie in behind wing. Two hackles are shown because this is a size 10 hook. It is wrapped standard style first behind and then in front of wing, dull side facing forward. Thread has been positioned at hackle tie-off area. Note stripped hackle stem at start.

16. Wrap hackle two to three times behind wing. Stroke wing back away from wing and place first wrap of hackle tightly against front of wing.

17. Hackle has been wrapped in front of wing. Trim butt close to hook shank.

18. Notice that there are no errant fibers protruding from front of fly and that we switched to cream thread. Place about six wraps of thread at head area. Fly is complete.

19. To tie Quill Gordon, repeat steps 1 through 13. Select wide and strong peacock herl from just below eye on tail.

20. Using your thumbnail and first finger, rub off the herl as shown.

21. Tie in tip end of herl at tail area and position thread at body tie-off area. To make a nice quill body, you must have a smooth underbody.

22. This peacock quill was too short to handle with fingers, so we used hackle pliers.

23. Tie in hackle and position thread at tie off area.

24. Wrap hackle, tie off, lacquer or Flexament body, and your Quill Gordon is complete.

Chapter 18

Blue Dun, Black Gnat, and Royal Coachman

Blue Dun
- Hook: 900BL, sizes 12-18
- Thread: Gray
- Wing: Gray duck quill, upright and divided
- Tail: Blue dun hackle fibers
- Body: Gray muskrat, Antron, or Superfine
- Hackle: Blue dun

Black Gnat
- Hook: 900BL, sizes 12-18
- Thread: Black
- Wing: Gray duck quill, upright and divided
- Tail: Black or red hackle fibers
- Body: Black Antron or Superfine
- Hackle: Black

Royal Coachman (John Haily, 1878)
- Hook: 900BL, sizes 12-16
- Thread: Black
- Wing: White duck quill, upright and divided
- Tail: Golden pheasant tippets
- Body: Royal three-part body: peacock, red floss, peacock
- Hackle: Coachman brown (original dressing); brown commonly used

The Blue Dun, Black Gnat, and Royal Coachman are the most popular patterns incorporating upright and divided duck quill wings. Quill wings are constructed with two sections from matching left and right duck wing primary quills (feathers). Most tyers have a phobia about tying quill wing flies, but I will describe a quick and easy method that almost guarantees a perfect wing every time.

Quill wings (duck wings, duck quill wings) are underrated and are more durable than most anglers believe them to be. When *lightly* treated at their base with Flexament, they hold together remarkably well. Upright and divided quill wings should not be treated until *after* they are in place. When a quill is tied on edge, its individual fibers contract and compress in response to thread pressure. If the fibers have been glued, they cannot do this. Quill wings that are tied downwing style (Henry's Fork Hopper) are not tied on edge and should be treated before they are tied in place.

The tips may split; if anything, this enhances the light pattern and does not detract from their effectiveness. Mike Lawson compares split quill wings to hair wings, which are essentially a group of split fibers, and asks why there should be a difference in effectiveness. Quill wings are buoyant and offer excellent translucence and water repellency. Anglers should note that bedraggled flies are easily restored by holding them over steam for a few seconds. Hackles, wings, and tails will return to their original condition as if by magic.

Beginning around 1970 standard quill wings began to lose their popularity. Many other easier-to-tie alternatives were available and came into vogue. This was due to the no hackle, match-the-hatch revolution. Today only a handful of quill wing dry flies are in use, including the Blue Upright, Blue Quill, Olive Dun, Olive Quill, Black Gnat, Black Quill, Ginger Quill, and Royal Coachman.

The Royal Coachman has been traced back to 1878 and is probably the oldest pattern described in this book. According to Harold Hinsdale Smedley in *Fly Patterns and Their Origins*, John Haily of New York created the Royal Coachman, and L. C. Orvis named it. It has the best name recognition and is the most often copied body color combination. The Royal Trude, Royal Wulff, Wright's Royal, Royal Parachute, Fan Wing Royal Coachman, Royal Elk Hair, and Royal Stimulator all have what has become known as a *royal* body. This plethora of patterns has pretty much put the old-time Royal Coachman out of business.

Nonetheless, the quill wing style fly is very productive, and I like to tie the hackle Catskill or western style and flare the tail. The following photos explain the proper preparation, placement and construction of standard upright and divided quill wings. Once this style of fly is mastered, you will be able to tie almost any upright and divided quill wing pattern. Note that the technique for tying fan wings is nearly identical to quill wings: match two feathers and strip *most* of the fluff (down) from the stem and proceed as if tying a quill wing. Another quill wing technique will be explained with our next fly, the No Hackle.

Olive Quill
- Hook: 900BL, sizes 14-18
- Thread: Olive
- Wing: Gray duck quill, upright and divided
- Tail: Olive hackle fibers
- Rib: Gold wire (optional)
- Body: Stripped peacock quill
- Hackle: Olive

Note: There are many gray-winged, olive-bodied mayflies for which this pattern can be called into action. In larger size (14) it works for smaller Green Drakes, same as the Olive Dun (olive Antron body). Consider using the Olive Dun for more robust-bodied hatches and this pattern for slimmer, more delicate mayfly bodies.

Blue Upright
- Hook: 900BL, sizes 12-18
- Thread: Gray
- Wing: Gray duck quill, upright and divided
- Tail: Blue dun hackle fibers
- Body: Stripped peacock quill
- Hackle: Blue dun

Note: Similar to Blue Dun but has a quill body. Standard style dry fly used to represent many hatches.

Ginger Quill
- Hook: 900BL, sizes 12-18
- Thread: Tan
- Wing: Gray duck quill, upright and divided
- Tail: Ginger hackle fibers
- Body: Stripped peacock quill
- Hackle: Ginger

Note: Popular in 1950s and 1960s, but dates way back. Useful for light brown hatches.

Pale Evening Dun (Charles Fox and Ray Bergman)
- Hook: 900BL, sizes 14-18
- Thread: Cream or tan
- Wing: Gray duck quill or blue dun hackle tips, upright and divided
- Tail: Light ginger or blue dun hackle fibers
- Body: Cream with yellow-orange highlights
- Hackle: Cream and/or cream and light dun

Note: Represents Ephemerella dorothea, an early season late evening hatch that offers midwestern and eastern anglers excellent surface action.

78 *Tying Dry Flies*

1. Position thread at 75-percent mark.

2. Select a left and right duck quill that have matching characteristics and that are fine-textured. Feather should have smooth edges. Split quills can usually be mended with your fingers.

3. Select wings from the bottom center of quill. Do not use coarse-textured fibers toward the top of the quill. Trim out a left and right pair of segments. Widths between 2/16″ and 3/16″ are about right for size 12-16 hooks.

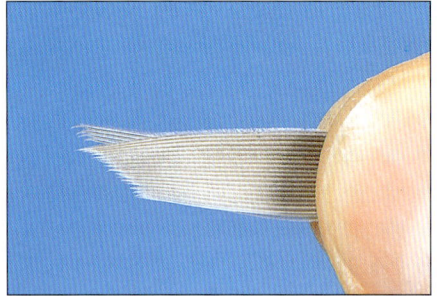

4. Place quill sections together with dull sides toward the inside. Tips should be even, and each feather should have a similar curvature and be same width.

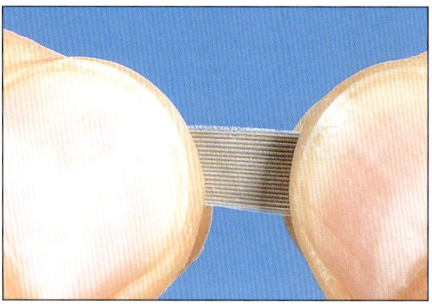

5. Straighten curvature slightly by gently stroking or pulling wings between your fingers. This lessens curvature once they are tied in place and straightens individual fibers.

6. Position wings over top of hook at tie-in location with your left hand. If you wish wing to be same length as hook shank, measure from tie-in location, not how far quill extends from your fingers.

7. Using up-between-the-fingers technique, take a loose wrap around hook and cinch it tightly. All succeeding tie-in wraps should be *behind* this wrap. Individual fibers come together at thread tie-in area. Wrapping forward disturbs this cinch point.

8. Wings are tied along top of hook. Trim butt ends.

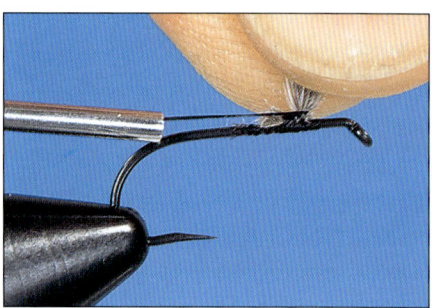

9. With your right hand, grasp wing tightly at the base and gently tilt to a vertical position. Take *one* horizontal wrap of thread up around the *front* of wing above hook and thread tie-in level.

10. Catch thread in wing butts. Remove your right hand and position wing at desired angle with thread leverage.

11. Take three to four turns of thread around hook, locking horizontal wrap of thread in place. Upright and divided quill wing is now perfectly positioned. Do not handle wing or adjust its divided angle until fly is finished.

12. Prepare hackle tail. Photo shows tail positioning with one wrap of thread in place. Fibers have been tied immediately behind wing butts and are spread apart. They are along the near side of the hook.

Blue Dun, Black Gnat, and Royal Coachman

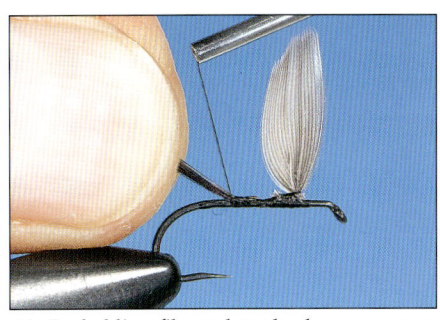

13. By holding fibers above hook as you wrap thread over them, fibers are properly placed along top of hook. They should be an extension of hook shank. To flare them, take a close turn of thread behind or underneath fibers.

14. Trim off tail butts. Tail and wing are 20-percent longer than hook shank and are oversized. It is difficult to keep proportions under control. Everybody gets carried away, but learn to recognize the problem.

15. Dub and construct body. When you have a level underbody and dub material evenly onto thread, you will be able to form a proper body quickly. Do not make dubbing strand too long. It is easier to add more than to take some off.

16. Finished body. If space is not a problem, dubbing can be wrapped in front of wing. Thread is positioned to tie in hackle. Hackle, which will be tied medium-heavy, occupies 30 percent of hook. Feather and quill wing flies are usually dressed much lighter.

17. Note hackle tie in closely. It has been tied in behind the wing on edge, shiny side facing you. Fibers have been stripped slightly beyond location where thread secures stem in place. Thread is positioned at hackle tie-off area.

18. Hackle has been wrapped tightly against back and front of wing and tied off. Note clear space left for head. Try to trim hackle taper with one cut.

19. Once the fly is completed, carefully separate wings and arrange their angle. You are finished.

20. A drop of Flexament can be placed at inside base of wings, but be careful not to get any on hackle. I generally do not treat hackled quill wings, but if you do, treat and dry wings before you hackle them.

21. Finished Blue Dun, showing position, angle, and curvature of wings. After practicing this method, your wings should look like this every time.

Railroad Ranch, Henry's Fork of the Snake, Last Chance, Idaho.

Chapter 19

No Hackle

Mike Lawson

No Hackle (Doug Swisher and Carl Richards)
- Hook: 900BL, sizes 16-18
- Thread: Yellow
- Wing: Gray duck wing quill
- Tail: Blue dun hackle fibers, split
- Body: Yellowish-olive Superfine

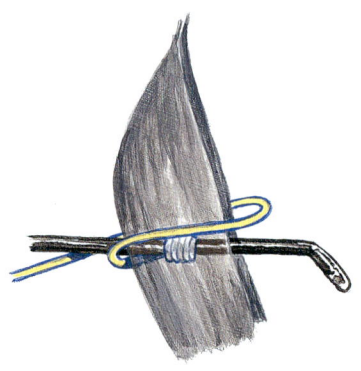

Completely encompass wings with your thumb and first finger, pinching them against sides of hook, holding wings in the position as shown. Thread is wrapped between fingers—you cannot see the tie-down process.

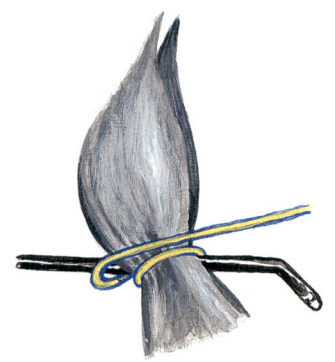

Tie down butt ends along sides of hook, wrapping thread underneath and over top of hook.

Divide wings as shown. Thread lifts up back of wing—hooks in tie-down butts.

When fish are feeding with abandon, neophytes can catch them, but, when fish are discriminating, even the most skilled anglers can have a tough time coaxing fish to the fly. When this is the case, it is a good bet your fly is not convincing enough. You could have the wrong size or color or *shape*. Think about it: If you can spot your bogus fly amid naturals from 20 feet away, what do you think fish see from three inches? You might as well laugh at yourself because the fish probably are.

Doug Swisher and Carl Richards initiated the No Hackle mania in the late 1960s and forever changed the way we view the surface film world of trout, form our imitations, and decipher multiple compound hatches. Swisher and Richards concluded that mayfly wings are the primary trigger, followed by the body. The No Hackle presented here is the product of their research and reasoning. It is tied with body, wings and a realistic forked tail, much like the natural. This method of construction allows the fly to float flush on the surface film and presents an unobstructed view of the body and wings. Its primary value is for selective feeders in slow, clear water, especially spring creeks. Anglers interested in learning more about this fascinating aspect should read their books, *Selective Trout* and *Fly Fishing Strategy*.

No Hackle-style wings extend out and up from the underside of the body. This offers fish a very realistic outline and helps stabilize the fly. Many anglers subscribe to the theory that when wings are slanted back they appear shorter and less obvious to fish, especially just before fully entering their "window" of vision. Therefore, highly visible wings should be a bit exaggerated and more upright.

Standard-style bushy tails probably look like an extension of the body on some surface imitations. Delicate split tails on flies like the No Hackle do not extend the body. Because the body is the secondary trigger it should sometimes be slightly exaggerated. When you are fishing a No Hackle with wings that have been chewed up or purposely reduced to imitate a hatching dun or surface emerger, the body becomes your primary trigger.

The wings are the major stumbling block in tying the No Hackle. You may have difficulty perfecting this technique, but, with a little perseverance, it will become easy. When you can tie them perfectly, you might try the Sidewinder (Double No Hackle). Simply tie in a double wing on each side. Be certain the width and length of all wings are identical and tie them all at once. Note that adult mayflies have a double wing. The outside wing is much smaller than the primary wing and goes unnoticed by many anglers. Vary the colors and sizes of No Hackles to duplicate the adult mayfly duns you are imitating.

No Hackle

1. Dub and wrap a short section of body. This is incorporated into body taper, so keep it small. It looks large here because this is a size 10 hook. Split tail is tied along each side of this dubbing, which keeps it separated (split).

2. Select two to three hackle or Micro Fibetts fibers and secure them along one side of hook. Do the same on the other side, forming a split or V tail. Tail angles vary from 30 to 90 degrees.

3. Wrap body to about the 70-percent mark and position thread at the 60-percent mark.

4. Prepare two matching pairs of duck quill wings. These need to be much wider than usual—about half the length of hook shank. It is difficult to tie these wings in large sizes; they are usually reserved for size 14 and smaller hooks.

5. Tying occurs between the fingers, and it is not visible. See illustrations on page 80 for detailed tying techniques. At this time wings angle back too far. Carefully open them up. Wrap thread as closely as possible to back base of wing and finish body.

6. If wings split when you are tying them in place, you might be able to repair them with your fingers. Otherwise, you might wish to start over. Spread wings with bodkin or scissors.

7. Notice that wings are angled nicely and have not split. A drop of Flexament can be applied to inside base of wings to keep them from splitting as you finish fly. Allow to dry before continuing.

8. Dub material onto thread and take a wrap or two against inside of quill, which causes it to flare at a wide angle and stand more upright. Work dubbing in and out as well as you can.

9. Finish thorax, or front portion, of body. That's it!

10. Finished size 16 No Hackle with perfect wings. Notice individual fiber curvature of wing—rear fibers have the most radical curve.

11. Front view, showing wing angle. Notice how wings exit from side and bottom of body, which creates stability and realistic visuals. Also, notice split tail fibers.

12. Top view.

Chapter 20

CDC Callibaetis Spent Spinner

Renè Harrop

CDC Callibaetis Spent Spinner (House of Harrop)
- Hook: 900BL, sizes 12-16
- Thread: Tan
- Tail: Light blue dun hackle fibers, five to eight stiff, flared
- Body: Tan turkey biot
- Wing: Blue dun CDC tied spent (underwing)
- Overwing: Brown Z-Lon fibers
- Thorax: Tan Superfine

CDC Blue-Winged Olive or Baetis *Spent Spinner.*

CDC Tricorythodes (Trico) *Spent Spinner.*

CDC Rusty *Spent Spinner.*

A late season snow squall blew up the canyon, engulfing the eastern Oregon lake in a cold, dense swirling cloud. It was a good time to paddle my float tube to shore, stretch, enjoy a bit of lunch, and relax. Reclining in the grass, I watched as the squall blew over the distant ridge. A small patch of blue sky appeared overhead, and suddenly the sun shone brightly. I closed my eyes and soaked up the bright warmth.

A few minutes later, as I was about to stand, I caught the motion of a rainbow that was feeding about three feet from shore. I eased back down and noticed several *Callibaetis* duns and spent spinners floating on the glassy surface. I crawled to the shoreline and, enchanted, watched *Callibaetis* hatch from their nymphal cases while yesterday's hatch deposited eggs and became spent spinners. Most were eaten by monster rainbow inches from my face. I could focus on the tiny eyes of the duns and spent spinners and see the iridescence in the eyes of the rainbow. More *Callibaetis* popped up, and swallows began swooping on them, hovering, hesitating in flight and plucking them from the water. What a show!

In a 10-minute period I did not observe one newly-hatched dun or spent spinner survive. How could these insects maintain their population numbers? An hour later, tens of thousands began hatching. *Callibaetis*, swallows, and rainbows were everywhere! I crouched on the bank and caught and released two chunky four-pounders on two casts not more than two feet from shore. I broke my hook point off and continued to cast to feeders. Upon feeling the resistance, they would dart off, drop the fly, and continue feeding! I was easy on them because they are my friends. They provide me with immeasurable pleasure and insights into nature's complexity.

Tyers imitate spinner wings with poly yarn, Antron yarn, hen hackle tips, and Z-Lon. All work to a degree, but when Renè Harrop showed me his CDC spinner patterns, I knew they would be the most successful of all.

The techniques discussed include split, or V, tails, spent wings incorporating CDC and Z-Lon, and a turkey biot body. You will also practice tying a spent hackle-tip wing. Turkey biot is the short fibers (about an inch long) found on the short side of the first flight feather of a turkey wing. As you construct your imitation, remember that naturals are extremely delicate and transparent. Underdressing them is difficult. The tying sequence can also be altered to wing, tail, body, thorax.

CDC Callibaetis *Spent Spinner*

1. Before tying CDC Spent Spinner wings, practice tying a spent hackle-tip spinner wing. Select two matching hen hackle tips and tie onto the hook as you would a hackle tip downwing (Mosquito).

2. Stand wings up as you would when tying a divided hackle-tip wing (Adams).

3. Spread the wings flat so they extend 90 degrees. Wrap thorax tightly against back and front of wing. **Sometimes** thorax can be wrapped between wings without altering their shape. That's it!

4. A poly or Z-Lon wing is easily tied. If necessary, material can be positioned forcefully. Cut a length of material and tie it across top of hook as shown. One thread wrap has been placed over wing in this photo.

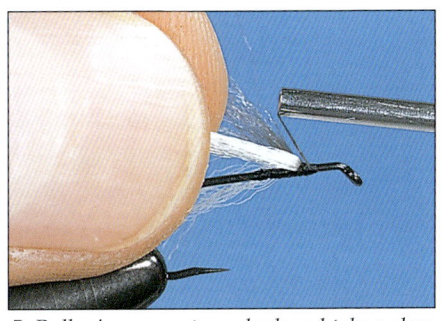

5. Pull wing nearest you back and take a close wrap of thread against it. This secures it at the proper 90-degree angle. Work thread around other wing so it is also secured in place. A figure-eight, or X, design also works well.

6. Spread and flare wing in a flattened position as shown. Trim any unwanted fibers and shape wing with scissors. This style of wing will be tied over top of the following CDC Spinner, only it will be much sparser.

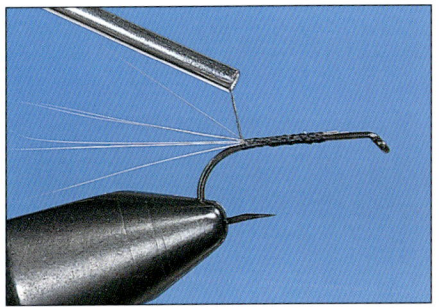

7. Tie in and flare tail fibers, keeping a level underbody. Moose is being used for visibility.

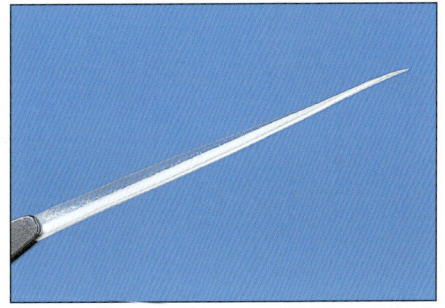

8. A single turkey biot, or quill. Tie onto hook tip first at tail area. Careful inspection will reveal a short ridge of fibers along leading edge of underside of each quill. This side should be wrapped down, shiny side facing out.

9. Secure turkey biot by **tip**. Use hackle pliers and wrap biot forward, forming body. Tie in a matched pair of CDC feathers like upright and divided hackle-tip wings (Adams), shiny sides facing inside. I usually tie the wings before the body.

10. Lift wings to vertical position. Wrap thread against front to stand wings up. Spread wings apart carefully and bring down to spent position. Do not fight CDC feathers or twist center stem; go with the flow. Do not wrap thread between wings.

11. Secure section of Z-Lon over top of CDC wing. Only a few fibers are necessary to produce desired sparkle. Dub thorax, wrapping between wings only if it does not twist them out of shape.

12. Finished CDC Callibaetis *Spent Spinner*. Note the flared tail.

Chapter 21

Blue-Winged Olive Thorax

Blue-Winged Olive Thorax
- Hook: 900BL, sizes 12-22
- Thread: Olive
- Wing: Blue dun turkey flat, thorax style
- Tail: Four to 10 blue dun hackle fibers, split
- Body: Olive to olive-brown Superfine or Antron
- Hackle: Blue dun, thorax style

Callibaetis Thorax
- Hook: 900BL, sizes 12-18
- Thread: Tan
- Wing: Mottled brown clump of hen saddle or brown partridge fibers
- Tail: Blue dun Micro Fibetts, split
- Body: Gray-tan Antron
- Hackle: Grizzly, thorax style

Black Thorax
- Hook: 900BL, sizes 18-26
- Thread: Black
- Wing: White turkey flat, thorax style
- Tail: Dark blue dun Micro Fibetts, split
- Body: Black Superfine
- Hackle: Natural grizzly, thorax style
- Note: Represents *Tricorythodes* mayfly adults

Dr. Edgar Burke wrote about thorax-style dry flies in the 1930s, but Vincent Marinaro refined, expanded, and popularized them with his classic book, *A Modern Dry Fly Code,* published in 1950. From close observation and experimentation on his home stream, the Letort in Pennsylvania, Marinaro concluded that trout keyed upon the wing above all other facets of adult mayflies. The thorax-style mayfly that is popular today is not like the one Marinaro describes in his book, but the centered single upright wing remains the same.

In sizes 12-14 the Olive Thorax is useful for Blue-Winged Olives, *Ephemerella cornuta,* and, in small sizes (16-22), for *Baetis,* which are long lasting and wide spread. Almost every unpolluted river and creek from sea level to the alpine zone is populated with these prolific, mostly olive and olive-brown-colored mayflies. They are usually most abundant when there would otherwise be little else to keep anglers and trout tuned toward the surface. Depending on climate zones, *Baetis* can be found hatching someplace in North America during every week of the year. I have seen huge hatches in Montana during September and October and in Alaska during August. *Baetis* are especially prolific in fast mountain streams. Anglers on the Deschutes River in Oregon see excellent *Baetis* hatches during the winter months between storms and spells of sub-freezing weather. When winds are calm, the small flies are out during midday. I like to scout the banks for feeders and usually find the trout receptive to adult *Baetis* in the back eddies.

During the off season, I usually have miles of river, or so it seems, to myself; while I don't always hook great numbers of fish, I find I don't need to. It is enough to watch the spectacle of duns easing off the water, hovering low for awhile and finally settling in the alders. Their glassy wings reflect the cool, low-angled sunlight, and I am reminded that spring will again overcome the short, shadowy days of winter. It is indeed a treat to enjoy dry fly fishing in January.

Baetis are small and go unnoticed by many anglers. Sometimes that "mystery hatch" is *Baetis*. At other times fish ignore the adults and secretly feed on the ascending nymphs. Anglers who hope to fish the *Baetis* hatch successfully often need small, nearly exact imitations. From a distance, adult duns appear dark olive in color, but, up close, their bodies are usually seen to have strong brown overtones.

Thorax-style mayfly imitations can be very effective, especially when fish are feeding selectively in shallow water or are hovering near

Blue-Winged Olive Thorax

the surface, looking through a narrow window. Because fish have a smaller window in shallow water, they naturally inspect any offering up close. Thorax flies have a reputation for fewer up-close refusals; once fish have a look, chances are good they will accept the fly. A useful formula for judging the window opening is to multiply the depth of the fish's lie by one-and-a-half. If a fish is holding two feet deep, its window will extend three feet to the front.

The techniques new to this pattern include a thorax-style wing, which is a single upright wing mounted near the center of the hook. Turkey flats, or shoulder feathers, are usually used to construct the wing, but a clump of soft hen hackle fibers or poly yarn is also popular. For aerodynamic and imitative purposes, single upright wings should be flattened with your fingers. When viewed from the front, they should be narrow. When viewed from the side, they should be wide. Upright and divided wings can be incorporated into thorax flies. These are often constructed from hen saddle or neck hackle and are burned to shape with wing burners.

Thorax-style hackle differs from standard hackle in that it is spaced out through the thorax area instead of being densely packed. A V is usually trimmed in the hackle on the underside, which allows the fly to ride low on the water. This in turn presents a bolder body outline.

Tiny Baetis *and* Trico *mayflies offer challenging fishing. Hatches can be prolific. It is easy for the angler's fly to be one of millions. During such times, fish feed at* their *leisure, and your fly must be at the right place at precisely the right time.*

Brookies!

86 Tying Dry Flies

1. Turkey shoulder (turkey flat) feathers make an excellent thorax-style wing. Tying technique is identical to tying a parachute wing, only a thorax wing is positioned more toward the center of hook shank.

2. Trim out center stem. If center stem is included in wing, it controls many fibers and acts independently of other individual fibers. Strip off all short fibers. Fibers that remain should all be about same length.

3. Position thread at about the 60-percent mark. Bunch turkey and measure correct distance against hook shank. Hold in position at tie-in area. Notice clump is narrow and wide (see Photo 7).

4. Correct tie in. Use up-between-the-fingers technique. After first wrap of thread is in place, wrap thread toward rear. Remember to make every wrap of thread count. Exert as much pressure as you can without breaking thread. Trim butt ends at angle.

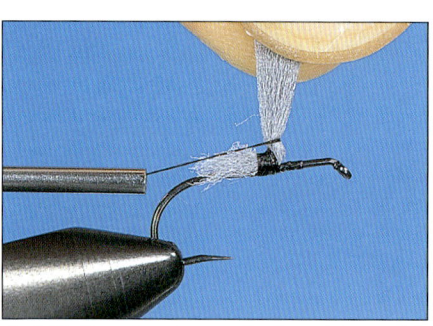

5. Lift the wing to vertical position with your right hand and take a horizontal wrap around and slightly up the base of wing.

6. A close-up of wing stand-up procedure. No other wraps of thread are necessary.

7. Complete wing tie down and dub a short section of body. Tie in a split tail at this location, two to three fibers along each side of dubbed clump.

8. Split tail is in place, and underbody is tapered.

9. Body is in place up to hackle tie-in position.

10. Term "thorax-style" hackle means hackle is tied standard style, shiny side facing back, except that it is evenly spaced throughout thorax area and is usually trimmed flat on underside. Prepare and tie in a hackle, shiny side facing back.

11. Remainder of body has been installed, and thread is at hackle tie-off position.

12. Wrap hackle through thorax area four to six times. Tie hackle off and finish thread head. If desired, wing can be started at 50-percent mark, leaving room for a dubbed thorax in front of hackle.

Blue-Winged Olive Thorax 87

13. Trim hackle on underside slightly shorter than hook gape. This allows fish to see a bold view of body and wing. Uncut hackle represents legs and helps balance fly. This is a front view.

14. Side view of finished Blue-Winged Olive Thorax.

15. Underside view.

16. Poly yarn also makes an excellent thorax-style wing. Tie-in technique is same as described in Photos 3 through 6. Tie in a section of poly yarn.

17. Trim off butt end.

18. Stand wing up and flatten it with your fingers before and after securing it in place.

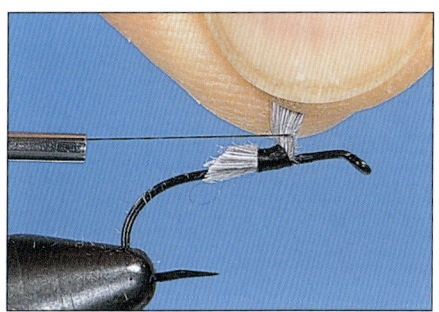

19. Once wing is in position, you can manipulate it to shape with your fingers and scissors. This style of wing also makes an excellent parachute-style fly. Thorax-style wings are secured at the 50- to 60-percent mark.

20. Stand up wing; lock into place. Wing is parallel to the hook, broadside to the side view.

21. Trim to shape.

22. Finished wing. This style wing could be incorporated into a mayfly drake iimitation, either with standard style or parachute hackle, or a thorax-style pattern. Other materials can be used for the wing.

Chapter 22

Parachute Adams

Parachute Adams
- Hook: 900BL, sizes 12-18
- Thread: Gray
- Wing: White calf, parachute style
- Tail: Grizzly and brown, or grizzly hackle fibers
- Body: Gray dubbing—muskrat, Antron, or Superfine
- Hackle: Grizzly and brown, parachute style

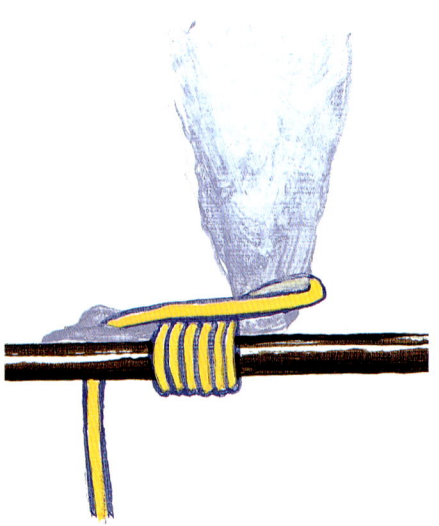

Place thread wrap around base of wing higher than level of thread.

Catch thread in butts and lock into place with three to four wraps of thread.

According to Ray Bergman, the original parachute was called a gyrofly and was introduced by A. C. Mills, Sr., through the former sporting goods dealer William Mills and Son of New York. The flies were under patent by William Avery Brush of Detroit in 1934 and were tied on a hook made especially for the purpose or hackle was wrapped around its own stem. Like many other original ideas and patterns, parachutes have evolved nicely and have been vastly improved upon and adapted to many other styles of tying.

Today parachute-style flies have a well-deserved permanent place in the angler's fly box. Their unique horizontal hackle construction usually allows them to flutter down lightly and land in an upright position without sacrificing floating qualities. They float flush in the surface film, emphasizing body size, color, and wing silhouette. They seem to represent a variety of food sources, including stoneflies, mayflies, caddisflies, and craneflies. Specifically, parachute-style hackle represents the spread legs of insects as they sit on the water's surface. Parachutes are also a possible representation of spent mayfly spinners and are useful to represent drowned and otherwise disabled duns.

Over the years I have added many effective parachute patterns to my fly boxes. I especially like a tannish-dun parachute that has consistently provided me with fine angling on Oregon's Deschutes River. I believe that fish take it for an adult cranefly of the family *Tipulidae*, which goes unnoticed by most anglers. Craneflies are often found by the hundreds clinging onto a single stone right at the water line.

Anglers love the Parachute Adams. Its gray-brown color combination is close enough to entice fish during many hatches. As an added bonus, it floats well and the white wing is relatively easy to follow, even in fast, choppy water. Apparently fish see it, too, because they eat lots of them.

When first seen, the technique for tying parachute hackle always elicits comments like, "so that's how it's done," or "isn't that tricky?" Parachute hackle is usually wound horizontally around a single upright wing. Each succeeding wrap of hackle is taken *under* the last wrap. If the wing base is not rigid, you must hold onto the wing when you wrap the hackle or the hackle will slip off over the top of the wing.

Once mastered, parachute flies will become a favorite at the tying bench and on the water. As you will learn in the following four chapters, this style of fly is versatile, and I encourage you to experiment on your own.

Parachute Adams

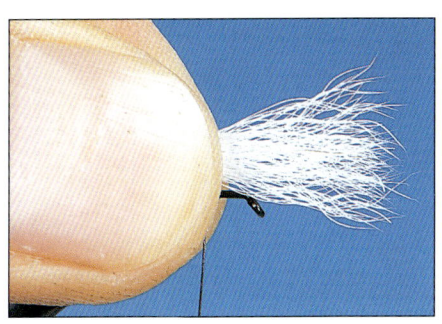

1. Position thread at the 80-percent mark. Select and stack some straight white calf hair. Take a loose wrap up-between-the-fingers and cinch it tightly. Wrap about 10 turns of thread back toward tail.

2. Wing should be secured as shown. Trim butts at an angle, but not too closely or it will be difficult to catch butts with thread when you stand the wing up.

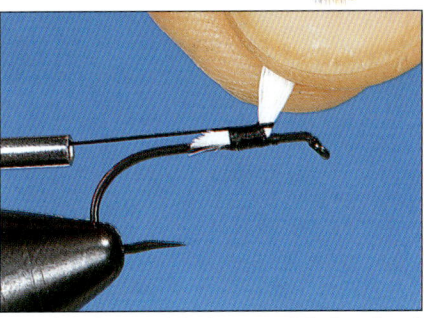

3. Hold wing upright in your right hand and bring thread around horizontally in front of wing. Wrap must be placed high on wing at position shown, or it will not stand up. If thread is placed too high, wing will slip away.

4. Once thread is wrapped in front of wing, it is brought around and through butts, as seen here. Next, take three to four standard wraps and lock stand-up horizontal wrap in place.

5. Select a few hackle fibers and tie them in just behind wing butts. Tie tail down back to tail area and trim off butt ends. Resulting underbody should look like this.

6. Dub and wrap body. Front part of body can be wrapped now or after hackle is tied in place. A touch-up turn or two of thinly-applied dubbing is often needed to cover up any noticeable thread wraps. Gray thread would not be noticeable through dubbing.

7. Tie hackle in behind wing flat, not on edge, with shiny side facing up. Hackle stems that are tied down can extend in front of wing. If needed, wrap more body in front of wing.

8. Parachute-style hackle is wrapped horizontally around base of wing. Hold onto wing as you wrap hackle. Wrap first turn of hackle at bottom of wing. Succeeding turns are placed below last wrap, pushing preceding turn of hackle up the wing.

9. To tie off hackle, sweep all fibers back between your fingers. Attach hackle pliers to hackle, freeing up your right hand. Tie off hackle at rear of thread head area. Notice bare hook behind hook eye. Do not crowd head area.

10. Place scissors against hook shank and make one clean cut. Pull hackle back with your left hand and finish thread head. Work hackle and wing into desired position.

11. Finished Parachute Adams.

12. Underside view. Note symmetrical hackle and tapered body.

Chapter 23

PMD Parachute

Pret Frazier

PMD Parachute (Pret Frazier)
- Hook: 900BL, sizes 16-18
- Thread: Yellow
- Wing: Mallard, parachute style
- Tail: Two blue dun Micro Fibbets or Betts' Tailing Fibers, split
- Body: Pale yellow to chartreuse yellow Superfine
- Hackle: Light ginger, parachute style, extending slightly beyond the body

PMD is short for Pale Morning Dun, which is short for *Ephemerella inermis* and its twin sister, *Ephemerella infrequens*. These two mayflies are responsible for much of the wonderful dry fly fishing encountered on the western fishing circuit, including Silver Creek and the Fire Hole, Deschutes, Big Horn, and Madison rivers. Duns begin to show in May and last through mid-August on some waters. They hatch routinely between 10 and 11 a.m. Fish can be seen at their feeding stations awaiting their daily fix well in advance of the hatch, but they are discriminating. These dainty insects are sizes 16 and 18 and are mostly pale yellow with overtones of brighter yellow, olive, and even chartreuse. *E. inermis* is more profuse and slightly smaller than *E. infrequens*.

Anglers should not overlook any stages, which will lengthen productive fishing time by three times or more. To take advantage of the many insect stages and angling opportunities they offer, fish your way *up* through the water column—bottom to top. Tie some nymphs, emergers, stillborn-cripples, adult duns, and spent spinners.

All surface stages of all mayflies do not provide fish and anglers with equal opportunity to capitalize upon them. PMD and *Callibaetis* duns and spinners are equally important, but Green Drake duns far outshadow spinners. *Trico* duns are less important than spinners, and Gray Drake duns are not nearly as important as the spinners. Such knowledge will aid tyers in stocking their fly boxes and help anglers prepare their angling strategy.

In recent years tyers have refined parachute-style flies to more closely imitate mayfly duns. The PMD Parachute, as tied by Pret Frazier, is indicative of this style. Pret lives in Sun Valley, Idaho, and, during the past 35 years, has fished his parachutes on Silver Creek. He explains that there are many advantages to his style of fly: prominent wing, thin body, realistic tails, good flotation, visibility, and durability. I like it because it creates an excellent low-floating silhouette complete with a scattering of legs. Pret's style of parachute is easily adaptable to most mayfly duns. Just plug in the size and color to suit your needs.

Techniques are about the same as for the Adams Parachute, with the exception of the forked tail and the use of mallard or teal for the wing. The wing tips can be trimmed to shape, and the thorax is pronounced.

Risers! Depending on their construction, parachutes fish well on any type of water and are visible to anglers. PMDs are found in almost all western streams. Somewhere in Montana, the big sky country.

PMD Parachute

1. Select a mallard flank feather with even tips and contrasting colors (good barring or mottling).

2. Strip off short fibers, leaving a feather with even tips as shown here. Not all feathers have even tips. Sort through them, put two or three feathers together, or prepare a clump of fibers as you would for a tail.

3. Cut out center stem so all fibers react individually.

4. Tie in a parachute-style wing and secure in place. Notice position of the horizontal thread wrap in front of wing. Proper position (on wing) for this wrap is just above top of butt tie-in, which creates leverage needed to hold wing upright.

5. Begin wrapping body. Stop at position shown.

6. Select two tail fibers and tie them in along each side of hook shank and body. Body helps separate fibers, forming a split, or V, tail.

7. Dub and wrap body. Tie in hackle. Parachute flies are often tied on size 14 and smaller hooks, and smooth dubbing (Antron or Superfine) is generally used.

8. Dub a pronounced thorax around wing.

9. Wind hackle and tie it off. Dub a little more fur to cover tie down. Finish thread head, which is very small. Trim wings to shape.

10. Finished PMD Parachute.

11. Finished PMD Parachute from below. Note body and thorax taper and hackle.

12. Frontal view—note shape of wing.

Chapter 24

Parachute Caddis

Ed Schroeder

Parachute Caddis *(Ed Schroeder)*
- Hook: 900BL, sizes 10-18
- Thread: Cream or color to match body
- Wing: White calf, parachute style
- Body: Blended natural hare's ear or other color to suit
- Wing: Mottled turkey clipped to V and tied tent-wing style
- Hackle: Grizzly, parachute style

Parachute Hare's Ear.

Parachute Stone.

Parachute Hopper.

California angler and tyer Ed Schroeder became frustrated with his friends and clients (and himself) not being able to see caddisfly imitations on the water under poor light conditions. Ed came up with the Parachute Caddis while fishing the Madison River in Montana. The Parachute Caddis is similar to Buz Buszek's King's River Caddis with the addition of a parachute wing and parachute hackle. It is one of only a few dry flies that have two different style wings: a parachute and tent-style wing. The addition of the parachute wing on the King's River Caddis greatly enhances fly visibility. The brownish gray color scheme allows the Parachute Caddis to effectively imitate many species of caddisflies, plus various stoneflies.

Spurred on by the success of the Parachute Caddis, Ed soon added the Parachute Mayfly, Parachute Hare's Ear, Parachute Olive Hare's Ear, Parachute Golden Stone, Parachute Emergent Caddis, Parachute Ant, and Parachute Hopper. This gives Ed a visible fly for almost every situation. According to Ed, his optometrist advised him that he has about 10 to 12 years left with his "Coke bottle" lenses before he'll need a red-tipped cane and a tolerant guide.

Many anglers use a bright piece of yarn or cork as a strike indicator when fishing nymphs. This allows anglers to detect the subsurface take. When the bright indicator quickly disappears from view, the chances are good that a fish has taken the nymph. Ed fishes the Parachute Caddis as an indicator. Fishing a dry fly and a nymph combination is not a new technique but few anglers employ it. The advantages of fishing a dry fly as an indicator are many. When a surface fly and subsurface fly are fished simultaneously, two feeding zones and two food sources are being covered. The floating fly can also act as a depth regulator for the nymph, allowing you to present your nymph at a specific and controlled depth. And, there is always the chance of hooking two fish at once! This can be both amusing and frustrating, especially when fish swim in different directions.

Tying the Parachute Caddis will show you how to construct a tent wing, which is very effective for imitating caddisflies. The parachute wing and hackle should not give you any trouble.

After this parachute course you should be ready for some experimentation of your own. Think about the various wing materials in conjunction with the tail, body, and hackle. Put together a parachute package that suits your needs. Good tying and good parachute fishing.

Parachute Caddis 93

1. Secure parachute wing at the 80 percent mark.

2. Install dubbed body.

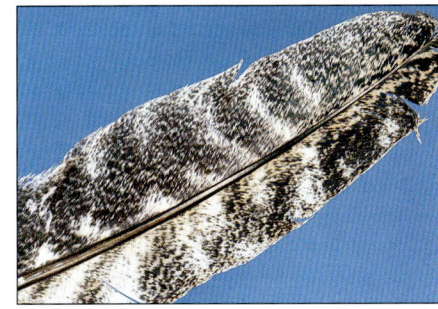
3. Select fine turkey quill fibers as they are less likely to split. Fibers close to stem (toward top of tail primaries) are coarse (thick), and split easily. Do not use coarse fibers. Choice turkey wing quill is shown.

4. To prepare turkey tent wing, apply Flexament to a turkey quill with bodkin or small brush and allow to dry. Flexament stiffens feathers slightly, but feathers remain flexible.

5. Trim a section of turkey wide enough to fold part way down sides of body.

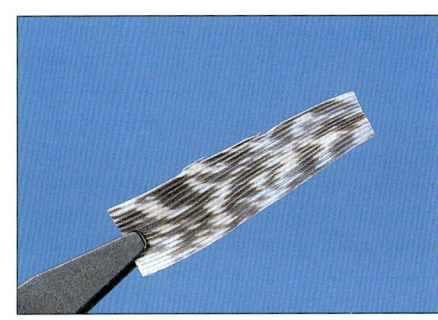
6. Trim the tip of the feather square.

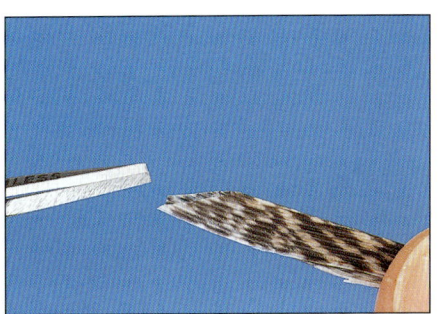
7. Fold it in half and cut feather at a 45-degree angle. Round pointed ends if desired.

8. The feather should look like this.

9. Position turkey wing flat over body behind parachute wing with your left hand and secure it, forming a tent-style wing. Wing should extend beyond bend of hook and fold slightly down along sides of body.

10. Wrap a little dubbing over tie-in area. Wrap several turns of thread up wing, forming a base for hackle, which will be wrapped from top down. Wrap dubbing in front of wing, finishing body. Tie in hackle.

11. Wrap hackle, taking several turns, making a tall and dense hackle. Keep hackle shorter than body.

12. Tie hackle off and finish a thread head. Finished Parachute Caddis.

Chapter 25

Green Drake Paradrake

Mike Lawson

Green Drake Paradrake (Carl Richards and Doug Swisher)
- Hook: 900BL, sizes 8-12
- Thread: Olive, yellow, or golden olive
- Wing: Natural dark gray or black elk
- Tail: Moose
- Body: Golden olive or olive elk, extended paradrake style
- Hackle: Grizzly dyed olive

Mike Lawson

Hexagenia *Paradrake*
- Hook: 900BL, sizes 6-10
- Thread: Yellow
- Wing: Dyed gray deer or elk
- Tail: Moose
- Rib: Yellow thread
- Body: Dyed yellow deer or elk
- Hackle: Grizzly dyed golden tan (substitute dark blue dun)
- Note: Represents Hexagenia limbata, a very large mayfly (1-1/4 inches long) that is found in lakes and slower streams.

Brian O'Keefe

Newly-hatched black drakes facing into the breeze and sun, ready to begin the mating ritual. Trout and birds will both begin a feeding frenzy.

Like many other anglers, I first encountered green drakes on the Henry's Fork at the Harriman Ranch in Idaho during an Independence Day weekend. Formally classified as *Ephemerella grandis*, green drakes are now classified as *Ephemerella drunella* or *Ephemerella drunella/grandis*. These beautiful, captivating insects drifted tall on the silent, slick current and were picked off at will by rainbows enjoying a hearty mid-morning brunch. Some of the largest trout are taken at the surface during this time. The green drake hatch offers anglers the best possible classic adult mayfly fishing; those who have not experienced it owe it to themselves to do so.

Some of my favorite Green Drake waters include the Big Wood in Idaho and quiet reaches of the Yellowstone River in Yellowstone National Park. Oregon's Metolius River has the longest hatch that I know of, with insects hatching over a six-week period during May and June. Best fishing often occurs on cool, damp, overcast, windless days.

During one memorable day at Copper Basin in Idaho, a loud summer thunderstorm battered the canyon. The combination of thousands of green drakes helplessly drifting on the surface, caught between exploding rain bombs, and merciless fish frantically devouring them created chaos. Imagine how the drakes must have felt, being bombed from above and sucked down from below!

The extended-body dry fly creates a realistic representation of the graceful and sometimes pronounced upright body curvature of larger mayfly adults, or drakes as they are sometimes called. Other large mayflies that lend themselves to the extended-style body include brown drakes, *Ephemera simulans,* which coincide with or closely follow green drakes; great yellow drakes (giant Michigan mayfly), *Hexagenia limbata*; and, to a much lesser degree because they usually crawl out onto the bank to hatch, gray drakes, *Siphlonurus occidentalis*.

The paradrake-style fly was originally designed and popularized by Carl Richards and Doug Swisher in their revolutionary book, *Selective Trout*. Mike Lawson and Renè Harrop refined the tying technique. This is not an easy fly to tie and make look good. The extended body that encompasses the tail and folds around the wing may require some practice and demands attention to detail. Green Drake bodies should be relatively short and robust. Take your time tying a few. Once you have the technique down, you will find this fly very satisfying to tie and to fish.

Green Drake Paradrake 95

1. Prepare a bunch of elk hair, which is tied onto hook parachute style at 60-percent mark. Cover hook shank with thread and secure wing in place. Work wing flat so that it spreads wide when viewed from side, narrow when viewed from front.

2. Select a dozen moose fibers. Even tips with stacker. Tie in tail as shown, which should be one-and-a-half-times as long as hook shank. You will eventually trim all but three fibers, which will extend from extended body, forming tail.

3. Prepare a bunch of elk hair about twice length of hook shank. Tie onto hook immediately behind eye with tips facing forward from hook. To secure, use the up-between-the-fingers technique, but allow hair to encompass hook as you secure it with thread.

4. Trim off butt ends in front of wing. Don't concern yourself that wing has been pushed out of shape. Bring it back to desired position with your fingers.

5. Bring elk fibers back along and around hook as shown, being certain that hair encompasses hook shank. Pull hair tight. This forms extended body.

6. Take two to three secure wraps of thread in front of wing and wrap thread back toward tail area as shown.

7. Hold tail and continue wrapping thread beyond hook shank. When rear position is reached, take two to three turns of thread and begin wrapping forward, crossing thread in an X pattern.

8. Position thread at front of wing. Trim butt ends of extended body and all but three tail fibers.

9. Prepare a hackle and tie it in parachute style in front of wing.

10. Wind hackle parachute style around base of wing. Use hackle pliers, freeing both hands.

11. Pull hackle away from tie-down area as shown and tie off. Minimize thread turns.

12. Trim hackle leftovers close to body. All tie downs should be on near side of hook so you can see them. Finish two half-hitches where thread is positioned and rearrange wing and hackle. You are finished.

Chapter 26

E/C Caddis

E/C Caddis (Ralph Cutter)
- Hook: 900BL, sizes 14-20
- Thread: Olive
- Tail (Shuck): Tan Antron or Z-Lon
- Body: Tan Antron dubbing
- Thorax: Olive green Antron dubbing
- Wing: Tan elk
- Hackle: Grizzly, parachute style

Note: *Ralph spent three seasons in scuba gear perfecting this pattern so that it presented the proper "dent" in the water exactly like an emergent caddis cripple. Ralph likes to loop the shuck because it creates a more effective surface impression.*

Caddis are found in nearly all waters. Spring Creek in New Zealand.

The Deschutes River in Oregon is known for its blizzard caddis hatches.

Lakes, ponds and slow moving waters also produce caddis. Lake Taupo, New Zealand.

My favorite dry fly fishing on Oregon's Deschutes River begins in late June after the big stoneflies and the angling crowds they attract are gone. After the sun slips below the canyon rim, the sweet odor of desert humidity and the flutter of swarming caddisflies suddenly fill the air. As the sky fades to dark purple, river sounds are amplified in the canyon's still evening air, and caddisflies sometimes reach blizzard proportions.

Caddisflies constantly bounce off my face, but it is a pleasant, reassuring sensation that signals the peak in surface activity. Rainbows boil to the feast. It doesn't last long, but it is intense. I prefer to fish choppy water because the rainbows quickly appear from nowhere and attempt to catch my bouncing and skittering offering. Many fish miss the fly, but it doesn't matter. It is exciting just to witness the chase. Once in awhile I get lucky and land a fish. I sometimes like to gently touch them and admire their beauty up close. I always wet my hands and release them carefully, gently, and quickly. To some readers it may sound like I have been affected by the scorching desert heat, but, when action is fast, I break my hook point off and laugh as fish play tug or war. It sometimes takes several seconds for them to lose interest in my game.

A hookless fly allows me more time to enjoy the sights, sounds, and smells and to observe hatching insects, which is truly amazing if you stop to think about it. The transformation of a water-breathing, swimming nymph into an air-breathing, winged insect is as incredible as a fish turning into a bird!

Caddisflies belong to the order Trichoptera, which means "hairy wings." Until Gary LaFontaine published his revolutionary book, *Caddisflies*, in 1981, caddisflies were confusing and only of passing interest to most anglers. Today anglers realize their importance to trout but imitations are mostly in the generic stage.

The E/C Caddis was designed by Ralph Cutter, who is an innovative tyer, freelance writer, adventure angler and author of *Sierra Trout Guide*. When not adventuring in far-off lands, Ralph and his wife Lisa live in Truckee, California, where they operate the Callifornia School of Fly Fishing.

E/C stands for emergent cripple caddis. The E/C Caddis is an excellent emerging caddis and adult caddis cripple. It is an effective mayfly dun/cripple imitation. It lands upright, rides flush on the surface, and is easily visible to anglers. I believe you may be pleasantly surprised by its effectiveness and versatility. Alter the color and size to suit your needs.

This pattern demonstrates tying a shuck and a unique style of parachute downwing.

E/C Caddis   97

1. Cover the hook shank with thread. Tie in Antron at the 75 percent mark on top of the hook and wrap thread back towards the bend of the hook. This will create the shuck.

2. Grasp the Angron between your thumb and first finger and hold it up and back over the top of the hook as you secure it in place. This allows specific placement of the material. Antron is tied directly on top of the hook shank. This maintains a level foundation.

3. The shuck can be trimmed to length now or later, or trim it part way to keep it out of your way and trim to exact length after fly is finished. Dub and wrap the abdomen (body) to the 65 percent mark, keeping it tight and slightly tapered.

4. Dub and wrap thorax. It should contrast in color with the abdomen and occupy roughly the 60-80 percent space along the hook shank. Do not crowd the hook eye. Position the thread at the tie-in location for the wing, which is at the 75 percent mark.

5. Select a bunch of medium-soft deer hair fibers about 1fi inches or longer in length so they are easy to handle. Soft hair ties down and flares more easily than stiff hair. This will form a down hairwing—see page 101 for more detail. Do not trim the butt ends.

6. Depending on the thorax taper, the hair may slip off the front. Even out the taper with dubbing or fill in slightly with thread. When wing is secure, wrap thread immediately in front of butt ends to stand them up. This helps facilitate installing the hackle.

7. Select, prepare and tie in a hackle. Note that black thread is used for photo visibility. Match thread to thorax color—it is much easier to cover and blends with the fly. Note the position of the wing and thread in relation to the hook eye.

8. Dub and wrap the thorax, covering thread wraps. Position thread immediately in front of hair butts as shown. This is where the hackle will be tied off. Note the empty space between the thorax and hook eye. Do not crowd this area.

9. Install the parachute hackle and tie off. Depending on the hook size, three to five turns should do it. Be careful not to tie down any hackle fibers. When the hackle is tied off, the thread only ties or wraps over the stem, not individual hackle fibers.

10. Once the hackle is secure and the tiny thread head is tied off, hold the wing butts as shown and trim close to hackle. One clean cut should do it.

11. Finished E/C Caddis, side view.

12. Finished E/C Caddis, top view. Note proportions of shuck (tail), wing and hackle. Use other color combinations to suit.

Chapter 27

Braided Butt Damsel

Blue Braided Butt Damsel
- Hook: 900BL, sizes 10-12
- Thread: Black
- Wingcase: Poly yarn; tie long (tall) parachute post, which will be folded forward to form wingcase, which will hold hackle back from hook eye
- Abdomen: Braided leader material colored with your choice of Pantone marker (olives, blues with black highlights)
- Thorax: Dubbing to match abdomen
- Hackle: Blue dun, parachute style
- Eyes: Burned monofilament

Note: Alter size and color for damsel or dragonflies.

Adult Damsel, Stalcup

Umpqua Feather Merchants

Damsel Country

A newly hatched adult damsel rests on floating vegetation. Colors range from tan to red, and olive to bright blue.

Heading for the patches of open water within the extensive weed beds on the windward shore of Oregon's Williams Lake, I propel my float tube purposefully. It is July, summer in high desert country, and damselfly time. Hatching adults crawl onto my float tube as I kick along. At first, I carefully remove and release them back into the water so they can hatch successfully, but soon there are so many that I am unable to keep up and I observe them as they seek a secure drying platform. They are all over my stripping apron and arms, face, and hair. Several are hanging from my rod and fly line, soaking up the warm sun, which hardens their wings so they can take flight. I like them. They are beautiful, friendly insects and mean me no harm. They provide some of the wildest trout fishing to be found.

As I cautiously approach the edge of the weeds, I can see tens of thousands of newly hatched damsels on top of the floating weeds. Hundreds are struggling on the water, and trout are enjoying the food orgy, pushing an enormous amount of water in their gluttony. I know they are big. They are all big here and very strong. I knot an adult damsel to my 3X tippet and pitch the offering inches from the weeds. My olive imitation parachutes gently onto the water and instantly disappears into a huge whirlpool. The fish surges into the weeds, pulling my rod tip into the water. I let it go, but the 3X tippet breaks like gut. I smile, open my fly box, and select another fly. I am well stocked and expect to lose a dozen or more flies today and am glad of it. I cannot think of a better use for them.

I like to fish adult damsels. Who wouldn't? The nature of the insect is such that they attract the big boys who know what they want and are not afraid to take it. Despite the heady action, adult damsel fishing is misunderstood and unknown to many anglers. The actual hatch or shoreward migration of damsels is well attended by anglers retrieving nymphs with intermediate lines, but little attention is paid to adults.

Look for adults on the water near floating vegetation, along shorelines, and adjacent to hatching areas. They become readily available to fish during windy conditions. It is not uncommon to see rafts of adults on the surface and trout sucking them down. Recently hatched adults may be light blue or olive in color. Mature adults are often bright blue, but pale blue and tan are common. Red damsels are common in New Zealand.

Construction of the wingcase, abdomen, and parachute hackle post are all a variation of the norm and unique to this pattern. This is also one of the few dry flies with monofilament eyes. Doubles for adult dragonflies. Alter color and size to suit.

Braided Butt Damsel

1. Tie a standard parachute wing in place at the 50- to 60-percent mark. Wing is tied with poly yarn.

2. Install a short section of dubbing as shown. This holds the extended body up at an angle.

3. Tie in a 1-1/4-inch section of braided leader butt material that has been colored with Pantone markers. Seal extended end with a match and tie in other end as shown.

4. Dub and install body to back of wing.

5. Tie in a hackle at the wing. Hackle should extend slightly beyond bend of hook when it has been wound in place. Hackle is wrapped parachute style.

6. Wind hackle in place around base of wing parachute style. Each succeeding wrap of hackle should be below last wrap. Tie hackle off at front of hook.

7. Dub and install body to the 90-percent mark.

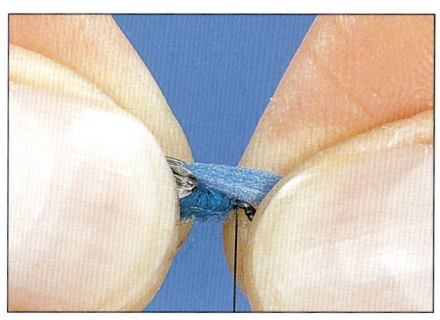

8. Stroke hackle fibers back away from wing. Pull wing tightly over top of hackle.

9. Tie wing down on top of hook at the 90-percent mark. Trim wing butts even with hook eye and apply Flexament to top of yarn.

10. Secure monofilament eyes onto top of hook.

11. Finished Braided Butt Damsel. This particular size is more suited for dragonfly adults. Slim down for adult damsels.

12. Olive Braided Butt Damsel

Chapter 28

Elk Hair Caddis

Umpqua Feather Merchants

Elk Hair Caddis, Tan *(Al Troth)*
- Hook: 900BL, sizes 10-20
- Thread: Tan
- Rib: Fine gold wire
- Body: Tan Antron
- Hackle: Blue dun, brown, or natural grizzly, palmered
- Wing: Light to medium natural elk

Umpqua Feather Merchants

Olive Elk Hair Caddis
- Hook: 900BL, sizes 10-20
- Thread: Olive
- Rib: Fine gold wire
- Body: Olive Antron
- Hackle: Olive grizzly, palmered
- Wing: Natural elk, color to suit

Umpqua Feather Merchants

CDC Caddis, Laible's
- Hook: 900BL, sizes 10-16
- Thread: Tan
- Rib: Fine gold wire or thread
- Body: Antron, color to suit
- Hackle: Natural dun CDC, palmered
- Wing: Elk

Note: Developed by European CDC Master Gerhard Laible. CDC is appreciated in Europe more than in the U.S. Give it a try.

The Elk Hair Caddis is to dry fly anglers what the Gold-Ribbed Hare's Ear is to nymph anglers. It works any place, almost any time, and is one of the most popular flies in the fishing world. It can be tied in endless color combinations and all sizes. I have an oversized plastic box with hundreds of assorted Elk Hairs. . .big ones, small ones, tiny ones, dark ones, light ones; just about every possible caddisfly color imaginable. I like to fish them, and equally important, I like to tie them. They are fast to construct, and I catch two dozen fish at the vise for every dozen flies that I tie!

Many anglers consider the Elk Hair Caddis to be the most productive general purpose adult caddisfly pattern. It fishes well in all water conditions—slow and fast water. Depending upon conditions, omit the hackle or beef it up to skate across the surface.

Al Troth developed the Elk Hair Caddis and first fished it on Pennsylvania's Loyalsock Creek in 1957. Al was fishing with Dick Leaver, who had been using a Skues' pattern, the Little Red Sedge. The tying technique of securing the palmered hackle with wire on the Skues' pattern fascinated Al, and he replaced the woodduck wing with elk hair and changed the body color to suit his needs.

The new pattern was supposed to sink, but, during the first trip astream, Al found that it floated like a cork and drove the fish crazy. Al believes the pattern is successful because it effectively represents a readily available and recognized food source and because it offers a small silhouette for the hook size. Compared to a size 10 Royal Wulff, which is about an inch long and has hackle an inch in diameter, a size 10 Elk Hair Caddis is nine-sixteenths of an inch long with about a quarter-inch of hackle extending below the hook shank. Additionally, it is an excellent floater, easy to see and to cast accurately.

You may find this fly easy to tie, but it allows practice tying a down hairwing and palmered hackle. The flies pictured on this page show a couple of variations. Al suggests tying a no-hackle Elk Hair Caddis for tough flat-water trout and a Royal Elk Hair Caddis for fast, choppy riffle water.

Elk Hair Caddis 101

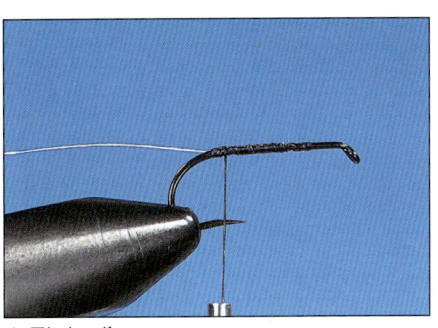
1. Tie in rib.

2. Dub body to position shown.

3. The Elk Hair Caddis has a palmered hackle, previously practiced on the Griffith Gnat. Prepare a hackle and secure as shown, shiny side facing forward. Tie-down area is short; secure hackle stem tightly.

4. Take two to three turns of hackle at head area, then begin wrapping it toward back in evenly spaced turns.

5. Use the over-the-top and hold-it technique and rest bobbin over top of your right hand. Size 14 to 18 hooks require four to six turns of hackle.

6. Secure hackle with two turns of wire at rear of hook.

7. Wrap wire rib forward to head area and tie off. Do not cut wire—work it back and forth until it breaks off. Broken end has a slight curl that prevents it from slipping out from under tying thread.

8. Select and prepare (stack) a clump of elk hair, which is tied downwing style. Wing should extend to about bend of hook, and tips should all be same length.

9. Proper tie-in location for wing. You do not need to keep head area completely free of thread because wing is tied at head area and butts are trimmed short. Do not crowd head area.

10. Wing is secured in place. Wrap a few turns of thread under, or in front of, wing and tie off.

11. Trim the hair even with the hook eye. Try to accomplish this with one scissors cut. Flare wing 180 degrees with your thumb.

12. Finished Elk Hair Caddis.

Chapter 29

Stimulator

Yellow Stimulator (Randall Kaufmann)
- Hook: 200R, sizes 6-18
- Thread: Fluorescent fire orange
- Tail: Light elk, flared wide
- Rib: Fine gold wire
- Abdomen: Fluorescent yellow Antron palmered with badger or ginger hackle
- Wing: Light elk, flared wide and tall
- Hackle: Grizzly, three to five turns through thorax
- Thorax: Amber goat

Orange Stimulator.

Rubber-Leg Stimulators. The peacock version has a CDC underwing.

Green and Tan Stimulators. White calf overwing allows angler visibility.

The Stimulator is my favorite dry fly, and I constantly find myself knotting it onto my leader. I fish it as an attractor, an exciter, and as a midday dredger when nothing else seems to be happening. I fish it in slow and fast water, lakes, spring creeks, and freestone rivers from Patagonia to the Arctic. I especially like it for imitating caddis in broken water and for skittering across the surface of a lake during a travelling caddis (sedge) hatch. It is also my favorite stonefly imitation, and I adapt it for all sizes and colors. In a pinch it will fish as a hopper, especially in faster water.

Fish view floating surface matter differently than we do. What looks like a perfect imitation to us might portray to fish neither the same image nor the impression (light pattern, water imprint) that denotes a specific food. We hypothesize what we *think* a fish sees and construct and fish our imitations accordingly, but these ideas are constantly changing.

I don't know why the Stimulator is so effective. Perhaps the light pattern or surface impression it creates is responsible. Maybe the silhouette or color combination is attractive, or possibly other characteristics, not yet contemplated, provide the magic. The Stimulator may be just different enough that fish do not remember having an earlier encounter with it and mistake it for real food.

The pattern is not unique, and it closely resembles many other downwing patterns. I have borrowed the "parts," incorporated some of my favorite materials and color combinations, and subtly improved on the tying style. I like to tie the Stimulator wide by spreading out the tail and wing. I also like it tall, and I spread the wing upward. This helps to stabilize the fly on the surface and creates the illusion of bulk and the blurred or fluttering image of wing movement. Palmered hackle adds to this illusion, and it should be stiff and tapered, smaller at the tail area. I like my Stimulators fresh, which ensures they react to tiny individual currents, portraying a buoyant, animated natural insect.

Much of the Stimulator's success can be attributed to versatility and the many size and color possibilities. Many anglers scoff at the importance of color, but I believe otherwise. Even a subtle change, like thread color, sometimes seems to make a difference.

The Golden Stimulator represents the Golden Stone, *Acroneuria californica*, and its sister species, *A. pacifica*, which is a favorite hatch throughout the West during June through mid-August. Oregon's Metolius River has perhaps the longest hatch; other favorite waters include the Williamson, Umpqua, McKenzie and Deschutes in Oregon, the Yakima in Washington, and all the famous waters in Idaho, Wyoming, Colorado, and Montana.

The Black Stimulator represents the giant *Pteronarcys californica,* commonly called a salmonfly, common in the Pacific basin from the west slope of the Sierras and Cascades to the Rocky Mountains. It also represents the largest of the stoneflies, *Pteronarcys dorsata,* which is important throughout the midwestern and eastern states. In the West, *P. californica* hatches just prior to *A. californica* and *A. pacifica,* and they often overlap. In addition, the Black Stimulator is my favorite dusk and starlight pattern. Try dragging, waking, or skating a size 6 to 10. Normally hesitant daylight feeders often attack aggressively. Even wary spring creek residents find this action difficult to resist.

The Yellow Stimulator is the most popular. Anglers often call upon it to represent the Little Yellow Stone, *Isoperla patricia, I. mormona,* and other related species. In most western waters, this hatch begins in June and often lasts through August. Anglers seldom see clouds of insects, but fish know what they are and seem to relish them.

Fish often take up a position along vegetation-lined banks, ready to accept any adult stonefly that haplessly falls onto the water. This is especially true of the larger species. When anglers continually pound the banks, fish move offshore; on the Deschutes this is often just beyond wading and casting distance. Fish may become wary of larger stonefly imitations and refuse or veer away from them at the last second. For this reason I like to fish an imitation one or two sizes smaller than the natural.

If I had one dry fly to fish in New Zealand, it would be the Green Stimulator, followed by the gold, peacock, black and tan patterns. There are many green stoneflies, beetles, and cicada, and this pattern generally does the trick. I once "hooked" the same fish five times in five minutes using a size 8 hookless Green Stimulator. It would pull the fly down three to six feet before letting go. You would think a five-pound rainbow would know better—or at least learn after the second mistake!

Adapt the Stimulator to your local needs. Numerous medium to small stonefly hatches throughout North America are imitated by a green, olive-brown, or other color Stimulator. Peacock is effective, too!

A Stimulator selection also provides *excellent* caddisfly fishing. My favorite colors include tan, green, olive, rust, and gray, sizes 14-18. Tie a small amount of calf body hair over the elk wing for better visibility. A size 8 Orange Stimulator is a good choice for the huge October caddis, *Dicosmoecus,* that hatch during late August through mid-October in the Northwest. Both steelhead and trout dine on these gorgeous three-quarter to one-inch caddisflies. Often a skating or dragging fly is just the ticket to action. Add rubber legs for animation and twitch it along.

The Seducer is a Stimulator with an added Shimazaki Fly Wing underwing, Krystal Flash and CDC. It looks real, and guides on the South Fork of the Snake River, Idaho, complain that seagulls pick it up!

The tying sequence of the Stimulator combines many previously discussed techniques, including a down hairwing and standard palmered hackle. Misjudging proportions and overdressing this style of fly is easy. The flared hairwing and tail create the appearance of bulk, but you want the fly to be dressed somewhat sparsely. Be especially careful to dub a small diameter body and to select a palmered hackle one or two sizes smaller than your hook would normally dictate. Rubber legs can be added.

Golden Stimulator
- Hook: 200R, sizes 6-10
- Thread: Fluorescent fire orange
- Tail: Golden-brown elk
- Rib: Fine gold or copper wire
- Abdomen: Golden blend of goat (gold, ginger, amber, yellow) and golden brown Hare-Tron, palmered with blue dun hackle
- Wing: Golden-brown elk
- Hackle: Furnace
- Thorax: Fluorescent fire orange Antron
- Note: Designed for the *Acroneuria* or golden stonefly hatch which occurs throughout the West.

The Black Stimulator represents dark stoneflies and is an excellent nighttime attractor.

Royal Stimulator—one of the favorites.

Black and Yellow Seducer.

Tying Dry Flies

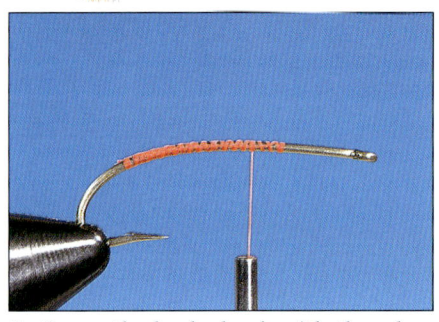

1. Cover the hook shank with thread as shown. Thread base is where body will be installed and where tail will be tied down.

2. Stimulator tails should be short, about the length of hook gape. After fly is completed, spread fibers wide with your fingers.

3. Stack a bunch of elk fibers and tie in tail, keeping it above hook shank as you secure it down along hook shank.

4. Finished tail. Design of Tiemco 200R hook is such that tail is properly positioned when thread hangs at hook point. Butt ends have been trimmed closely, at an angle.

5. Tie in rib at tail and dub body to the 60-percent mark.

6. Tie in hackle, with shiny side facing front. Hackle is tied palmer style.

7. Wrap palmered hackle, shiny side facing forward, taking two turns adjacent to each other at beginning.

8. Secure hackle with wire rib. Notice tie-down area. No unnecessary thread has been built up. Wrap a few more turns of thread forward on bare hook so wing has a good base.

9. Prepare wing and measure its length against hook shank. Wing should extend to about bend of the hook.

10. Secure wing in place as shown. Trim butt ends at an angle. If you forget to do this, compensate by building up a thread taper (step 12). After fly is finished, spread wing with your fingers so it is tall and wide.

11. Tie hackle in place and wrap with shiny side facing forward. This is contrary to standard-style hackling, but it matches the angled direction of the palmered hackle.

12. Taper wing tie-down with thread, eliminating abrupt drop off that would cause dubbing and hackle to slip or fall off this edge.

Stimulator 105

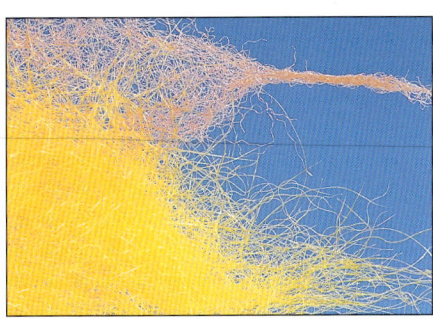

13. Goat is relatively coarse and must be handled differently than smooth, fine-textured materials such as Antron and Superfine.

14. Wax thread and spread a little goat along thread. Roll your fingers over dubbing two to three times. It will not be tight, but it will look okay when it is wrapped in place.

15. Goat is unruly when first tied in place.

16. Sweep all fibers back and take two to three turns of thread against thorax, angling any wild fibers away from hook eye. Using your fingers, pull out or trim away any remaining wild fibers.

17. Wrap hackle (shiny side forward) through thorax three to five times. Stroke hackle and thorax back after each wrap of hackle. Take last wrap of hackle at very front of thorax, which fills in space at front of hook. Tie off.

18. Capture and pull all goat fibers away from head area and finish thread head. This head is a bit large because of thread diameter; 6/0 would be much smaller. Finished Stimulator.

19. To tie the Seducer, complete steps 1-8. Trim hackle flat on top. Tie in a few strands of fluorescent yellow and pearl Krystal Flash.

20. Trim suitable section of Shimazaki Fly Wing and tie in downwing style, flat over top of body.

21. Install elk hair wing. Tie-in area looks bulky because of the large diameter thread we are using. Size 6/0 would greatly reduce bulk.

22. Tie in hackle and peacock herl.

23. Wrap peacock herl, forming thorax. Then, wrap hackle.

24. Finished Seducer. Other Stimulator variations include clipped hair bodies and rubber legs.

Chapter 30

Royal Wulff

Royal Wulff (Lee Wulff)
- Hook: 900BL, sizes 8-18
- Thread: Black
- Wing: White calf, upright and divided
- Tail: Elk or moose body
- Rib: Gold wire (optional)
- Body: Royal body (peacock, red floss, peacock)
- Hackle: Brown

Ausable Wulff (Francis Betters)
- Hook: 900BL, sizes 8-14
- Thread: Red
- Wing: White calf
- Tail: Moose
- Body: Dark tan or gray-tan Antron
- Hackle: Grizzly and brown
- Notes: Designed for the Ausable River, New York.

Grizzly Wulff (Dan Bailey)
- Hook: 900BL, sizes 8-14
- Thread: Black
- Wing: Medium elk
- Tail: Medium elk
- Body: Yellow floss or Antron
- Hackle: Grizzly and brown mix
- Note: Developed while Dan camped on the Madison at Hutchin's Bridge in 1936. Based on the original Wulff patterns, it was used extensively on the Yellowstone, Madison, Snake, and Flathead rivers. Today, 65 years later, the Grizzly Wulff is still popular on those waters and many others, from Alaska to Patagonia.

Lee Wulff, pioneer angler, tyer, and author, was the first to incorporate animal hair into wings and tails, which forever changed the construction of flies. The first Wulffs were tied with bucktail. At the urging of Dan Bailey, Lee Wulff called his new style of fly a Gray Wulff. A White Wulff soon followed. Dan Bailey and Lee Wulff first popularized the Wulff in 1929. Dan Bailey added two more to the series in 1936, naming them the Grizzly and Black Wulff. He continued to popularize the Wulff pattern through his famous angling shop in Livingston, Montana, which he opened in 1938.

Today the Wulff is considered a style of dry fly, and many standard patterns have been converted to this hairwing design, including the Irresistible, Green Drake, Adams, and Royal Coachman. The Royal Wulff is the most popular. Wulffs are versatile, durable, practical, and pretty. They were designed to float and be seen in fast-moving water. They were originally tied with bulky bodies to give fish something for which to rise, and this style of Wulff is still very popular. They can also be tied sparsely for slow water use. They are effective for all species of freshwater fish, from panfish to Atlantic salmon.

The Royal Wulff commands space in *every* fly box. Many anglers consider it an attractor fly, enticing fish under a wide range of water and light conditions.

The theory of attraction continues to entertain and elude tyers and anglers. Entering into the equation is color, or, more specifically, *light*. There is bright, dull, visible, and invisible (infrared) light, and there is no light at all. Size, shape, and animation of an imitation, as well as where, when, how, and what species is being angled for must all be considered. There are many possible shapes: tall, wide, narrow, low, bulky, or slim. A pattern can be designed to sit up off the water, rest flush on the surface film, or ride both on and in the surface film. It can offer a solid, or stationary, wing outline or that of a blurred, or moving, wing. All of these possibilities and more combine with water type to direct the tyer-angler in the quest for the best attractor pattern.

Gary LaFontaine, in his book *The Dry Fly, New Angles*, presents the best theory of attraction that I have read, and I recommend that all tyer-anglers read it. Regarding the Royal Wulff, Gary says, "It is not bright, it is half bright. . .under most conditions the Royal Coachman [Wulff] is a fly possessing both dull and bright materials. . .It is a rough simulation, either a mayfly in upwing variations or a caddisfly in downwing variations (Royal Trude), that has touches of brightness that focus attention and attract trout. As well as any fly, it stretches reality without breaking it in most situations on trout streams."

Royal Wulff

Wulffs are not difficult to tie. The most common problem is overdressing, or trying to crowd too much into too little space. Practice tying a sparse wing *before* you attempt the fly. Gradually increase the amount of wing material until you are satisfied with its bulk, remembering that too much bulk will cause the fly to fall forward. As with most dry flies, hackle is the other critical aspect. Leave plenty of room for hackle, which can encompass nearly half the hook shank. *This hackle area should be free of body material and unneeded thread wraps.*

Tying the Royal Wulff will explain how to construct a hair tail and upright and divided hairwings, plus the best method for tying a royal body, which consists of three equal parts of peacock, red floss, and peacock.

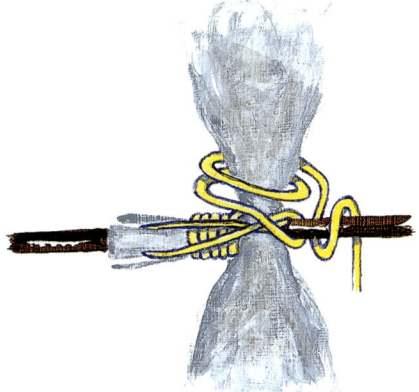

Wrapping thread around the base of the wings pulls all the fibers together and permanently separates them. Place thread at base of wings.

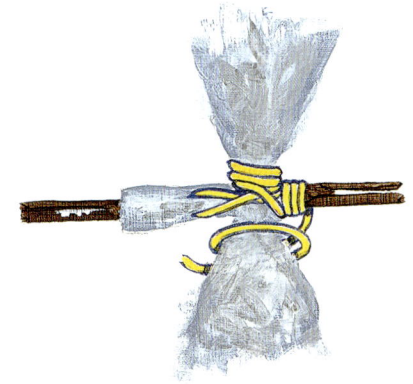

Grayling feeding in fast water are usually game for a Wulff pattern.

108 *Tying Dry Flies*

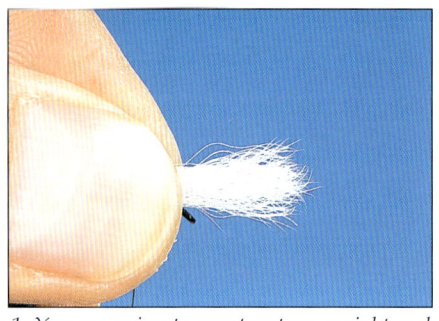

1. You are going to construct an upright and divided hair wing. Prepare a bunch of calf hair as you would for a parachute-style fly. Stack tips and remove all short fibers. Wing should be as long as hook shank.

2. Using the up-between-the-fingers technique, secure hair on top of hook shank at the 70-percent mark.

3. Trim butts at an angle as shown. Wing should be as long as hook shank, and all fibers should be same length.

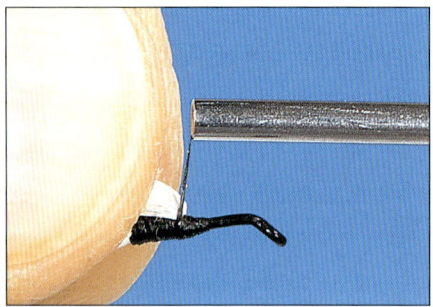

4. Pull all wing fibers back between your fingers as shown and wrap thread against front of wing. Do not take unnecessary wraps of thread that do not directly hold wing in a vertical position.

5. Wing has been positioned vertically. If your wing looks like this, you are ready to proceed.

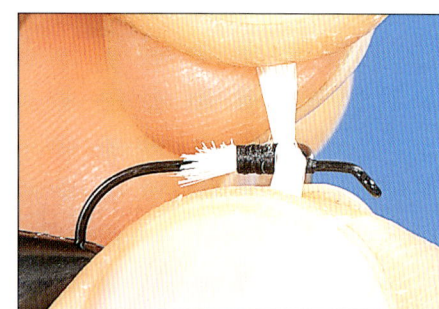

6. Split wing in half with your fingers.

7. Cross thread in an X between wing halves. Catch thread in butts on near side of hook and cross over between wing halves to far side of hook in front of wing.

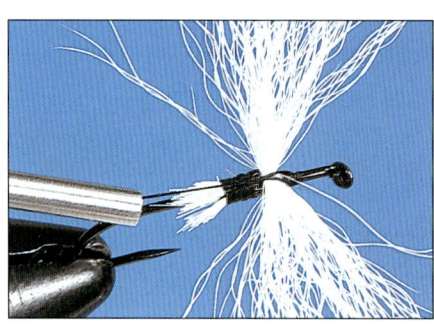

8. Wrap a turn of thread in front of wing.

9. Cross between wing halves to far side of hook, catching thread in butts. This completes the X between wings, and they are divided.

10. Lock the X wrap of thread in place by taking a couple of turns of thread around the wing butt area. Next, group the wing fibers together by wrapping thread around their base.

11. Thread is wrapped around base of each wing about six times (called "posting"). Hold one wing with thumb and index finger and throw bobbin around wing with your other hand, catching it as it comes around.

12. Wings are finished, and butts are tied down. Notice smooth body taper and where wing has been posted with thread. Tie in the tail.

Royal Wulff 109

13. Tail butts should taper into tapered underbody as shown. Once thread is wrapped to end of tail taper at the 50-percent mark, underbody will be smooth. See step 14. Tie in peacock.

14. Wrap peacock, forming rear third of body. Peacock herl must be thick. If desired, tie in a section of fine gold wire as a reinforcing rib. Thread is positioned at peacock tie-off area.

15. Peacock is in place and has been tied off. Do not trim off end. Same piece is used for rear third and front third of royal body. Tie in red floss.

16. Wrap red floss and tie off, forming middle section of body.

17. Wrap peacock, forming front third of body.

18. Front third of royal body is in place. It appears that peacock is crowding wing and hackle area, but once peacock is swept back and first turn of hackle is taken through or over last wrap of peacock, there is plenty of room.

19. Wrap the rib and trim the ends of the rib and peacock. Two saddle hackles have been tied on edge, and thread has been positioned at hackle tie-off position. Note bare hook shank behind eye where thread head will be placed.

20. The hackle has been wrapped densely behind and in front of wing to tie-off area. Hackle is tied down. Note position of tie down on top facing side and that three wraps are in place back from eye.

21. Hackle tips have been trimmed close. Note that no wild hackles point forward over the hook eye. Finish thread head.

22. Finished Royal Wulff. Notice proportions, hackle density, and wing height. Note royal body and thickness of peacock herl.

23. Top view. Note posted wings, density of hackle, and general proportions.

24. Front view. Note symmetry of wings.

Chapter 31

Irresistible

Umpqua Feather Merchants

Adams Irresistible
- Hook: 900BL, sizes 8-18
- Thread: Black or tan
- Tail: Moose or Adams (grizzly and brown mix) hackle fibers
- Body: Caribou, trimmed to shape
- Wing: Grizzly hen hackle tips, upright and divided
- Hackle: Adams (grizzly and brown mix)

Umpqua Feather Merchants

Wulff Irresistible
- Hook: 900BL, sizes 8-18
- Thread: Black or tan
- Tail: Moose
- Body: Caribou, trimmed to shape
- Wing: White calf body or calftail, upright and divided
- Hackle: Brown or Adams (grizzly and brown mix)

Heading out, circa August, 1966: Jack, Jay, and Lance at the trailhead. Note the gear and packs. Jack carried the raft, oars, and steel pump. Jay had too much unneeded dunnage and couldn't make the pass. Lance and I carried photo gear and food. We struggled, improvised, laughed at adversity, and tested our freedom. Wilderness teaches many things, especially the value of wilderness.

The Irresistible is said to be the most dreaded dry fly to tie, especially if hair wings are incorporated. It is difficult to tie well, and years ago few tyers could or would supply them on a commercial basis. Jack Dennis is one of the best, and he always had orders for all he could produce. When my brother, Lance, and I first met Jack in the summer of 1966, we were on high school vacation, and Jack was tying Irresistibles in his father's combination liquor-sporting goods store outside Lander, Wyoming. Lance and I were heading into the high country of the Wind River Mountains and stopped in to get acquainted. Jack was covered with caribou hair from his feet to his teeth. Even though Jack sold us a king's ransom in unneeded tackle, we still invited him to join us on our golden trout adventure. He was unable to leave until he finished a big Irresistible order, so Lance and I helped him. In the process, we learned how to tie Irresistibles and began a life-long friendship.

Soon four of us were headed up the trail from Dickinson Park. Lance and I had down mummy bags, Jack's friend, Jay Martin, had an old army bag that weighed too much, and Jack was packing a space blanket that didn't weigh enough but which he claimed would keep him warm. I remember Jack saying, "The astronauts use these in space. They're great. It's all I'll need." He *almost* convinced Lance and me to buy space blankets and leave our mummy bags behind. The first night, we camped at 11,100 feet, and Jack didn't get much sleep because he was busy walking back down the trail for wood to keep the fire going. Fortunately for Jack, Jay decided the price of golden trout was too steep and hiked out, leaving Jack his bag. The three of us had the type of adventure all kids should have time and time again. In retrospect I understand what Aldo Leopold said when he wrote, "I am glad I shall never be young without wild country to be young in. Of what avail are 40 freedoms without a blank spot on the map?" Unfortunately, wild places continue to disappear, and they cannot be replaced.

The Irresistible style of fly has been around for many years. Ray Bergman reports that, as far as he knew, Joe Messinger of Morgantown, West Virginia, originally put a clipped hair body together with wings on a dry fly. In 1939, the legendary Catskill tyer Harry Darbee and a friend, Percy Jennings, arrived at a pattern dubbed the Rat-Faced McDougall. It was a clipped deer hair hackle-tip wing pattern similar to the Irresistible of today. Many new patterns are refinements or variations of older ones, and the Irresistible has been reworked and refined many times. Hank Roberts of Boulder, Colorado, refined and tapered the body in the early 1960s, and Jack Dennis has made other subtle improvements and helped to popularize it.

Trimming the Irresistible is the most difficult aspect. Jack likes to trim the bottom first, making certain it is flat and that the body will not block the hook gape. I like to trim around the tail so I don't accidentally trim it in the shaping process. Trim the top and sides into an oval, or wedge, shape. Consider tying an Adams Irresistible with hackle tip wings before progressing to the Irresistible Wulff with hairwings.

Once mastered, there is a great deal of satisfaction in tying Irresistibles, and you will enjoy showing them off to other anglers. It is a fine floating fly and an excellent fish getter.

Irresistible water!

A rainbow prowls the surface.

112 Tying Dry Flies

1. Wrap a thread base. Prepare and stack moose tail and secure in place. If tail rotates easily around hook, start over. Foundation must be solid. Position thread at tail.

2. Trim section of caribou. Choice portion of hair is next to skin. Trim hair close to skin and trim off tips. You should have about a one-inch-long bunch of hair that is about the diameter of a pencil.

3. Hold caribou in your left hand and position it on top of and parallel to hook. Pinch caribou with your fingers and hold it down against hook shank.

4. Take loose wrap of thread between your fingers and cinch straight down. Take another wrap at same location. Back your fingers off slightly. Hold caribou in place and wrap four to five turns forward through caribou to bare hook shank.

5. First one or two turns of thread spin and flare caribou. Succeeding wraps secure it in place. When wrapping forward through caribou, be certain not to tie down individual fibers. Using thumbs and forefingers, pack caribou tightly toward first wrap of thread.

6. Small flies require one clump, larger flies two or three clumps. Tie in a second clump. Repeat first tie-in process. Work with shortest possible bunch of hair because it is less likely to get caught around hook point or in bend of hook.

7. Second clump is in place. Notice length of hair. For this pattern, body should occupy 50 to 60 percent of hook shank.

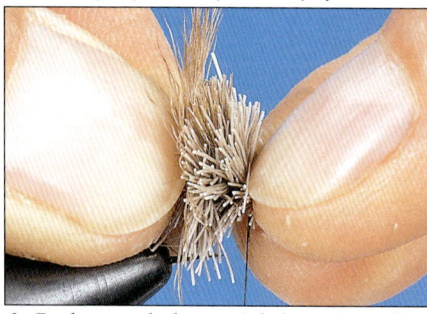

8. Pack second clump tightly against first clump. Packing caribou is a very important aspect of tying clipped hair flies. If hair is not packed tightly, it will not look right when it is trimmed to shape. Half-hitch thread twice and trim it off.

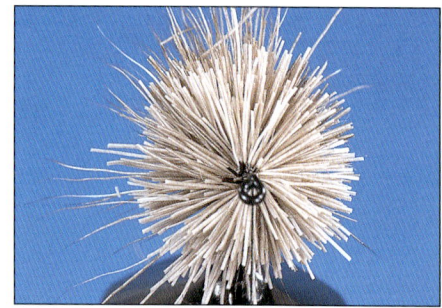

9. A front view of spun caribou. Remove hook from vise.

10. Trim around tail first; it is less likely that tail fibers will be cut with ensuing cuts. Slide scissors point down tail at a right angle to base of caribou and make a cut. Continue to cut around tail.

11. This photo shows tail cut clear of all fibers. Body can be trimmed to any shape. Try a flat bottom with a rounded taper on top and sides. Trim bottom next. Trim it flat and close to hook shank.

12. The body has been trimmed flat. There must be plenty of space between the body and hook point. From this point it is easy to round and taper remaining fibers along top and sides.

Irresistible 113

13. Finished body with thread positioned to tie in upright and divided hair wings. Body occupies about half the hook shank.

14. Prepare a calf wing and secure at the 70-percent mark.

15. The wing has been tied in place. Note position.

16. Position wing upright by wrapping a thread "wall" directly in front. (See Royal Wulff, page 108.)

17. Trim butt ends of wing.

18. Divide wings and position thread at hackle tie-in location as shown.

19. Two hackles have been prepared and tied in place. Thread has been positioned at hackle tie-off area. Notice bare hook shank where thread head will be placed.

20. Hackle has been wound in place, and thread head has been tied off. Finished fly is half hackle and half body.

21. Front view, showing wing angle and hackle length. Notice that wing is slightly longer than hackle. This is standard proportion for a hair-wing dry fly.

Hunting trout, South Island, New Zealand.

Chapter 32

Humpy

Fluorescent Green Royal Humpy
- Hook: 900BL, sizes 8-18
- Thread: Fluorescent green 6/0 or single strand floss
- Wing: White calf body or calftail, upright and divided
- Tail: Moose
- Overbody: Moose
- Body: Fluorescent green thread or floss
- Hackle: Brown and grizzly

Yellow Royal Humpy
- Hook: 900BL, sizes 8-18
- Thread: Bright yellow
- Wing: White calf body or calftail
- Tail: Light elk
- Overbody: Light elk
- Body: Bright yellow thread
- Hackle: Ginger, badger, or brown
- Note: Most popular Royal Humpy color. Fished throughout the angling world with spectacular results. Especially useful for fishing pocket water.

Red Humpy
- Hook: 900BL, sizes 8-20
- Thread: Bright red
- Wing: Elk
- Tail: Elk
- Overbody: Elk
- Body: Red thread
- Hackle: Brown, Adams, or badger

The Humpy is the paradox of fly patterns and is one of the greatest surface flies ever devised. It represents nothing and everything. It is not a specific representation of any food source; yet, depending on its construction, the Humpy can represent caddisflies, stoneflies, mayflies, midges, and terrestrials. It floats low and rides high, offering excellent visibility to both fish and fisherman.

Its origin is cloudy, but Jim Quick, in *Trout Fishing And Trout Flies*, claims an all deer-hair fly called the Algonquin was used by Indians in northern Michigan decades ago. The Horner Deer Hair, or Little Jack Horner, a cousin to the current Humpy, was created by San Francisco tyer Jack Horner in the early 1940s.

Pat Barnes, along with his wife Sig, guided and operated a fly shop in West Yellowstone, Montana, for 36 years. Pat relates how he was fishing Cliff Lake with George Fay, a friend of Jack Horner's. Pat picked up George's rod, made a cast, hooked a fish, and lost it. Borrowing another fly, Pat cast again and hooked the fish he had just lost! Before releasing it, he removed a length of leader and the fly. Pat placed the fly in his hat. The next day several shop customers asked about the fly in his hat with the leader attached; before long the Barneses were producing a fly called the Little Jack Horner. No one would accept the name, and people began to ask for "a few of those goofy looking deer-hair flies that fooled a rainbow twice in 10 minutes." Goofy looking was shortened to goofy bug and then to Goofus Bug.

In the early 1950s Dan Bailey cataloged an identical fly and called it the Poor Man's Wulff but tied it with red, yellow, and green floss underbodies. In the mid 1960s, I recall seeing Goofus Bugs in West Yellowstone and Humpies in Jackson Hole. They were one and the same, and both areas claimed it as their local pattern.

Jack Dennis, a master at tying hair flies and the author of three fine tying books, *Western Trout Fly Tying Manual*, *Western Trout Fly Tying Manual, Volume II,* and *Tying Flies With Jack Dennis and Friends,* refined and popularized the Royal Humpy in the 1970s. Jack relates how the Royal Humpy came about: "I worked out the mechanics of tying the Royal Humpy, but the man responsible for its existence is a former guide, friend, and companion of mine, the late Charles Ridenour."

Jack and I spent the summer of 1968 tying flies at Dick Boyer's Rod and Reel shop in Jackson, Wyoming, and I learned many hackle and hair tricks. Today Jack operates Jack Dennis Sports in downtown Jackson, produces fishing and fly tying videos, and lectures throughout the world.

My earliest fishing experience with the Humpy was during our family summer vacations in the early to mid-1960s on Montana's Madison River below Quake Lake and later on the Green River outside Pinedale, Wyoming. Since those quiet glory days of angling, the Humpy has provided me with wonderful fishing from the small brush and seldom-fished canyon streams along the eastern Sierra and Andes mountains to the cold rainbow rivers of Alaska.

I like the Royal Humpy best because it is usually easier to see, and it is pretty. The fluorescent green pattern is my favorite, but yellow, red, black, dun, and orange are all good. Ultra violet light activates fluorescent material, making it visible under low light conditions, which probably helps to account for the success of the Fluorescent Green pattern. Gary LaFontaine, in *The Dry Fly, New Angles,* has some interesting thoughts about green flies.

I often fish a size 6 or 8 Royal Humpy in waters where there is not an abundance of insects, especially throughout Alaska, Argentina, and New Zealand. Fish in food-poor waters are seldom selective (but they are spooky) and are usually delighted to find a large morsel coming their way. Perhaps big flies have a heavy "imprint," which allows fish to see them underwater before they would otherwise become visible in a trout's window. At other times, when trout are settled in deeper water and their window is wider, they are tantalized by a big gulp and finally succumb!

One of my most memorable days fishing a big Humpy was at a stream junction near Makarora, New Zealand, a favorite hangout of mine. I had the entire river canyon to myself and rose a two- to four-pound rainbow on every other cast with a size 6 or 8 Humpy. I have revisited this location several times since and have not found fishing nearly as fast as on my first visit. For once I was in the right place at the right time—a welcome change from the proverbial "you should have been here yesterday," or "wait until tomorrow."

I have also encountered rampaging British Columbia summer steelhead on big Humpies, which is a thrill never to be forgotten. The point is, don't limit yourself to what, where, and how everybody else fishes. Be a geek. Think for yourself. . .break on through to the other side.

The techniques presented here include a review of upright, divided wings, plus how to form a smooth humped back, or overbody. There are a couple of methods of tying the overbody, but I feel the most effective and easiest is to tie the wing in first. The tail and overbody are one section of hair. This allows you to tie a near-perfect fly every time. Tyers who are having trouble making a neat body or securing hair with size 6/0 thread should try 3/0.

Jack Dennis Humpies. Note Jackson Hole style and dubbed bodies.

Orange "steelhead" style Humpy. Tie this style on TMC 7989 or 7999 hook.

Blonde Humpy. Use your imagination—there are many color combinations.

Royal Humpies: Yellow, tied with elk and calf body; Red, tied with moose and calf tail.

Snake River cutthroat are native to Jackson Hole and love dry flies.

Grand Teton National Park offers fine angling and spectacular scenery.

Double Humpy, popular in the Jackson Hole country.

116 Tying Dry Flies

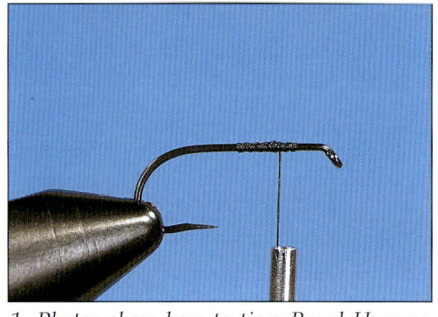

1. Photos show how to tie a Royal Humpy, which has upright and divided white calf wings instead of the deer or elk wings called for on a regular Humpy. Secure thread at the 70-percent mark and prepare wing.

2. A properly prepared wing; all fibers are same length.

3. Measure wing length and secure in place.

4. Trim butt ends at an angle and proceed to stand up and divide wing, same as you did for the Royal Wulff wing.

5. Holding wing upright with your fingers, wrap thread in front of wing to keep it in an upright position.

6. Divide wing. Wrap thread around base of wing. Cover hook with thread (foundation for tail). Position thread at tail tie-in location. Bulk is built up because we are tying with nylon floss for visibility.

7. Prepare section of moose or elk about five times length of body. All fibers should be same length. Tie tail in place at the 30-percent mark. Wrap thread back to tail area and back to original tie-in area at 30-percent mark.

8. Wrap thread forward to 50-percent mark, covering body area with thread.

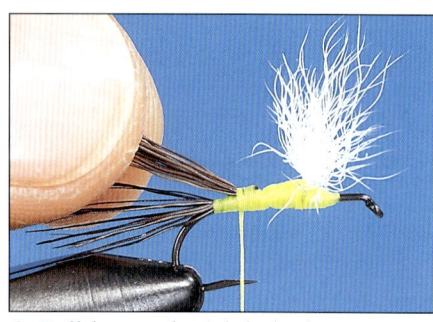

9. Pull butt ends tightly back over top of body, and wrap thread back to tail area.

10. When moose is pulled forward, forming overbody, there should be no thread showing between tail and overbody. If there is thread showing, moose has not been secured back far enough on top of tail.

11. Position thread at the 50-percent mark and pull moose over top of body, forming overbody. Keep moose directly over top of body. Pull overbody tight.

12. Hold overbody in place with your right hand and secure temporarily. Don't worry about pushing wings forward. Change hands and hold overbody in place with left hand and secure tightly.

13. Trim butts at an angle behind wing. Overbody is directly over top of hook. There are no fibers along side of body. Thread body is smooth, and thread is positioned to tie in hackles.

14. Two saddle hackles have been prepared and tied on edge. Thread has been positioned at huckle tie-off area. Note empty space reserved for thread head.

15. Wrap three to four turns of hackle behind wing. If hackle is placed tightly against back of wing (and it should be), wing angles slightly forward.

16. Stroke wings back and place first wrap of hackle immediately in front of wing. This first tight wrap stands wing back up. Wrap three to four turns of hackle in front of wing.

17. Hackle is in place and tied off. Sweep all hackle fibers back between your fingers. This allows a clear view of thread head area. Trim tips and take four to six turns of thread to finish head.

18. Side view of finished Royal Humpy. Notice proportions.

19. Top view, showing wing angle and overbody. Wings are stacked evenly, and hackle is packed densely.

Humpies are a multi-purpose attractor and can be productive in both lake or stream. Mini humpies double for midge. Magnum humpies can work for cicada, which are common in New Zealand, where the water is like the air—transparent.

118 *Tying Dry Flies*

Umpqua Feather Merchants

MacSalmon *(Al Troth)*
  Hook: 5263 or 200R, sizes 4-6
  Thread: Fluorescent fire orange
  Body: Braided macrame cord, color to suit (orange, rust, gold)
  Underwing: Black, pearl and fluorescent orange Krystal Flash and Shimazaki Fly Wing, tied tent-wing style, extending slightly beyond cord body
  Overwing: Light and dyed orange elk, downwing style
  Collar: Dark moose
  Head: Dark moose
  Legs: Black round rubber
  Note: Pattern can also be tied with a bullet head and rubber legs as pictured here. See page 132 for original dressing.

Al Troth

MacHopper *(Al Troth)*
  Hook: 5263, size 8
  Thread: Orange
  Body: Yellow braided macrame cord
  Underwing: Golden yellow Fly Wing, trimmed to shape
  Overwing: Yellow deer or elk
  Legs: Flat yellow rubber; keep three strands together, knot and tie in place along each side of body; trim off two strands at end knot joint (legs beyond knot are smaller diameter than front section)
  Collar: Olive or olive-yellow deer
  Head: Olive or olive-yellow deer, trimmed to shape, or bullet-head style

Chapter 33

MacSalmon

Al Troth is a master fly tyer and angler living in Dillon, Montana, where he guides and ties some of the prettiest and most exact flies you will ever see. The MacSalmon and MacHopper are two of his most unique patterns.

Stoneflies belong to the order Plecoptera. They probably received their name because the nymphs are commonly found in rocky sections of streams and often crawl out of the water onto rocks, where they transform into adults. Except for isolated cases, stoneflies are restricted to moving water. Species preferring fast-water habitat are best known, although many species inhabit slower water. In many fast-water streams such as the Madison and Big Hole in Montana, the Deschutes in Oregon, and the Gunnison in Colorado, stoneflies are believed to be the primary or secondary food source of trout. In many streams stoneflies are especially important to trout during winter months, when small, dark species are sometimes abundant.

Because nymphs crawl out onto the bank to hatch and mate, they do not create the feeding opportunities that mayflies and caddisflies do. Nonetheless, nymphs provide anglers with year-round action. When adults become available, both fish and anglers become very excited. Adult stoneflies become available to fish when females run across the water or dip their abdomens onto the surface of the water to deposit eggs. Spent and drowned insects provide many meals. When strong winds blow adults onto the water from their streamside vegetation, action can be explosive.

There are many adult stonefly imitations. Several incorporate various braided yarns or macrame cord to represent the long abdomen of the adult. This style of imitation is very effective for the larger *Pteronarcys* and *Acroneuria* species. It is also an excellent catcher of anglers.

The macrame body is easy to install, and the technique for the over and under downwing and clipped head has been discussed previously. A bullet head can be substituted for the trimmed hair head (see Henry's Fork Hopper, Chapter 35). Rubber legs can also be added to the bullet head. In addition, we are adding some Krystal Flash to the wing. The *original* MacSalmon as tied by Al Troth is pictured and described on page 132. This style of fly also lends itself nicely to hopper imitations.

MacSalmon

1. Cover hook shank with thread. Tie two half-hitches and cut thread. Cut a 7/8- to one-inch section of 3.5mm (3/16-inch) diameter macrame cord. Using a match or lighter, melt end to prevent it from fraying.

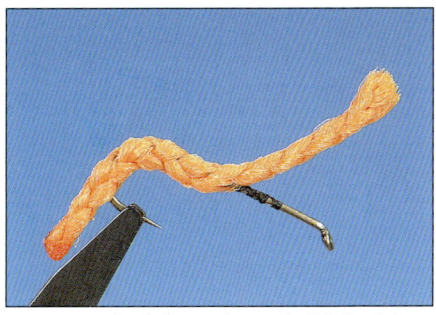

2. Remove hook from vise and slide hook into the cord about 3/8-inch from melted end. Replace hook in vise.

3. Attach tying thread. Secure macrame at the 60-percent mark with about 10 tight wraps of thread. Apply Zap-A-Gap to tie-down area and allow to dry. Tie in Krystal Flash.

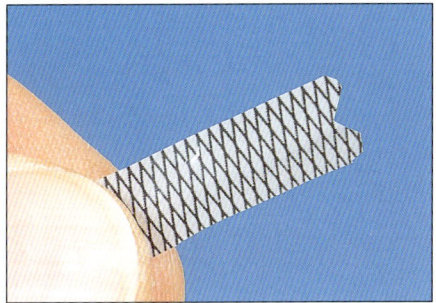

4. Trim out a section of Shimazaki Fly Wing material about twice as wide as macrame cord and trim in a heart shape at end.

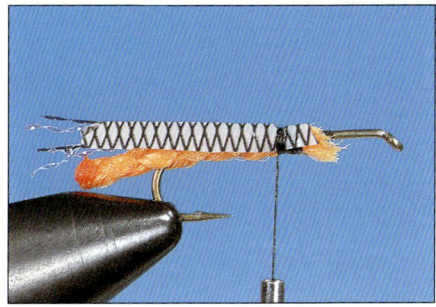

5. Wing should extend to, or slightly beyond, extended macrame body and out from sides or top of body. Position wing with your right hand. Change hands and tie in downwing style.

6. Tie in elk hair wing. If it flares, take a few turns of thread on top of wing and body. Collar will cover these wraps, and trimmed or bullet-style head will cover sharp drop-off.

7. Tie in orange deer or elk. Don't be too concerned about the tie-in space. The bullet head will cover it. Cover remaining hook shank with thread and position thread at eye of hook.

8. Hold moose hair in your right hand and slip it over hook eye so it encompasses body 360 degrees. Change hands and tie it in at the eye of hook.

9. Collar is in place, and butts have been trimmed. Apply Zap-A-Gap to tie-down area for a secure head.

10. We are changing thread color and are using fluorescent fire orange single strand nylon floss for visibility. This is the required color.

11. Sweep back butts and secure them, forming the collar 360 degrees around the fly.

12. Tie in a section of rubber along each side of the head. You are finished!

Chapter 34

Dave's Hopper

Umpqua Feather Merchants

Dave's Hopper (Dave Whitlock)
- Hook: 5212, sizes 4-12
- Thread: Brown
- Tail: Red deer or elk, tied short
- Rib: Yellow thread
- Body: Yellow Antron yarn (or closed-cell foam), palmered with brown saddle hackle
- Underwing: Pale yellow deer, tied downwing style over body
- Overwing: Turkey quill tied downwing style, flat over underwing and body (lacquered and trimmed)
- Legs: Yellow grizzly hackle, trimmed and knotted
- Collar: Natural dun-brown deer
- Head: Deer or caribou, trimmed

Dave's Cricket (Dave Whitlock)
- Hook: 5212, sizes 8-14
- Thread: Black
- Tail: Moose or black deer or elk
- Rib: Black thread
- Body: Dark chocolate brown Antron, palmered with black hackle clipped on top
- Wing: Black goose quill, treated with Flexament
- Legs: Black hackle stems, trimmed and knotted (lacquer knots)
- Collar: Black deer
- Head: Black deer, trimmed to shape

Dave's Hopper, tied with closed-cell foam, offers excellent flotation.

Dave Whitlock, noted angling author, artist, and fly innovator, designed the Dave's Hopper in the late 1960s. Today, it is the standard hopper imitation.

Grasshoppers have been a favorite hatch with American anglers for a long time, but only fairly recently have anglers, especially western anglers, gone hopper mad. During prolific hopper years, nearly every low- to mid-elevation stream plays host to a hopper population that bulges the stomachs of trout. Sometimes they are so full that hoppers fall from their mouths, but feeding continues like it was their last supper. I call such trout "grasshopper pigs." This gluttony has attracted a large population of anglers eager to cash in on the comparatively easy fishing that takes place during the otherwise mid-day doldrums.

Hoppers do not like cool or cloudy weather, and the hottest part of the hottest days offers the hottest angling. If a stiff wind is blowing, so much the better because hoppers blown off the banks will be floundering on the water in large numbers. August and September are the best months. Montana waters are legendary for their hopper hatches. Along the Madison River I have seen hoppers so large that one thinks twice about picking them up because they shoot an incredible wad of stinky juice! Mountain meadow waters can also have dense hopper populations, and I have enjoyed excellent action in the Cascade, Sierra, and Rocky mountains.

When good hopper years coincide with good steelhead years, anglers are in for some big-time action. Imagine dropping your hopper alongside a mid-stream hummock in Oregon's Deschutes River and twitching it along expecting a 14-inch trout, but instead a seven-pound summer steelhead slams the hopper and tail walks your fly line off the reel before breaking off. Now, *that* is fishing!

Hoppers belong to the order Orthoptera, which is formed from the Greek words "straight" and "wing" and includes crickets, katydids, and our favorites, cockroaches.

The standard Dave's Hopper calls for a yarn body (poly or Antron), but I like to use closed-cell foam. New techniques include a feather downwing, hackle stem legs, and a clipped hair head, which can be tricky. If you can tie and trim this head, a Muddler-style head will be easy. Use a razor blade for trimming the head. The Dave's Hopper is easily converted into a Cricket by using chocolate brown or black materials. Use golden, green, or brown materials, and you have a Cicada imitation.

Dave's Hopper

1. Cover body area of hook shank with thread. Tie in a short tail at the 50- to 60-percent mark and secure it. Trim butt ends at an angle and position thread at tail area.

2. We will tie a palmered hackle with a method not previously shown. It is wrapped back to front (shiny side back). It requires no rib, but it is not as durable or neat. Tie in wire rib, and use standard palmered method if you like.

3. Tie in a loop of poly yarn and secure a length of poly yarn along top of hook shank. You can tie in a section of closed-cell foam in lieu of poly loop and body. It is important to keep front of body tapered.

4. Wrap poly yarn, forming body, and tie off. Wrap hackle with shiny side facing toward back. Secure at front of body. Trim hackle along top of body. This allows the wing to lie flat.

5. Trim out a section of turkey quill that has been treated with Flexament and trim the tip round. It should be wide enough to fold slightly down along sides of body. If desired, underwing of pale yellow deer can be tied prior to turkey wing.

6. Note downwing tie-in location and that wing folds slightly down or over side of body. Also, note tapered tie-down area where hair head will be installed.

7. Tie in two pre-formed, trimmed, and knotted hackle stem legs along each side. Trim hackle even with hook gape or shorter along underside of body.

8. Prepare a bunch of deer hair, which is tied 360 degrees around body to form collar. Hold hair in right hand between thumb and first finger and slip it down over top of body so it encompasses entire fly.

9. Holding collar in your left hand, secure in place at back of available tie-down area. Do not trim butts. Stroke them backwards and take a couple of wraps of thread to hold them back.

10. Collar butts have been secured and incorporated into the trimmed head. Remaining area becomes trimmed head. Prepare and tie in a bunch of caribou or deer as you did for the Irresistible.

11. Caribou or deer has been secured in place, and thread has been tied off at head area, which is very short. You are now ready to trim head to shape.

12. Using scissors or razor blade, trim head flat on bottom, removing collar. Trim sides flat. Next, trim top flat, but angle it up toward eye. This is basically a rectangle with an angled top. That's it!

Chapter 35

Henry's Fork Hopper

Mike Lawson

Henry's Fork Hopper (Mike Lawson)
- Hook: 5212, sizes 6-14
- Thread: Yellow
- Body: Light elk, reverse style, secured (ribbed in an "X" pattern) with tying thread
- Underwing: Yellow elk, downwing style, extending to end of body
- Overwing: Mottled brown hen saddle feather treated with Flexament, worked to shape with fingers and tied down over top of yellow elk
- Head: Elk, reverse style bullet head; natural ends form collar
- Legs: Yellow rubber, knotted and tied along each side, extending to end of body; legs are tied at bullet head tie-down area and extend forward to hook eye

Mike Lawson

Henry's Fork Cricket (Mike Lawson)
- Hook: 5212 or 5263, sizes 6-14
- Thread: Brown
- Rib: Brown thread
- Body: Dark brown elk
- Underwing: Dark brown elk
- Overwing: Black hen saddle treated with Flexament
- Head: Black deer or elk (bullet head); natural ends form collar
- Legs: Black rubber, knotted and tied along each side

Umpqua Feather Merchants

Henry's Fork Hopper with built-in strike indicator.

The Henry's Fork in Idaho was the best-kept spring creek angling secret 30 years ago. Today it is the world's most popular spring creek. During this time, the Henry's Fork has been the working laboratory for many of the most innovative angler-tyers of our time. Mike Lawson, one such angler, founded Henry's Fork Anglers at Last Chance, Idaho, just a long cast from the famous Harriman Ranch waters.

Fishing surface flies on slow water over finicky fish always presents a challenge, especially if the flies are large. Twenty years ago, standard hopper patterns were not consistent on The Fork, and Mike felt that improvements were needed. After careful observation, he concluded that hoppers rest both in and on the water's surface, much like an iceberg. Because hoppers often become available to fish as a direct result of wind, any imitation needed to be castable, or streamlined, in appearance, yet capable of landing with a characteristic "splat." It also had to be durable and convincing to selective feeders. With these thoughts in mind, Mike created the Henry's Fork Hopper. This style of fly can be adapted to an excellent cicada imitation.

The next time you are fishing a hopper, or any other hatch, set your rod aside and indulge in some careful observation. Besides observing the usual physical habits, characteristics, and responses of fish, ask yourself some "what if" questions. This is a powerful way to get your imagination going and might just dispel a common belief or improve on current knowledge. Remind yourself that past and present tyer-anglers have brought you to this level of enjoyment and ask yourself what you can do to help protect and enhance fragile angling environments. Remember, nature is not making any more pristine rivers, ancient forests, or wetlands, and we cannot afford to degrade, lose, or compromise in any way what little is left. More to the point, we are not so poor that we need to sacrifice any more of our precious heritage.

I have saved this fly for last because it is an all-hair pattern and it can be difficult. Two new techniques are discussed: the bullet head and a reversed-hair body. We will also discuss rubber legs. Once this fly is mastered (assuming you have progressed in sequence to this point), you will have the skills to tie every fly listed in the pattern directory. Congratulations; may you spend many enjoyable and innovative hours at the tying bench and astream chasing wild trout in wild places!

Henry's Fork Hopper

1. Prepare a bunch of elk about three times length of hook shank. Hold tail with your left hand and spiral thread around tail. Take three extra turns at end of extended body and X pattern back to hook.

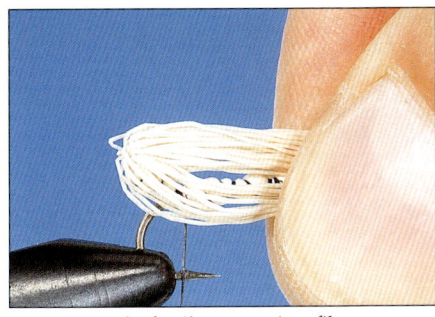

2. Press end of tail, separating fibers so you can pull them forward. Fibers should encompass tail 360 degrees. Take three secure wraps at tail area and wrap forward, forming body.

3. Tie off at about the 65-percent mark and trim hair tips, unless they are proper length to form underwing (as shown here), in which case they can be folded back to form underwing. Otherwise, tie in underwing.

4. Body and underwing are in place. Note proportions of extended body, wing and unused hook area. Normally, yellow thread would be used.

5. Select a wide and rounded, mottled-brown hen saddle feather. Apply Flexament and stroke to shape. Allow to dry.

6. Position flat over body and secure in place. It should fold down slightly along each side of body. Double downwing (underwing and overwing) is complete. Position thread at hook eye.

7. Install a bullet head, similar to Green Drake Paradrake extended body. Measure hair against hook shank. It should be same length. Switch hands and, holding hair between right thumb and first finger, slip hair around hook eye as shown.

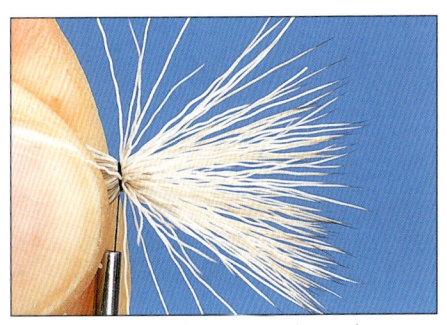

8. Change hands and, using the up-between-the-fingers technique, secure in place immediately behind hook eye.

9. Elk hair is secured in place, 360 degrees around hook. Thread is positioned at next tie-down position for bullet head. Hair butts have been trimmed.

10. Sweep all hair back between your fingers and secure in place.

11. Tips of bullet head form collar. It is important to judge length of hair properly before you secure it onto hook. Notice proportions.

12. Tie in a section of knotted round rubber along each side of bullet head, forming legs. Henry's Fork Hopper is finished.

Chapter 36

Tying With Speed And Efficiency

Most tyers, especially beginners, will work through this book and tie at a leisurely pace. Eventually, some tyers may become more serious about stocking their fly boxes and might begin to tie for their friends or, perhaps, their local sports shop. If this happens to you, consider increasing your speed and efficiency.

The following ideas are a look into the tying and thought process of a professional tyer. See what might benefit you and how clever you can be at omitting unnecessary moves. The underlying idea is to have fun.

Once you have command of your hand-eye-mind coordination and the basic tying techniques become automatic, you are ready to increase your speed without sacrificing fly quality or enjoyment. Tying flies is not a race to be won, but your enjoyment and level of satisfaction will probably increase proportionally to the number of flies tied.

When I was tying commercially, I routinely took orders for 100 dozen or more of the same pattern. A typical order might read: Blue Dun, 48/12 (48 dozen size 12), 48/14, 48/16. This order for 144 dozen was perfect because it allowed me to tie the same pattern for two weeks, eliminating the time and bother of setting up for other patterns. I also could use up three sizes of hackle.

Repetition builds speed, and speed means more flies in your box—or more money in the bank—for the same time spent at the vise. Building speed is very difficult when tying only one or two dozen of a pattern. When you spend six to eight hours per day for two weeks tying the same fly, you become proficient. I recommend that tyers choose a favorite fly that is relatively easy and tie up to 10 dozen in sequence. Such repetitive tying will be a big boost in increasing your speed for all patterns—and your stock of flies!

To begin, I cleared my desk of all other materials and distractions and laid out enough hooks for a day's work, say 16 dozen size 14s. Next, I pulled out all the size 12 hackles from a neck so they were ready to pick up, prepare, and tie in place. I started with the 14s, because I was certain to pull some larger and some smaller; these I set aside to use for the other sizes. Finally, I laid out the tail, abdomen, and wing material. I began work on the 14s, moved to the tougher 16s, and ended with the easier 12s. The flies would be finished in 10 days, or about 80 hours at the vise.

I recommend that you tie at a pace that feels comfortable. Incorporate the following ideas into your tying routine, and your production will automatically increase.

1. Tie against a smooth, light-colored background. Light blue poster board is perfect.
2. Clear all non-essential items from your tying area.
3. All tools should be in perfect working order. Tools that you do not carry on your hand (hackle pliers, threader-cleaner, stacker, bobbin) should always be placed in the same location.
4. Carry the scissors on your hand. Picking them up and setting them down after every tie in and tie off is time consuming.
5. Have extra bobbins threaded.
6. Tie under a high intensity lamp or one with a cool, concentrated beam of light. Good visibility is crucial in preventing eye fatigue.
7. Use only the best materials. They quickly pay for themselves.
8. Set up for several flies of the same pattern by laying out the hooks (smashing the barbs first) and all materials, which should be prepared for immediate use. You should never hunt for or prepare anything once you begin tying.
9. Material pick up and tie in should be *immediate.*
10. Material handling should be *minimized.*
11. *Minimize* thread turns. Thread placement should be fast, exact, and effective. Except when dubbing, the bobbin should be about one inch from the hook. Wrapping a one-inch circle is much more efficient than wrapping a three-inch circle.
12. Think ahead to the next step. Force your hands to move faster. Get into a comfortable pace as you would in jogging.
13. Use two half-hitches to finish a fly. If done properly, they will outlast the fly and are much faster than a whip finish.
14. Lacquer all the heads at one time.

Tying 12 to 18 dry flies per hour is not difficult. Many tyers could easily accomplish more with a few subtle changes in their tying style. Most tyers waste time preparing and securing materials. They also take too many wraps of thread, which not only takes up time but produces unwanted bulk. Set up a clock with a second hand at your tying bench and see how your tying schedule compares to mine.

How long should it take to dub a few fibers of Antron onto the thread and wrap it around the hook 10 times? Probably a lot less than you think. Try doing it in 20 seconds. The following instructions detail how long each step should take to tie a 90- and 180-second size 14 Blue Dun. It also details how many (or how few) thread wraps are needed. If you fall into the 180-second column, that is 20 flies per hour!

Remember, all hooks must be spread out, and all material must have been selected and prepared before you begin tying. All wing segments should be cut before you start tying. Tail material that will last for several flies should be quickly accessible. *You are only picking up and tying materials onto the hook.* Searching for materials and looking for tools has been eliminated. Thread must be wrapped as tightly as possible, just short of breaking. When thread is wrapped tightly, very few wraps are required to secure material.

If you are to increase your speed, every move at the vise must accomplish its goal on the first attempt. "Economy of motion" is the key phrase. When you open the vise jaws and insert the hook, it must be properly placed immediately. If you have to lift it up, move it forward, etc., you will never increase your speed. The same applies to every other tying step. If you cannot do it right the first time, practice until you can.

Tying Dry Flies

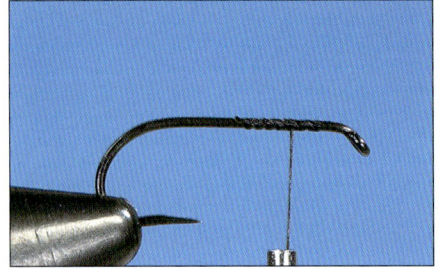
Step 1

Step 2

Step 3

Step 4

Step 5

Step 6

Speed Schedule	Thread Wraps	Time (Seconds)	Time (Seconds)
Step 1: Pick up and insert the hook in the vise. Attach thread to hook at wing tie-in area with ten wraps of thread. Cut the thread with the scissors, which you are carrying in your hand, or pull the thread end off with your fingers. Black thread is being used for better visibility.	10	10	20
Step 2: Pick up a left and right duck quill segment. Match the tips, straighten the feather curvature with your fingers, and secure them onto the hook with seven wraps of thread. Trim off the butt ends and take one turn around the base of the wings to stand them up. Wrap the thread back to bend of the hook (seven to ten wraps), locking the turn of thread around the base of the wings in place and covering the hook shank in the process. Return thread to tail tie-in area as shown.	16	20	40
Step 3: Pick up the tail material (hackle) and prepare the tail fibers. Place the feather back on your tying bench if it still offers usable fibers. If not, throw it into your waste area. The thread should be at the mid-body area. Tie the tail fibers in place with six wraps of thread. Trim the butt ends of the tail just short of the wings where the hackle will be tied in. Thread should be at back of body area.	6	10	20
Step 4: Spread dubbing material along thread. Roll dubbing onto thread. This should be accomplished with five rolls or less. The dubbing should be started about a half-inch down the thread from the hook shank. It requires about five wraps of thread before the dubbing reaches the hook. Use these five wraps to secure the tail ends and to position the thread at the tail *when* the dubbing is ready to wrap around the hook. Take five to 10 wraps of dubbing (depends on dubbing diameter and body length). Wrap forward in one direction to just behind the wings, where hackle will be tied in. There should not be any dubbing left over.	15	10	20
Step 5: Pick up and prepare two hackles. Tie them in place with five wraps of thread and position the thread at the hackle tie-off area. Wrap both hackles at once (accomplished much faster without hackle pliers). Tie hackles off—three wraps of thread will do it. Trim hackle ends closely with *one* snip of the scissors. (*All* scissors cuts should be accomplished with one snip.) Note that the head area is free of all materials.	8	25	50
Step 6: Finish off the thread head with three to five wraps of thread. Half-hitch twice, cinch knots backwards until they tighten up, and cut the thread. Arrange the wings with your fingers if needed. Lacquer heads later.	5	15	30
Total Thread Wraps	60		
Total Tying Time in Seconds (1-1/2 minutes)		90	
Total Tying Time in Seconds (3 minutes)			180

Part III

Pattern Directory

Part III is the pattern directory. If you have progressed carefully through Part II, you will be able to tie any of the 80 patterns listed here. These patterns represent the most frequently used and popular dry flies in North America, if not the fishing world. They are all proven "fish getters" and have also been known to "hook" a few anglers. This fact can be confirmed by the many anglers who collect far more patterns than they will ever have time to fish. Collecting and tying new patterns provides much pleasure and is an intrinsic part of the escape from the ordinary offered by fly tying. Fly tying is an extension of fly fishing that can be enjoyed any day of the year without leaving the house.

Dressings are given in the order in which they are *tied* onto the hook. This is not necessarily the order in which they are *wrapped* around the hook or manipulated into final position. As an example, the wingcase material for the Hatching Midge is tied *onto* the hook before the thorax and hackle, but the actual wingcase is not formed or positioned until after the thorax and hackle are in place.

By now you should be able to "read" any dry fly dressing and not only understand the tying sequence and associated tying technique, but also visualize the finished fly. If you have any trouble remembering how to handle a particular technique, check the index and refer back to the appropriate page. Unless otherwise specified, all hook numbers are Tiemco.

Nearly all pattern dressings are authentic, many having been supplied by the originators. All other dressings are today's accepted commercial standard. As new ideas and materials become available, some patterns will change. In many cases, the fly pictured was also tied by the originator. Credits to the right of photos designate the person who tied the fly shown. Fly photos without credits were tied by the author.

This plump golden trout couldn't resist a Golden Stimulator.

John Muir Wilderness, High Sierra, California.

Mary along the John Muir Trail, High Sierra, California.

Ansel Adams Wilderness, High Sierra, California.

128 *Tying Dry Flies*

Adams (Leonard Halladay, 1922)
  Hook: 900BL, sizes 10-20
  Thread: Gray
  Wing: Grizzly hen hackle fibers, upright and divided
  Tail: Grizzly or grizzly and brown hackle fibers or moose
  Body: Muskrat or gray Antron or Superfine
  Hackle: Grizzly and brown mix (Adams)
Note: See page 70.

Adams Parachute
  Hook: 900BL, sizes 12-18
  Thread: Gray
  Wing: White calf, parachute style
  Tail: Grizzly and brown hackle fibers
  Body: Muskrat or gray Antron or Superfine
  Hackle: Grizzly and brown, parachute style
Note: Currently the most popular standard parachute pattern. See page 88.

Beetle, Foam
  Hook: 900BL, sizes 6-18
  Thread: Black
  Overbody: Black foam trimmed to desired width
  Body: Black thread or dubbing to suit
  Legs: Black deer or round rubber tied in X pattern
  Indicator: Glo-Bug yarn, color to suit
Note: Realistic, durable, easy to tie, and easy to see. See page 42.

Beetle, Krystal Flash
  Hook: 900BL, sizes 12-20
  Thread: Black
  Overbody: Black foam trimmed to desired width
  Body: Peacock herl
  Legs: Red Krystal Flash or color to suit
  Indicator: Fluorescent fire orange Glo-Bug yarn or other to suit
Note: A great mini-beetle or tie it giant size.

Bivisible
  Hook: 900BL, sizes 12-18
  Thread: To match hackle color
  Tail: To match hackle color
  Hackle: Any color, with three turns of white at front, wrapped standard style over entire hook shank
Note: Originated by Edward Hewitt, whose writings included *Nymph Fly Fishing* and *Better Trout Streams*. Hewitt was an angler far ahead of his time.

Black Gnat
  Hook: 900BL, sizes 12-18
  Thread: Black
  Wing: Gray duck quill, upright and divided
  Tail: Black hackle fibers (red fibers are also popular)
  Body: Black Antron or Superfine
  Hackle: Black
Note: At one time a very popular dark pattern, but specific patterns have somewhat reduced its popularity. See page 76.

Blue Dun
  Hook: 900BL, sizes 12-18
  Thread: Gray
  Wing: Gray duck quill, upright and divided
  Tail: Blue dun hackle fibers
  Body: Muskrat or gray Antron or Superfine
  Hackle: Blue dun
Note: See page 76.

Blue-Winged Olive
  Hook: 900BL, sizes 14-20
  Thread: Olive
  Wing: Dark blue dun hen hackle tips, upright and divided
  Tail: Dark blue dun hackle fibers
  Body: Medium olive to brown olive Superfine
  Hackle: Dark blue dun
Note: Most popular "standard" imitation of *Baetis vagans*, east to west, and *Ephemerella cornuta*.

Brown Drake
  Hook: 900BL, sizes 10-12
  Thread: Brown
  Wing: Medium or light elk, upright and divided
  Tail: Moose
  Rib: Yellow floss
  Body: Golden olive-brown Antron
  Hackle: Dyed brown grizzly
Note: Current favorite *Ephemera simulans* imitation for fast water. See Paradrake, Brown, for another effective imitation.

Pattern Directory 129

California Mosquito
- Hook: 900BL, sizes 12-18
- Thread: Black
- Tail: Grizzly hackle fibers
- Rib: White thread
- Body: Black floss
- Wing: Grizzly hackle tips, downwing style
- Hackle: Grizzly

Note: Most effective mosquito pattern; especially popular in western America. See page 64.

CDC Caddis Adult, Tan (House of Harrop)
- Hook: 900BL, sizes 12-20
- Thread: Tan
- Abdomen: Tan Antron or Superfine
- Underwing: Tan, yellow or amber Z-Lon
- Overwing: Tan CDC, flat over body
- Thorax: Same as abdomen; more of a "head" than thorax
- Legs: Tan CDC—incorporate stem

Note: Renè and Bonnie Harrop and family operate the House of Harrop, purveyors of fine flies prized by anglers and collectors.

CDC Callibaetis Comparadun (Shane Stalcup)
- Hook: 900BL, sizes 12-16
- Thread: Tan
- Wing: Natural dun CDC with natural mallard or teal flank
- Tail: Dun Betts' Tailing Fibers
- Abdomen: Tan turkey biot
- Thorax: Tan Superfine

Note: See page 46.

CDC Callibaetis Spinner (House of Harrop)
- Hook: 900BL, sizes 12-16
- Thread: Tan
- Underwing: Light blue dun CDC tied "spent" style
- Overwing: Brown Z-Lon
- Tail: Light blue dun hackle fibers, three to five, flared wide
- Body: Tan turkey biot
- Thorax: Tan Superfine

Note: See page 84.

CDC Spinner, Rusty (House of Harrop)
- Hook: 900BL, sizes 16-20
- Thread: Brown
- Underwing: Light blue dun CDC tied spent
- Overwing: Light blue dun Z-Lon
- Tail: Light blue dun hackle fibers, three to five stiff, flared wide
- Body: Rust turkey biot
- Thorax: Rusty Superfine

Note: See page 82.

Chernobyl Ant
- Hook: 5263BL, sizes 6-12
- Thread: Yellow or color to match body
- Body: Yellow closed cell foam
- Overbody: Tan closed cell foam
- Legs: Sili Legs, color to suit
- Indicator: Closed cell foam, colors to suit

Note: An unorthodox pattern but it works. Especially popular in Wyoming and Montana. *Developed by Mark Forslund and Alan Woolley. Popularized by Emmett Heath, a highly-respected guide on Utah's Green River.*

Clark's Cicada (Clark Reid)
- Hook: 200RBL, sizes 6-8
- Thread: Color to match abdomen
- Eyes: Burned monofilament
- Abdomen: Olive or dark brown deer, trimmed to shape
- Underwing: Pearl Krystal Flash
- Overwing: Fly Wing
- Legs: Olive or dark brown deer
- Thorax: Olive or dark brown deer

Note: Designed by New Zealand angler/tyer Clark Reid to imitate cicada, which is anxiously awaited each season by both angler and fish.

Comparadun (Al Caucci and Bob Nastasi)
- Hook: 900BL, sizes 10-20
- Thread: Color to match body
- Wing: Mottled brown (or color to match natural) deer; single upright and flared
- Tail: Blue dun hackle fibers, stiff, split wide
- Body: Color to match natural, Antron or Superfine

Note: See page 46.

Cripple (Bob Quigley)
- Hook: 900BL, sizes 14-20
- Thread: Yellow
- Shuck: Brown Z-Lon over brown marabou or pheasant hackle
- Rib: Copper wire or omit
- Body: Ringneck pheasant tail
- Thorax: Yellow Superfine or other
- Wing: Natural deer or elk
- Hackle: Grizzly or color to suit

Note: Adapt this pattern to any mayfly hatch. It is deadly! Keep small sizes sparse.

Tying Dry Flies

Damsel, Braided Butt
- Hook: 900BL, sizes 10-12
- Thread: Black
- Wingcase: Poly yarn; tie long (tall) parachute post which will be folded forward to form wingcase
- Abdomen: Braided leader material colored with Pantone marker
- Thorax: Dubbing to match abdomen
- Hackle: Blue dun or grizzly
- Eyes: Burned monofilament

Note: See page 98.

Dark Cahill
- Hook: 900BL, sizes 12-16
- Thread: Gray
- Wing: Mallard flank dyed woodduck, upright and divided
- Tail: Brown hackle fibers
- Body: Muskrat or gray Antron
- Hackle: Brown

Note: Believed to have been developed by Theodore Gordon. See page 72.

Dave's Hopper (Dave Whitlock)
- Hook: 5212, sizes 4-12
- Thread: Brown
- Tail: Red deer or elk, tied short
- Rib: Yellow thread
- Body: Antron yarn or foam, palmered with brown saddle hackle
- Underwing: Pale yellow deer
- Overwing: Turkey quill
- Legs: Yellow grizzly hackle
- Collar: Natural dun/brown deer
- Head: Deer or caribou

E/C Caddis (Ralph Cutter)
- Hook: 900BL, sizes 14-20
- Thread: Olive
- Tail (Shuck): Tan Antron or Z-Lon
- Body: Tan Antron dubbing
- Thorax: Olive green Antron dubbing
- Wing: Tan elk
- Hackle: Grizzly, parachute style

Note: Ralph spent three seasons in scuba gear perfecting this pattern so that it presented the proper "dent" in the water exactly like an emergent mayfly cripple.

Elk Hair Caddis, Original (Al Troth)
- Hook: 900BL, sizes 6-20
- Thread: Tan
- Rib: Fine gold wire
- Body: Hare's ear dubbing
- Hackle: Medium to dark brown palmered through body
- Wing: Cream or bleached elk

Note: See page 100.

Elk Hair Hopper (John Bailey)
- Hook: 5212 or 5263, sizes 6-10
- Thread: Black
- Tail: Red hackle fibers or red deer or elk
- Body: Yellow foam, palmered with brown hackle
- Rib: Yellow thread or gold wire
- Wing: Elk
- Hackle: Grizzly and brown

Note: John Bailey owns and operates world-famous Dan Bailey's Fly Shop in Livingston, Montana.

Flying Ant, Black
- Hook: 900BL, sizes 10-20
- Thread: Black
- Back: Black deer
- Abdomen: Black Antron or Superfine
- Wing: Dark blue dun hackle tips tied *delta wing* style
- Hackle: Brown, blue dun, or black
- Thorax: Same as abdomen; black deer pulled over top is optional

Note: Excellent ant imitation. Overlooked by most anglers. See page 68.

Goddard Caddis (John Goddard and Cliff Henry)
- Hook: 900BL, sizes 10-16
- Thread: Tan
- Body: Tan (or color of choice) caribou or soft deer
- Antennae: Brown or other color hackle stem, stripped
- Hackle: Adams Brown or color of choice

Note: John Goddard and Brian Clarke co-authored, The Trout And The Fly. It offers excellent insight.

Green Drake (Mike Lawson)
- Hook: 900BL, sizes 10-12
- Thread: Olive
- Wing: Dyed black elk or black calf, upright and divided
- Tail: Moose
- Rib: Yellow floss
- Body: Olive Antron or Superfine
- Hackle: Olive grizzly

Note: The most popular standard-style Green Drake.

Pattern Directory 131

Griffith Gnat (George Griffith)
- Hook: 900BL, sizes 12-22
- Thread: Black or to match body
- Rib: Thread or fine gold wire
- Body: Peacock or other to suit
- Hackle: Grizzly or other to suit, palmered

Note: See page 60.

H and L Variant
- Hook: 900BL, sizes 8-16
- Thread: Black
- Wing: White calf, upright and divided
- Tail: White calf
- Body: Stripped peacock herl and peacock herl
- Hackle: Brown

Note: A striking fly that offers excellent visibility and floatability. Also called a House and Lot. Was a favorite of President Eisenhower when he fished in Colorado.

Hairwing Dun, Hendrickson (Renè Harrop)
- Hook: 900BL, sizes 12-16
- Thread: Brown
- Tail: Medium to dark blue dun hackle fibers, split
- Hackle: Medium to dark blue dun
- Body: Gray brown Antron, Hare-Tron, or Superfine
- Wing: Brown elk

Hatching Midge (Randall Kaufmann)
- Hook: 900BL, sizes 12-18
- Thread: Black
- Shuck: Gray or black CDC and Z-Lon
- Rib: White thread
- Body: Black thread or Superfine
- Wingcase: Gray or black CDC
- Hackle: Grizzly
- Thorax: Peacock
- Antennae: Gray or black CDC

Note: See page 62.

Henry's Fork Hopper (Mike Lawson)
- Hook: 5212 or 5263, sizes 6-14
- Thread: Yellow
- Body: Light elk, reverse style and ribbed with tying thread
- Underwing: Yellow elk, downwing style
- Overwing: Speckled hen saddle
- Head: Elk, reverse style (bullet head); natural ends form collar
- Legs: Yellow rubber, knotted and tied at bullet head tie down

Note: See page 122.

Henryville Special (Hiram Brobst)
- Hook: 900BL, sizes 12-20
- Thread: Olive
- Rib: Fine gold wire (optional)
- Body: Light olive floss or dubbing with palmered grizzly hackle
- Wing: Mallard flank dyed woodduck; overwing of matched pair of gray duck wing quills, referred to as a split quill downwing
- Hackle: Brown

Note: Sometimes called a Henryville Caddis.

Hot Butt™ Caddis (Randall Kaufmann)
- Hook: 900BL, sizes 12-18
- Thread: Black or to match body
- Butt: Fluorescent red Glo-Bug yarn or other color to suit
- Rib: Fine gold or copper wire
- Body: Peacock herl or dubbing to suit
- Hackle: Grizzly, or other color to suit, palmered through body
- Underwing: Natural gray CDC tied full and thick
- Overwing: Natural gray elk tied sparse

Humpy, Double
- Hook: 5262, sizes 6-12
- Thread: Bright yellow
- Wing: Natural deer
- Tail: Natural deer
- Overbody: Natural deer
- Body: Tying thread
- Hackle: Grizzly

Note: Jackson Hole, Wyoming, favorite. Local anglers prefer a slightly scraggly tie—it should not be too perfect. Other colors to suit. See page 114.

Humpy, Royal Fluorescent Green
- Hook: 900BL, sizes 8-18
- Thread: Fluorescent green, 6/0, or single strand floss
- Wing: White calf tail or calf body, upright and divided
- Tail: Moose
- Overbody: Moose
- Body: Fluorescent green thread
- Hackle: Brown and grizzly

Note: See page 114.

Humpy, Royal Red (Jack Dennis and Charles Ridenour)
- Hook: 900BL, sizes 8-18
- Thread: Bright red
- Wing: White calf tail or calf body, upright and divided
- Tail: Moose
- Overbody: Moose
- Body: Bright red thread
- Hackle: Brown or Adams

Note: One of the most beautiful attractor flies of the day. See page 114.

Humpy, Yellow
- Hook: 900BL, sizes 8-20
- Thread: Bright yellow
- Wing: Elk, upright and divided
- Tail: Elk
- Overbody: Elk
- Body: Bright yellow thread
- Hackle: Adams, badger, brown, or furnace

Note: Standard Humpy. Available at almost every fly fishing establishment. See page 114.

Improved Sofa Pillow (Pat and Sig Barnes)
- Hook: 200R or 5263, sizes 4-10
- Thread: Black or orange
- Tail: Elk
- Rib: Orange thread or gold wire
- Body: Burnt orange poly yarn or Antron yarn or dubbing, palmered with brown or furnace hackle
- Wing: Elk, full and bushy
- Hackle: Brown

Irresistible, Adams
- Hook: 900BL, sizes 8-16
- Thread: Black or tan
- Tail: Moose or Adams hackle fibers
- Body: Caribou trimmed to shape
- Wing: Grizzly hen hackle tips, upright and divided
- Hackle: Grizzly and brown

Note: See page 110.

Irresistible, Wulff
- Hook: 900BL, sizes 8-16
- Thread: Black
- Tail: Moose
- Body: Caribou trimmed to shape
- Wing: White calf, upright and divided
- Hackle: Brown

Note: Popular all-hair high-floating fly difficult to beat for dredging up big fish in big water. Often used for Atlantic salmon and steelhead. See page 110.

King's River Caddis (Wayne "Buz" Buszek)
- Hook: 900BL, sizes 12-18
- Thread: Tan
- Body: Tan Antron
- Wing: Turkey wing quill section, apply Flexament and clip in V
- Hackle: Brown

Note: Buz and his wife, Virginia, ran Buz's Fly Shop, a mail order house in Visalia, California. When I began tying in the mid-1960s, they were my main source of materials.

Light Cahill (Dan Cahill)
- Hook: 900BL, sizes 12-20
- Thread: Pale yellow
- Wing: Mallard flank dyed woodduck
- Tail: Light ginger or cream hackle fibers
- Body: Cream Antron or Superfine
- Hackle: Light ginger or cream

Note: In the East and Midwest the *Stenonema canadense* emergence usually begins in early June and can continue into August. Western hatches are much more sporadic.

MacSalmon (Al Troth)
- Hook: 5263 or 200R, sizes 4-8
- Thread: Orange
- Body: Orange, rust, or gold braided macrame cord
- Underwing: Mottled dark gray Fly Wing
- Overwing: Light elk, downwing style
- Collar: Brown deer, heavy
- Head: Brown deer, trimmed to shape

Note: Pattern can also be tied with a bullet head and rubber legs. See page 118.

Madam X (Doug Swisher)
- Hook: 5263, sizes 6-10
- Thread: Yellow, or color to suit
- Tail: Deer
- Body: Yellow thread, or color to suit
- Wing: Deer
- Head: Deer tied reverse style; natural ends form wing
- Legs: Rubber, color to suit, adjusted to X pattern, two along each side

Note: Originally designed and fished on the Bitterroot River, Montana.

Pattern Directory   133

March Brown *(Preston Jennings)*
- Hook: 900BL, sizes 10-14
- Thread: Yellow
- Wing: Mallard flank dyed woodduck, upright and divided
- Tail: Brown hackle fibers
- Body: Fawn-colored fox
- Hackle: Grizzly and brown

Note: Catskill-style imitation that is popular during the **Stenonema vicarium** hatch. Art Flick adapted the Jennings pattern slightly and popularized it beginning in 1950.

March Brown, American
- Hook: 900BL, sizes 12-14
- Thread: Brown
- Wing: Mottled brown hen or turkey quill
- Tail: Brown hackle fibers
- Rib: Yellow floss, twisted tightly
- Body: Medium-brown Antron
- Hackle: Brown

Note: A favorite quill wing, standard style March Brown **Stenonema vicarium** imitation.

No Hackle, Olive *(Doug Swisher and Carl Richards)*
- Hook: 900BL, sizes 16-20
- Thread: Olive
- Wing: Gray duck wing quill, no-hackle style
- Tail: Blue dun hackle fibers, split
- Body: Olive or olive-brown Superfine

Note: Represents almost all olive mayfly duns. Vary to suit your needs. See page 80.

Para Wulff, Royal *(Jack Dennis)*
- Hook: 900BL or 101BL, sizes 10-16
- Thread: Black
- Wing: White calf, upright and divided
- Tail: Moose body
- Body: Three-part royal body
- Hackle: Brown or furnace tied parachute style

Note: Designed by Jack Dennis of Jack Dennis Sports in Jackson, Wy., legendary angler, author, video master, fly innovator, and entrepeneur. Others to suit.

Parachute, Baetis *(Pret Frazier)*
- Hook: 900BL, sizes 16-22
- Thread: Olive
- Wing: Mallard
- Tail: Blue dun Micro Fibetts, two, split
- Body: Olive to olive-brown Superfine
- Hackle: Dyed olive grizzly or natural grizzly

Note: One of the better **Baetis** patterns. See page 90.

Parachute, Black Gnat
- Hook: 900BL, sizes 14-18
- Thread: Black
- Wing: White calf, parachute style
- Tail: Black hackle fibers
- Body: Black dubbing
- Hackle: Black, parachute style

Note: The black and white color combination offers anglers visibility under most light conditions. See page 88.

Parachute, Dun Brown
- Hook: 900BL, sizes 12-18
- Thread: Brown
- Wing: Dark blue dun turkey flats
- Tail: Two dark blue dun Micro Fibetts
- Body: Brown or rusty brown or chocolate Antron
- Hackle: Medium to dark blue dun

Note: Useful for many dun brown mayfly hatches, including **Epeorus**, **Rithrogena**, and **Cinygmula**.

Parachute, Gray *(Pret Frazier)*
- Hook: 900BL, sizes 14-16
- Thread: Gray
- Wing: Mallard or teal flank
- Tail: Blue Dun Micro Fibetts, two, split
- Body: Gray Antron
- Hackle: Grizzly, parachute style

Note: **Callibaetis** imitation for selective feeders. A tan and tanish-pink version is also good, especially for representing smaller crane flies.

Parachute, Light Cahill
- Hook: 900BL, sizes 12-18
- Thread: Yellow
- Wing: White calf, parachute style
- Tail: Light ginger or cream hackle fibers
- Body: Cream dubbing
- Hackle: Light ginger or cream, parachute style

Tying Dry Flies

Parachute, PMD (Pret Frazier)
- Hook: 900BL, sizes 16-18
- Thread: Yellow
- Wing: Mallard, parachute style
- Tail: Blue dun Micro Fibetts or Betts' Tailing Fibers, two, split
- Body: Pale yellow to chartreuse yellow Superfine
- Hackle: Light ginger or pale blue dun, parachute style

Note: See page 90.

Parachute, Red Wing Adams
- Hook: 900BL, sizes 12-18
- Thread: Gray
- Wing: Fluorescent red calf, parachute style
- Tail: Grizzly hackle fibers
- Body: Muskrat or gray Antron or Superfine dubbing
- Hackle: Grizzly and brown, parachute style

Note: Excellent visibility. Popular on Montana's Big Hole River

Parachute, Trico
- Hook: 900BL, sizes 18-24
- Thread: Black
- Wing: White hen hackle fibers
- Tail: Black hackle fibers or Micro Fibetts
- Body: Black or gray Superfine
- Thorax: Black Superfine
- Hackle: Grizzly, parachute style

Note: When these tiny mayflies get going literally millions can be seen swarming in the air.

Paradrake, Brown
- Hook: 900BL, sizes 10-12
- Thread: Brown
- Wing: Elk, parachute style
- Tail: Moose
- Rib: Golden thread
- Body: Medium golden brown deer or elk
- Hackle: Medium brown grizzly, parachute style

Note: Represents **Ephemera simulans**. See page 94.

Paradrake, Green Drake
- Hook: 900BL, sizes 8-12
- Thread: Olive, yellow, or golden olive
- Wing: Natural dark gray elk, or black elk or moose, parachute style
- Tail: Moose
- Body: Golden olive elk, extended style
- Hackle: Olive grizzly, parachute style

Note: Very successful pattern. Realistic outline and floats flush in the film. Represents **Ephemerella grandis** and, in smaller sizes, **E. flavilinea**. See page 94.

Power Ant (Guy Turck)
- Hook: 900BL, sizes 10-18
- Thread: Black
- Abdomen: Black dubbing
- Wing: White calf
- Legs: White round rubber tied in an X
- Hackle: Brown or furnace tied in center of hook
- Thorax: Same as abdomen

Note: A Jackson Hole, Wyoming creation used by many local anglers and guides. Twitch the fly to animate. See page 68.

Quill Gordon (Theodore Gordon)
- Hook: 900BL, sizes 12-18
- Thread: Gray
- Wing: Mallard dyed woodduck, upright and divided
- Tail: Blue dun hackle fibers
- Body: Stripped peacock quill
- Hackle: Blue dun

Note: One of the longest-surviving fly patterns. Represents **Epeorus pleuralis**. See page 72.

Renegade (Taylor "Beartracks" Williams)
- Hook: 900BL, sizes 10-16
- Thread: Black
- Tag: Flat gold tinsel
- Aft Hackle: Brown
- Body: Peacock
- Fore Hackle: White

Note: This is one of the few flies that has fore and aft hackle. One story is that "Beartracks" Williams first tied the Renegade in 1928. George L. Herter claimed the fly to be an English pattern tied by Mrs. Edith Cox in the late 1800s.

Royal Coachman (John Haily)
- Hook: 900BL, sizes 12-16
- Thread: Black
- Wing: White duck quill
- Tail: Golden pheasant tippets
- Body: Royal three-part body
- Hackle: Coachman brown

Note: According to Harold Hinsdale Smedley, John Haily of New York created the Royal Coachman in 1878 and L. C. Orvis named it. See page 76.

Pattern Directory 135

Royal Trude (Carter Harrison)
- Hook: 5212, sizes 10-16
- Thread: Black
- Tail: Elk, deer, or red hackle fibers
- Body: Royal (fine wire rib optional)
- Wing: White calf, downwing style
- Hackle: Brown

Note: In 1901, in Island Park, Idaho, Carter Harrison clipped some red hair from a spaniel and yarn from a rug and tied it onto a gaff-sized hook. He named and presented it to his host, A.S. Trude.

Seducer, Green (Randall Kaufmann)
- Hook: 200R, sizes 8-18
- Thread: Fluorescent fire orange
- Tail: Dark elk
- Rib: Fine gold wire
- Abdomen: Fluorescent lime or green Antron, palmered with brown hackle
- Wing: Dark elk over Shimazaki Fly Wing over green Krystal Flash
- Hackle: Grizzly
- Thorax: Peacock

Note: See page 102.

Seducer, Orange (Randall Kaufmann)
- Hook: 200R, sizes 8-18
- Thread: Fluorescent fire orange
- Tail: Light elk
- Rib: Fine gold wire
- Abdomen: Fluorescent fire orange Antron, palmered with furnace hackle
- Wing: Light elk over Shimazaki Fly Wing over orange Krystal Flash
- Hackle: Grizzly
- Thorax: Peacock

Note: See page 102.

Shimazaki's Caddis (Ken Shimazaki)
- Hook: 900BL, sizes 8-18
- Thread: Olive
- Body: Olive Superfine
- Wing: Gray CDC under gray Shimazaki Fly Wing, tent style
- Hackle: Partridge and grizzly, grizzly/white

Note: Other colors to suit. Ken Shimazaki is an artistic Japanese tyer, Tiemco hook designer, and inventor of Fly Wing.

Sparkle Dun, PMD (Craig Mathews and John Juracek)
- Hook: 900BL, sizes 16-20
- Thread: Yellow
- Wing: Dyed gray deer, single, upright and flared
- Tail: Olive-brown Z-Lon
- Body: Yellowish Superfine

Note: Represents *Ephemerella infrequens* and *E. inermis*. See page 46.

Spent Partridge Caddis (Sheralee Lawson)
- Hook: 900BL, sizes 14-18
- Thread: Olive
- Body: Tan or olive Superfine
- Wing: Mottled brown hen saddle fibers
- Hackle: Brown and grizzly, spaced through thorax area
- Thorax: Peacock

Note: The Lawsons operate Henry's Fork Anglers at Last Chance, Idaho.

Spent Spinner, Hen (Doug Swisher and Carl Richards)
- Hook: 900BL, size to match natural
- Thread: Color to match body
- Tail: Light blue dun Micro Fibetts
- Wing: Light to medium blue dun hen hackle tips tied spent (select broad hackle tips); continue dubbed body between wing to head
- Body: Color to imitate natural

Note: See page 82.

Stimulator, Peacock Rubber Leg (Randall Kaufmann)
- Hook: 200R, sizes 8-14
- Thread: Fluorescent fire orange
- Tail: Dark elk
- Rib: Fine gold wire
- Abdomen: Peacock, palmered with furnace hackle
- Wing: Nat. dark elk over nat. dark gray CDC, over Krystal Flash
- Hackle: Grizzly
- Thorax: Fluorescent fire orange Antron

Stimulator, Royal (Randall Kaufmann)
- Hook: 200R, sizes 10-16
- Thread: Fluorescent fire orange
- Tail: Medium or dark elk
- Rib: Fine gold wire
- Abdomen: Royal body (use fluorescent fire orange floss) palmered with furnace hackle
- Wing: Medium or dark elk and white calf body
- Hackle: Grizzly, three to four turns
- Thorax: Fluorescent fire orange Antron

Stimulator, Yellow (Randall Kaufmann)
- Hook: 200R, sizes 6-16
- Thread: Fluorescent fire orange
- Tail: Light elk
- Rib: Fine gold wire
- Abdomen: Fluorescent yellow Antron, palmered with badger or ginger hackle
- Wing: Light elk
- Hackle: Grizzly, three to four turns
- Thorax: Amber goat

Note: See page 102.

Thorax, Blue-Winged Olive
- Hook: 900BL, sizes 12-22
- Thread: Olive
- Wing: Medium to dark blue dun turkey flat, thorax style
- Tail: Four to 10 medium to dark blue dun hackle fibers, split
- Body: Olive to olive-brown Antron or Superfine
- Hackle: Medium to dark blue dun or olive grizzly, thorax style

Note: See page 84.

Thorax, Pale Morning Dun (PMD)
- Hook: 900BL, sizes 16-18
- Thread: Yellow
- Wing: Light blue dun turkey flat, thorax style
- Tail: Four to 10 light to medium blue dun hackle fibers, split
- Body: Yellow (light to chartreuse) Superfine
- Hackle: Light to medium blue dun, thorax style

Note: See page 84.

Trude, Lime
- Hook: 900BL, sizes 8-14
- Thread: Fluorescent green
- Tail: Moose
- Body: Peacock, fluorescent green floss, peacock
- Wing: White calf body
- Hackle: Brown and grizzly

Note: One of many Lime Trude variations—this is my favorite. It floats in heavy water and has good color.

Turck's Tarantula (Guy Turck)
- Hook: 5262, sizes 6-12
- Thread: Tan
- Tail: Amherst pheasant tippets
- Body: Hare's mask
- Wing: White calf, natural tan deer, and pearl Krystal Flash
- Head: Deer
- Legs: White round rubber

Note: Guy Turck guides out of High Country Flies in Jackson, Wyoming, where this fly is very effective. Other colors to suit.

Dan Bailey Flies

Wulff, Gray (Lee Wulff)
- Hook: 900BL, sizes 8-14
- Thread: Gray
- Wing: Elk or stiff deer
- Tail: Same as wing
- Body: Gray Antron
- Hackle: Medium to dark blue dun

Note: Especially useful for imitating Black and Gray Drakes, Siphlonurus occidentalis, an early season hatch in the far West and mid to late summer in the Rockies. Dress the Gray Wulff sparsely for this hatch.

Wulff, Royal (Lee Wulff)
- Hook: 900BL, sizes 8-18
- Thread: Black
- Wing: White calf, upright and divided
- Tail: Elk or moose body
- Body: Three-part royal body
- Hackle: Brown

Note: See page 106.

Wulff, White (Lee Wulff)
- Hook: 900BL, sizes 8-16
- Thread: Black
- Wing: White calf, upright and divided
- Tail: White calf
- Body: White Antron
- Hackle: Badger

Note: One of only two white surface flies readily available and worth having in your fly box. Highly visible. Use for salmon, trout, and steelhead. See page 106.

Craig Mathews

X Caddis (Craig Mathews and John Juracek)
- Hook: 900BL, sizes 12-18
- Thread: Tan or to match body
- Tail: Gold Z-Lon or to match body dubbing
- Body: Golden tan Antron or color to suit
- Wing: Light mottled deer hair, tied downwing style, butt ends clipped short

Untying Flies

As a teenager, I traveled with my family to Montana every summer. I always looked forward to visiting Otto Schultz, a grand German character who sold flies out of his house along Highway 2 south of Columbia Falls. Otto's place was brightly painted, and the front yard was decorated with antlers. Inside his wood-paneled station wagon was his permanent "passenger," a life-sized statue of an Indian maiden. Otto liked to talk about "them big cutthroats" in the Hungry Horse area and how the fishing and the country had been so much better before construction of the dam. Otto tied beautiful Trude-style flies, and I always collected a few and marveled at their construction, especially the hackle.

Another obscure but excellent tyer, Andrew "Buck" Bruckbauer, lived along the Santiam River in Oregon and tied the most beautiful duck quill wings I have ever seen. Dennis Black often ordered Ginger Quills from Buck, and we would admire their flawless construction. One day Dennis suggested we take one apart and see how he tied them.

Since then, I have learned a great deal about tying techniques simply by untying flies. Otto tied his Trudes with three saddle hackles and left plenty of room at the front of the hook to accommodate them. Buck's unique tie-in method for duck wings is still the method I use and is detailed in the Blue Dun chapter. Over the years, I have discovered many other subtle tricks and techniques.

Useful tools include a razor blade, tweezers, bodkin, and two or three hackle pliers. Begin by asking yourself what specifically you want to learn and proceed *slowly*. Take *explicit* notes about *everything*. It may be necessary to use a razor blade to get the thread unraveled, especially if a whip finish and hard lacquer was used on the head. Once you get an end, attach a hackle pliers so it does not unravel prematurely. After the thread head is removed, pick up the hackle tip (or tips) with another pliers.

Unravel each component intact and carefully lay it on your bench. Count every turn of thread and observe its placement closely. Note every wrap of dubbing and where all materials are tied in and tied off. Note the angle of scissors cuts. Make note of proportions, diameter of dubbing and hackle stems, width of hackle fibers, material density, number of tail fibers, *everything* you can think of. A subtle technique can be easily overlooked.

Once the fly is apart and your notes are complete, attempt to put the fly back together. You should be able to restore it to its original condition less one turn of hackle and a couple of turns of thread at the head. One never knows what will be found hidden beneath a perfectly-tapered body or a minute thread head!

Tying Dry Flies

Brian O'Keefe

Fish should always be kept in the water. **Minimize handling!** *If you take a photo, these are possible poses.*

Landing and Releasing Fish

The more quickly you land fish, the better their chances of survival. To do this, use the strongest leader possible, exert maximum sideways pressure on them, and strip or reel in the fish quickly.

A barbless hook helps ensure safe handling and facilitates a quick release. Slide your hand down the leader and back out the hook without touching the fish. If the fish is hooked deeply, use a forceps or smooth-nosed pliers. If the fly cannot be removed without damage to the fish, cut the leader.

Do not release a tired fish until it has *completely* recovered. Hold a tired fish firmly by the tail with one hand and gently support the fish from underneath just behind the head with your other hand. Face the fish upstream (when current is available) in an upright position in fairly calm water where there is enough oxygen to allow the fish to breathe easily. In lakes and slow water, it is mandatory to gently move fish back and forth to ensure the flow of oxygen-rich water through their gills.

When tired fish are released prematurely, they often swim strongly out of sight, lose their equilibrium, turn onto their side, and die. It does not hurt to revive fish a bit longer than you feel is necessary. This ensures a *complete* recovery without complications. This process usually takes a minute or two, but fish that are extremely tired can require several minutes. A fish which is bleeding slightly will probably survive. Even a fish that is bleeding profusely can usually be revived if *you* are patient enough.

Most fatal damage occurs to fish through improper handling, not during the actual hooking and playing of fish. *It is best not to handle fish or remove them from the water.* When a fish is removed from the water, it begins to suffocate immediately, and the risk is great that the fish will flop about on the bank, slip from your grasp, or be squeezed to death. If you must handle fish, be certain your hands are wet, for wet hands do not destroy the protective mucous film on fish (especially trout). Do not bring fish into a boat or onto a float tube. *Keep them in the water.* Do not lay fish on their sides. Do not put undue strain on fish by lifting them by the tail or in an unnatural position. Never put your fingers in their gills for this is like puncturing a lung. Gills also excrete toxins and are critical to a fish's ability to swim. Never squeeze fish; vital organs are easily damaged. Fish seldom struggle when handled gently or turned upside down. Never toss fish back into the water! Photos are best taken of fish in the water. *The important consideration is to release fish quickly and without harm.*

Bibliography

Books

Almy, Gerald. *Tying & Fishing Terrestrials*. Harrisburg, Pennsylvania: Stackpole Books, 1978.
Bergman, Ray. *Trout*. New York: Alfred A. Knopf, 1976.
Best, A. K. *Production Fly Tying*. Boulder, Colorado: Pruett Publishing, 1989.
Blades, William F. *Fishing Flies And Fly Tying*. Harrisburg, Pennsylvania: Stackpole Books, 1979.
Borger, Gary. *Designing Trout Flies*. Wausau, Wisconsin: Tomorrow River Press, 1990.
Brooks, Charles E. *Fishing Yellowstone Waters*. New York: Winchester Press, 1984.
Brooks, Joe. *Trout Fishing*. New York: Harper & Row, 1979.
Caucci, Al and Bob Nastasi. *Hatches II*. New York: Lyons & Burford, 1986.
Cordes, Ron and Randall Kaufmann. *Lake Fishing With A Fly*. Portland, Oregon: Frank Amato Publications, 1984.
Cutter, Ralph. *Sierra Trout Guide*. Portland, Oregon: Frank Amato Publications, 1984.
Darbee, Harry and Mac Francis. *Catskill Fly Tyer*. New York: J. P. Lippincott Company, 1977.
Dennis, Jack. *Western Trout Fly Tying Manual*. Jackson Hole, Wyoming: Snake River Books, 1974.
_____. *Western Trout Fly Tying Manual, Volume II*. Jackson Hole, Wyoming: Snake River Books, 1980.
Draper, Keith. *Trout Flies In New Zealand*. Wellington, New Zealand: A. H. & A. W. Reed, Ltd., 1971.
Flick, Art. *Art Flick's Master Fly Tying Guide*. New York: Crown Publishers, Inc., 1972.
_____. *New Streamside Guide*. New York: Crown Publishers, Inc., 1969.
Fling, Paul N. and Donald L. Puterbaugh. *The Basic Manual Of Fly Tying*. New York: Sterling Publishing, 1979.
Fothergill, Chuck. *Fly Tying 101, A Classroom Approach*. Woody Creek, Colorado: Stream Stalker Publishing, 1990.
Hafele, Rick and Dave Hughes. *The Complete Book Of Western Hatches*. Portland, Oregon: Frank Amato Publications, 1981.
Harder, John R. *The Orvis Fly Pattern Index*. New York: Penguin, 1990.
Harvey, George W. *Techniques Of Trout Fishing And Fly Tying*. Bellevue, Pennsylvania: Metz Hatchery, 1985.
Hellekson, Terry. *Popular Fly Patterns*. Salt Lake City, Utah: Peregrine Press, 1977.
Herter, George Leonard and Jacques P. Herter. *Professional Fly Tying And Spinning Lure Making Manual*. Waseca, Minnesota: Herter's, Inc., 1941.
Horn, Elizabeth. *Sierra Nevada Wildflowers*. Missoula, Montana: Mountain Press Publishing Company, 1998.
Inland Empire Fly Fishing Club. *Flies Of The Northwest*. Spokane, Washington: Inland Empire Fly Fishing Club, 1981.
_____. *Flies Of The Northwest*. Spokane, Washington: Inland Empire Fly Fishing Club, 1989.
Kaufmann, Randall. *The Fly Tyers Nymph Manual*. Portland, Oregon: Western Fisherman's Press, 1986.
_____. *Tying Nymphs*. Portland, Oregon: Western Fisherman's Press, 1994.
_____. *Fly Patterns Of Umpqua Feather Merchants*. Glide, Oregon: Umpqua Feather Merchants, 1995.
La Branch, George M. L. *The Dry Fly And Fast Water*. New York: Charles Scribner's Sons, 1914.
LaFontaine, Gary. *Caddisflies*. New York: Nick Lyons Books, 1981.
_____. *The Dry Fly, New Angles*. Helena, Montana: Greycliff Publishing, 1990.
Leiser, Eric. *The Book Of Fly Patterns*. New York: Alfred A. Knopf, 1987.
Leonard, J. Edson. *Flies*. New York: A. S. Barnes, 1960.
Marinaro, Vincent. *A Modern Dry Fly Code*. New York: Lyons & Burford, 1983.
_____. *In The Ring Of The Rise*. New York: Crown Publishers, Inc., 1976.

Mathews, Craig and John Juracek. *Fly Patterns Of Yellowstone*. West Yellowstone, Montana: Blue Ribbon Flies, 1987.
McCafferty, Patrick W. *Aquatic Entomology*. Boston: Science Books International, 1981.
McKim, John F. *Fly Tying, Adventures In Fur, Feathers And Fun*. Missoula, Montana: Mountain Press, 1982.
Migel, Michael. *The Masters On The Dry Fly*. New York: Lyons & Burford, 1989.
Patrick, Roy. *Pacific Northwest Fly Patterns*. Seattle, Washington: Patrick's Fly Shop, 1970.
Pequegnot, Jean-Paul. *French Fishing Flies*. New York: Nick Lyons Books, 1987.
Pobst, Dick. *Trout Stream Insects*. New York: Lyons & Burford, 1990.
Quick, Jim. *Trout Fishing And Trout Flies*. New York: Castle Books, 1957.
Richards, Carl, Doug Swisher, and Fred Arbona. *Stoneflies*. New York: Winchester Press, 1980.
Schwiebert, Ernest G., Jr. *Matching The Hatch*. New York: MacMillan Publishing Co., Inc., 1955.
_____. *Trout*. New York: E. P. Dutton, 1978.
Shaw, Helen. *Fly-Tying*. New York: John Wiley & Sons, 1979.
Stewart, Dick. *Universal Fly Tying Guide*. Westfield, Massachusetts: Universal Vise Corporation, 1979.
Swisher, Doug and Carl Richards. *Fly Fishing Strategy*. New York: Crown Publishers, Inc., 1975.
_____. *Selective Trout*. New York: Crown Publishers, Inc., 1971.
Usinger, Robert L. *Aquatic Insects Of California*. Berkeley, California: University Of California Press, 1956.
Wilson, Dermot. *Fishing The Dry Fly*. London: Adam & Charles Black, 1957; 1970 edition.
Wilson, Loring D. *Tying And Fishing The Terrestrials*. New York: A. S. Barnes & Co., 1978.
Wright, Leonard M., Jr. *Fishing The Dry Fly As A Living Insect*. New York: E. P. Dutton & Co., Inc., 1972.
Wulff, Lee. *Trout On A Fly*. New York: Nick Lyons Books, 1986.

Videos
Dennis, Jack. *Tying Western Trout Flies*. Jackson Hole, Wyoming: Jack Dennis Fly Fishing Video Library, 1988.
Lawson, Mike and Jack Dennis. *Tying Western Dry Flies*. Jackson Hole, Wyoming: Jack Dennis Fly Fishing Video Library, 1988.

Catalogs
Black's Custom Flies. Winchester, Oregon: 1970.
Buz's. Visalia, California: 1962, 1965.
Dan Bailey. Livingston, Montana: 1985, 1990, 1991, 1994.
Kaufmann's Streamborn. Tigard, Oregon: 1972, 1980, 1990, 1991.
Kaufmann's Streamborn, Inc. Tigard, Oregon: 1995.
Orvis Co. Manchester, Vermont: 1970, 1990, 1991.
Umpqua Feather Merchants. Glide, Oregon: 1995.

Articles
Barnes, Pat. "Flies For Float Fishing: Jug Head & Goofus Bug." *Fly Tyer*. Winter, 1979.
_____. "Goofus Bug Evolution." *American Angler & Fly Tyer*. Spring, 1990.
Gartside, Jack. "The Pheasant Hopper." *Fly Fisherman*. Winter, 1978.
Harrop, Renè. "Harrop's Hairwing Dun." *Fly Fisherman*. June, 1988.
Harvey, George. "New Dry Fly Wings." *Fly Fisherman*. December, 1990.
Leeson, Ted. "Natural Wings." *Fly Fisherman*. December, 1990.
Mathias, Dr. Eugene. "Buz Buszek's Western Coachman and King's River Caddis." *Fly Tyer*. Spring, 1984.
McCracken, Dave. "Renegade and Bear Paw Fore & Aft Flies." *Fly Tyer*. Fall, 1983.
Morris, Ray. "The Henryville Special." *Fly Fisherman*. May, 1986.
Neimeyer, Ted. "How To Untie A Fly." *Fly Fisherman*. Winter, 1976.
Puyans, Andrè. "Winding Hackle." *Fly Fisherman*. March, 1982.
_____. "Winding Hackles, II." *Fly Fisherman*. April, 1982.
_____. "Winding Hackles, III." *Fly Fisherman*. May-June, 1982.
Talleur, Dick. "The Wonderful Wulffs." *American Angler & Fly Tyer*. Winter, 1988.
Toman, Kevin. "Western Green Drake and Eastern Green Drake." *Fly Tyer*. Winter, 1979.
Troth, Al. "Elk Hair Caddis." *Fly Tyer*. Unknown.
_____. "The MacSalmon Fly." *Fly Tyer*. Summer, 1985.
_____. "Troth Salmon Fly and Gulper Special." *Fly Tyer*. August, 1980.
Woods, Craig. "Hackles." *Fly Fisherman*. Spring, 1981.

Index

A
A Modern Dry Fly Code, 42, 84
abdomen, 26, 27, 68, 98, 118
acetate, 68
Acroneuria, 103, 118
Acroneuria californica, 102, 103
Acroneuria pacifica, 102, 103
Adams, 12, **13**, 27, 28, 29, **70-71**, **128**
Adams, Charles, 70
Adams hackle, 70
Adams Hairwing Dun, 70
Adams Humpy, 70
Adams, Irresistible, 70, **110-111**, **132**
Adams Loop Wing, 70
Adams Parachute, 29, 31, 70, **88-89**, **128**
Adams Wulff, 70, 106
adult damsel, 98
Adult Damsel, Stalcup, **98**
adult dun, 12
adult dragonfly, 98
Adult Midge, 12
Advanced Strategies For Selective Trout, 11
aft hackle, **26**
Alaska, 106, 115
Algonquin, 114
Almy, Gerald, 42
Andes Mountains, 115
Ansel Adams Wilderness, High Sierra, California, **127**
Ant, Black Flying, 28, 29, 30, **68-69**, **130**
Ant, Brown Flying, 68
Ant, Foam, 68
Ant, Power, **134**
antennae, 26, **28**, 62
Antron, **20**, **21**, 22, 23, **25**
ants, 10, 68-69
application jar, 14
Arctic, 102
Argentina, 115
Atlantic salmon, 106
attraction, theory, 106
attractor, 12-13
AuSable Wulff, 106

B
back, **27**, **28**
Baetis, 70, 82, **133**
Baetis Parachute, **133**
Baetis vagans, 128
Bailey, Dan, 106, 114
Bailey, John, 130
barbless hooks, 18, 138
Barnes, Pat and Sig, 114, 132
base vise, **16**
basic tying techniques, 32-39
Beaverkill River, New York, 72
Beetle, Foam, 28, **42-44**, **128**
Beetle, Krystal Flash, **128**
beetles, 10, 42-43
bend, hook, **17**
Bergman, Ray, 12, 77, 88, 110

Better Trout Streams, 128
Betters, Francis, 106
Betts' Tailing Fibers, 23, **25**
Big Hole River, Montana, 118, 134
Big Horn River, Montana, 90
Big Wood River, Idaho, 94
biot, 82
Bitterroot River, Montana, 132
Bivisible, **128**
Black and Brown Flying Ant, **68**
Black and Yellow Seducer, 103
Black Ant, **68**
Black, Dennis, 41, 137
black drake, **70**, **94**, 136
Black Flying Ant, 28, 29, 30, **68-69**, **130**
black flies, 60
Black Gnat, 22, 31, **76-79**, **128**
Black Gnat, Parachute, **133**
Black Quill, 76
Black Stimulator, **103**
Black Thorax, **86**
Black Wulff, 106
blender, 14
Blonde Humpy, **115**
Blue Bottle, 12
Blue Damsel, Braided Butt, **28**, **98**
Blue Dun, 22, 29, **26**, 31, **76-79**, 128
Blue Quill, 76
Blue Ribbon Flies, 46
Blue Upright, 76, **77**
blue-winged olive, 84
Blue-Winged Olive, 70, **129**
Blue-Winged Olive Thorax, 29, 31, **84-87**, **136**
Blue-Winged Olive, CDC Spinner, **82**
Boardman River, 70
bobbin, 14, 125
bodkin, **15**
body, **20**, **26**, **27**, **28**, 45, 82
Boise River, South Fork, 134
Bonnett, Jim, 134
Borger, Gary, 98
Boyer, Dick, 114
Braided Butt Damsel, 29, **98-99**, **130**
British Columbia, 115
Brobst, Hiram, 131
brook trout, **41**, **43**, **85**
brown drake, 94
Brown Drake, **128**
Brown Flying Ant, 68, **69**
Brown Paradrake, **27**, **134**
brown trout, **43**
Bruckbauer, Andrew, 137
Brush, William Avery, 88
Bucktail Caddis, **12**
bullet head, **26**, 118, 122, 132
Burke, Dr. Edgar, 84
burned monofilament eyes, 98-99
Buszek, Virginia, 132
Buszek, Wayne "Buz," 12, 92, 132
Buz's, 132

C
C-clamp vise, **16**
Caddis, CDC Adult, Tan, **129**
Caddis, Elk Hair, 21, 23, **29**, 30, **100-101**, **130**
Caddis, Goddard, **130**

Caddis, Peacock, **134**
Caddis, Spent Partridge, **135**
Caddis, X, **136**
caddisflies, 10, 12, 13, 26, 43, 60, 70, 88, 92, 96, **100**, 103, 114, 118
Cahill, 12, 72
Cahill, Dan, 72, 132
Cahill, Dark, **130**
Cahill, Light, 31, 52, **72-75**, **132**
calf, 24, **25**
California Mosquito, 29, 30, **64-67**, **129**
Callibaetis, 12, 70, 82, 90
Callibaetis, Caddis Cripple, **13**
Callibaetis, Sparkle Dun, **13**
Callibaetis Spinner, **27**, 28
Callibaetis Thorax, **13**, **84**
caribou, 23, **24**, 25
Cascade Mountains, 120
catch and release, 138
Catskill Fly Tyer, 72
Catskill patterns, 72, 73
Catskill-style wings, **74**
Caucci, Al, 46, 129
CDC, **22**
CDC *Baetis* Spent Spinner, **26**, 82
CDC Blue-Winged Olive Spent Spinner, **82**
CDC Caddis, **100**
CDC Caddis Adult, Tan, **129**
CDC *Callibaetis* Comparadun, **47**, **129**
CDC *Callibaetis* Spinner, 28, 30, **82-83**, **129**
CDC Cluster Midge, 60-61
CDC Comparadun, 31, 46-49
CDC feathers, 22, 25
CDC Mahogany Comparadun, **47**
CDC PMD Comparadun, **47**
CDC Rusty Spent Spinner, 82, **129**
CDC *Tricorythodes*, 82
cements, 15
ceramic bobbin, **14**
Chandler, William, 72
Chernobyl Ant, 41, **129**
Chile, **9**, 85, 111
Chinese necks, **50**
chironomids, 10, 12, 60, 62
Christian, Herman, 72
cicada, 10, **117**, 120, 122
Cinnamon Flying Ant, **68**
Cinnamon Fur Ant, **68**
Cinygmula, 133
Clarke, Brian, 130
Clark's Cicada, **129**
Cliff Lake, Montana, 114
clipped hair body, 110
clipped hair head, 118, 120
closed cell foam, 20, 23, 25, 43
Cluster Midge, 60-61
Coachman, Royal, 22, 31, **76-79**, 106, **134**
Coleoptera, 42
collar, **28**, 29, 118-119, 120-121, 122-123
commercial tying, 124-125
Comparadun, 13, 23, 46, 49, **129**
Comparahatch, 46
Copper Basin, Idaho, 94
Cordes, Ron, 11

Covich, Jon, 40, 60, 79, 111, 113
Cox, Edith, 134
craneflies, 26, 60, 88
Cricket, 120
Crinkle Z-Lon, 23
cripple, 12, 13
Cripple, **129**
Crystal Epoxy, 15
Cutter, Ralph, 130
cutthroat trout, **47**, **115**

D
Dai-Riki hooks, 17
Daiichi hooks, 17
Damsel, Braided Butt, 29, **98-99**, **130**
damselflies, 10, 26, **98**
Dan Bailey's Fly Shop, 115, 130, 131, 136
Danville thread, 21
Darbee, Harry, 72, 110
Dark Cahill, **130**
Dark Flying Ant, **68**
Dark Hendrickson, **72**
Darlon, 25
Dave's Cricket, **120**
Dave's Hopper, **13**, 29, **120-121**, **130**
debarbing pliers, **16**
deer flies, 70
deer hair, 23, **24**, 25, 47
deer hair head, 30, 119, 120-121
delta wing, **31**, 68
Dennis, Jack, 11, **110**, 111, 114, 115, 132, 133
Deschutes River, Oregon, 11, 84, 88, 90, **96**, 102, 103, 118, 120
Dickinson Park, Wyoming, 110
Diptera, 10, 60, 64
Dicosmoecus, 103
divided hair wing, 27
double downwing, 19, **20**
double hackles, **58-59**
Double Humpy, **115**, **131**
Double No Hackle, 80
down hairwing, 100, 103
downwing, 13, **27**, **28**, **29**, 30, 45, 118
dragonflies, 26, 98
drakes, 28, 70, 90, 94, 136
Drunella coloradensis, 46
Drunella flavilinea, 46
Dry Falls Lake, Washington, 62
dry fly, 10
dry fly evolution, 12-13
dry fly fishing, 10
Dry Fly, New Angles, The, 11, 106, 115
dubbing, **20**, **21**, 22, 25, **38-39**
duck, **22**, 25
duck quill wing, upright, divided, **31**, 76
Dun Brown Parachute, **133**
Dusty Miller, 12
Dyna-King vise, **16**

E
E/C Caddis, **12**, **29**, **96-97**, **130**
Eisenhower, President, 131
elk hair, 23, **24**, 25, 100-101
Elk Hair Caddis, 21, 23, **29**, 30, **100-101**, **130**

Elk Hair Hopper, **130**
emergers, 12
Emerging Midge, 12
Epeorus, 133
Epeorus pleuralis, 72, **134**
Ephemera simulans, 94, 128, **134**
Ephemerella cornuta, 84, **128**
Ephemerella dorothea, 77
Ephemerella drunella, 94
Ephemerella drunella/grandis, 94
Ephemerella flavilinea, **134**
Ephemerella grandis, 94, **134**
Ephemerella inermis, 90, **135**
Ephemerella infrequens, 90, **135**
Ephemerella subvaria, 72
epoxy, 15
Erickson, Mary, **40**, **127**
Evolution Creek, California, 64, **65**
Evolution Valley, California, 64
extended body, **27**, **28**, 94, **99**
Extended Boby Spinner, 94
Extended Gray Drake, **13**
Extended Green Drake, **12**
eye, hook, **17**, 18
eyes, **28**
eyes, monofilament, 98-99

F
fan wing, 77
Fan Wing Royal Coachman, 76
Fay, George, 114
feather downwing, 120
feather wing, upright-divided, 31, 73
feathers, 25
Federation of Fly Fishers, 10
feeding rhythm, 60
feeding zone, 92
Female Adams, **70**
Fine and Dry dubbing, 22, 25
Fire Hole River, Montana, 90
Firefly, **43**
flared hair, 110-111
flared tail, 83
Flathead River, Montana, 106
Flexament, 15, 73, 75, 76, 79, 99
Flick, Art, 133
Flies, 12
float tube, 98
floss, 25
Fluorescent Green Royal Humpy, **27**, **114-115**
Fly-Fisher's Entomology, The, 42
Fly Fishing Made Easy, 11
Fly Fishing Strategy, 80
Fly Fishing Tips From The Traveling Fishermen, 11
Fly Patterns And Their Origins, 76
Fly Patterns Of Yellowstone, 46
Fly Tying Basics, 11
Fly Wing, Shimazaki, 23, 25
Flying Ants, **68-69**
FlyMaster thread, 21
Foam Ant, **68**
Foam Beetle, 28, **42-44**, **128**
foam, closed-cell, 20, 23-25, 43
food sources, 92
fore hackle, **26**
forked tail, 90
Formicidae, 68

Foster, James, **64**, **65**
fox, red, 25
Fox, Charles, 77
Francis, Mac, 72
Frazier, Pret, 90, 133, 134
front-to-back technique, 54

G
gape, **17**
genetic hackle, 50
giant Michigan mayfly, 94
Ginger Quill, 76, **77**
Glasser, Sam, 64
Gnat, Black, **76-79**, **128**
Gnat, Griffith, 21, **60-61**, **131**
gnats, 60, 70, 76-77
goat, **21**, 22, 25
Goddard Caddis, **130**
Goddard, John, 130
Gold-Ribbed Hare's Ear, 100
golden pheasant tippets, 25
Golden Stimulator, 25, 102, **103**, **127**
golden stone, 102, 103
golden trout, **64**, **65**, **127**
Goofus Bug, 114
goose, 22
Gordon, Theodore, 72, 130, 134
Grand Teton National Park, Wyoming, 115
grasshoppers, 10, 118, 120, 122
gray drake, **13**, 70, 90, 94, **136**
Gray Hackle Peacock, 12
Gray Hackle Yellow, **12**
Gray Slow Water Caddis, **135**
Gray Wulff, 106, **136**
grayling, **107**
great yellow drake, 94
green drake, **28**, 90, 94
Green Drake, **130**
Green Drake Paradrake, 28, 29, 31, 47, **94-95**, **134**
Green Drake, Small, Sparkle Dun, **46**
Green Drake, Wulff, 106
Green River, Utah, 129
Green River, Wyoming, 115
Green Seducer, **135**
Green Stimulator, **102**, 103
Griffith, George, 60, 131
Griffith Gnat, 21, 29, **60-61**, **131**
grizzly hackle, 51
Grizzly King, **12**
Grizzly Wulff, 106
Guard, Bob, 11
Gunnison River, Colorado, 118
gyrofly, 88

H
H & L Variant, **131**
hackle, 24, **25**, **26**, **28**, 29, **45**, 50-59, 62
hackle density, 52
hackle gauge, 15, **52**
hackle length, 52
hackle pliers, **15**, **58**, 125
hackle post, 98-99
hackle, reversed, 54
hackle stem legs, 120
hackle stems, 51
hackle stiffness, 51

hackle tail, **27**, 66, 75
hackle tip downwing, **27**, **30**, 65
hackle tip, spentwing, 82
hackle tip, upright-divided, **27**, 70-71
hackle width, **52**
hackling, 50
Haily, John, 76, 134
hair, 23-24, 25
hair body, reversed, 122-123
hair flies, 110-111
hair head, **28**, 118-119, 120-121, 122-123
hair tails, **27**, 107, 109, 116
Hairwing Dun, Hendrickson, **131**
hairwing, **28**, 29
hairwing, upright-divided, 106-109
half hitch, **34**, 125
Halladay, Len, 70, 128
Hardshell Ant, **68**
hare's ear, 25
hare's mask, 25
Hare's Ear Parachute, **92**
Hare-Tron, **21**, 22, 25
Harriman Ranch, 46, 94, 122
Harrison, Carter, 134
Harrop, Bonnie, 129
Harrop, Renè, 60, 82, 94, 129, 131
hatch breaking, 42
Hatches II, 46
Hatching Mayfly, PMD, **62**
hatching dun, 12, **13**
Hatching Midge, 12, **13**, **28**, **62-63**, 127, **131**
Hatching PMD, **13**
Haystack, 46
head, 28, **29**, 49, 68, 118, 119, 120, 121, 123
Heath, Emmett, 129
hen hackle, 25, 50
hen hackle tips, 82
hen neck, 25
hen saddle, 25
Hen Spent Spinner, **135**
Hendrickson, **72**
Henry, Cliff, 130
Henry's Fork Anglers, 122, 135
Henry's Fork Cricket, **122**
Henry's Fork Hopper, **13**, 23, **26**, 28, 29, 30, 76, **122-123**, **131**
Henry's Fork of the Snake, Idaho, 46, **79**, 94, 122
Henryville Caddis, 131
Henryville Special, 22, **131**
Herter, George L., 134
Hewitt, Edward, 72, 128
Hexagenia limbata, 94
Hexagenia Paradrake, 94
high intensity lamp, 125
High Country Flies, 136
High Sierra Mountains, California, **40**, **67**, **111**, 115, 120, **127**
Highland Flies, 99
Highland Lakes, Tasmania, 42
Hook and Hackle gauge, 15, **52**
hook, inserting in vise, 32
hooks, 17-19
hoppers, 10, 118, 120, 122
Hopper, Elk Hair, **130**

Hopper, Henry's Fork, **13**, 23, **26**, 28, 29, 30, 76, **122-123**, **131**
Hopper, Parachute, **13**, **29**, **92**
Horner Deer Hair, 114
Horner, Jack, 114
Hot Butt™ Caddis, **12**, **131**
House and Lot (H & L), **131**
House of Harrop, 82, 129
Humpy, 12, **13**, 20, 21, 23, 28, 31, 47, **52**, **114-117**, **132**
Humpy, Double **115**, **131**
Humpy, Royal, **12**, 28, 114-115, **116**, **131**, 132
Humpy, Royal Fluorescent Green, **131**
Humpy, Royal Red, **132**
Humpy, Yellow, **132**
Hymenoptera, 68

I
Improved Sofa Pillow, **13**, 23, **132**
Indian saddles, 25, **51**
infrequens, 21
inserting hook, 32
Iron fraudator, 72
Irresistible, 12, 28, 29, 31, **110-113**
Irresistible, Adams, 70, **110-111**, **132**
Irresistible, Wulff, 106, 110-111, **132**
Island Park, Idaho, 10, 134
Isoperla mormona, 103
Isoperla patricia, 103

J
Jack Dennis Sports, 114
Jack Horner, **12**
Jackson Hole, Wyoming, 114, 115, 136
Jay, **110**
Jennings, Percy, 110
Jennings, Preston, 133
Joe's Hopper, **13**
John Muir Wilderness, California, **67**, **111**, **127**
Jumping Beetle, **43**
Juracek, John, 46, 135, 136
JW Creekside, **16**
JW Pro, **16**

K
Kamloops lakes, British Columbia, 62
katydids, 120
Kaufmann, Lance, **110**
Kaufmann, Randall, 11, 62, 102, 131, 135, 136
Kaufmann Stimulator blend, 21
Kaufmann Stone, 14
Kaufmann's Streamborn, 12
Kevlar thread, 21
King's Canyon National Park, California, 64
King's River Caddis, 92, **132**
Kiwi Fleetle, **43**
Krystal Flash, 118
Krystal Flash Beetle, **128**

L
lacquer, 14

Index 143

LaFontaine, Gary, 11, 68, 70, 96, 106, 115
Laible, Gerhard, 100
Laible's CDC Caddis, **100**
Lake Fishing With A Fly, 11, 62
lake flies, 62
Lake Taupo, New Zealand, **60, 96**
lamp, 15
landing and releasing fish, 138
Lawson, Mike, 11, 76, 80, 94, 122, 128, 130, 131, 133, 134, 135
Lawson, Sheralee, 135
leaders, 62
Leaning to Fly fish for Trout, 11
Leaver, Dick, 100
legs, **26, 28, 29,** 43, 68, 118, 120, 123
Lenore Lake, Washington, 62
Leonard, Edson J., 12
Leopold, Aldo, 110
Letort, Pennsylvania, 84
light, 106, 115
Light Cahill, 28, 29, 31, 52, **72-75,** 132
Light Cahill, Parachute, **133**
Lime Trude, **136**
Little Jack Horner, 114
Little Red Sedge, 100
little yellow stone, 103
Loop Wing Adams, 70
loose-wrap-and-cinch technique, **36**
Loyalsock Creek, Pennsylvania, 100

M

MacHopper, **28,** 118
macrame body, 118
macrame cord, 23, 25, 118
macrame yarn, **25**
MacSalmon, 28, 29, **118-119,** 132
Madam X, **132**
Madison River, Montana, 92, 106, 115, 118, 120
Makarora, New Zealand, 115
mallard, **22,** 25
Manuka beetle, 42
March Brown, **133**
March Brown, American, **133**
Marinaro, Vincent, 42, 84
Martin, Jay, 110
Matarelli bobbin, 14
Matarelli threader-cleaner, 16
Matching The Hatch, 11
material clip, **15**
material tie in, 35-39, 124
materials, 20-25
Mathews, Craig, 46, 135, 136
mayflies, 10, 12, 60, 70, 84, 85, 88, 90, 114, 118
mayfly dun, 90, 133
mayfly spinner, 82-83, 88
McKenzie River, Oregon, 102
Messinger, Joe, 110
Metolius River, Oregon, 94, 102
Metz hackle, **50-51,** 53
Michigan mayfly, 94
Micro Fibetts, 23, **25**
Midge, Hatching, 12, **13,** 28, **62-63,** 127, **131**
midges, 10, 12, 13, 26, 28, **60, 62,** 114

Mills, A. C., Sr., 88
Mills, William & Son, 88
monofilament eyes, 98
moose, 23, **24,** 25
Mosquito, California, 30, **64-67, 129**
mosquitoes, 10, 60, 64-65, 70, 129
Muddler-style head, 120
multi-imitators, 13, 102-103
muskrat, **20,** 21, 25

N

Nastasi, Bob, 46, 129
neck hackle, **50, 51, 52**
Neversink River, New York, 72
New Zealand, 41, 42, 70, **96,** 98, 103, **111, 113,** 115, 117
No Hackle, 13, 31, **80-81,** 133
no hackle duck wings, 80-81
No Hackle, Olive, **133**
Nunnally Lake, Washington, 62
Nymph Fly Fishing, 128
nymphal case, 82
nymphs, 12, 92, 98, 118

O

October caddis, 103
O'Keefe, Brian, 85, 90, 94
Olive Braided Butt Damsel, **99**
Olive Dun, 76
Olive Elk Hair Caddis, **100**
Olive Quill, 76, **77**
Olive Thorax, **84-87**
Orange Humpy, **115**
Orange Seducer, **135**
orange sneezeweed, **64**
Orange Stimulator, **102,** 103
Orthoptera, 120
Orvis, L. C., 76, 134
over and under downwing, 118
over-the-top and hold-it technique, 36, **37**
overbodies, **28,** 43, 115
overwing, 118, 122-123

P

Pacific Northwest Fly Patterns, 12
Pale Evening Dun, **77**
Pale Morning Dun, **12,** 21, 46
Pale Morning Dun, Thorax, **29, 136**
palmered hackle, **29, 54-55,** 60, 100, 102, 103
panfish, 106
Para Wulff, Royal, **133**
Parachute Adams, 29, **88-89**
Parachute Ant, 92
Parachute *Baetis*, **133**
Parachute, Black Gnat, **133**
Parachute Caddis, 29, 30, **92-93**
Parachute, Dun Brown, **133**
Parachute, Emergent Caddis, 92
Parachute, Golden Stone, 92
Parachute, Gray, **133**
parachute hackle, **27, 29,** 88-89
Parachute Hare's Ear, **92**
Parachute Hopper, **13, 29,** 92
Parachute Light Cahill, **133**
Parachute Mayfly, 92
Parachute, Olive Hare's Ear, 92
parachute patterns, 88-99
Parachute, PMD, 29, **134**

Parachute, Red Wing Adams, **134**
Parachute, Stone, 92
parachute style wing, 13, **27, 29, 30,** 88-99
Parachute, Trico, **134**
paradrake, 23, 94, 134
Paradrake, Brown, **134**
Paradrake, Green Drake, 29, 31, 45, **94-95, 134**
partridge feathers, 23, 25
Partridge hooks, 17
parts of a dry fly, 26-31
Patagonia, Argentina, 40, 102, 106
Patrick, Roy, 12
pattern directory, 127-136
peacock, **23, 25,** 60, 72
peacock body, 60
Peacock Caddis, **134**
Peacock Stimulator, **135**
Peaslee, Chris, **64,** 65
Pezl, Bob, 98
pheasant, 23
Pink Lady, 12
Piute Creek, California, **64**
Plecoptera, 118
pliers, debarbing, **16**
pliers, smooth-nosed, 15
Plymouth Rock hackle, 50
PMD, **12,** 90
PMD Hatching Mayfly, 62
PMD Parachute, 29, 31, **90-91,** 133
PMD Sparkle Dun, **46, 135**
PMD Thorax, **136**
point, hook, **17,** 18
poly yarn, 87
Poor Man's Wulff, 114
Power Ant, **134**
preparing hackle, 53
proportions, 45
Pteronarcys, 118
Pteronarcys californica, 103
Pteronarcys dorsata, 103
Pteronarcys Stimulator, 103

Q

Quake Lake, Montana, 115
Quick, Jim, 70, 114
Quigley, Bob, 129
quill body, 73
Quill Gordon, 12, 28, **72-75, 134**
quill wing, 76-79

R

rabbit dubbing, 21
Railroad Ranch, Henry's Fork, **79**
rainbow trout, **64, 70,** 111
Rat-Faced McDougal, 110
razor blade, 120
Reading Trout Streams, 11
Red Humpy, **114**
Red Royal Humpy, **28, 115**
Red Tail Mosquito, **27,** 67
Regal vise, **16**
releasing fish, 138
Renegade, **26,** 29, **134**
Renzetti vise, **16**
reversed hair body, **26,** 122
rib, **27, 28**
Richards, Carl, 11, 13, 80, 94, 133, 135

Ridenour, Charles, 114, 132
ringneck pheasant, 23, 25
Rio Grande, Argentina, **40**
Rithrogena, 133
Riverton Flies, 42
Roberts, Hank, 110
Rocky Mountains, 120
Rod and Reel Shop, 114
rolled wing, 31
Ronalds, Alfred, 42
rooster hackle, 50
Rosborough, Polly, 58
Rosenbauer, Tom, 11
royal body, 76, 107
Royal Coachman, 22, 31, **76-79,** 106, **134**
Royal Elk Hair, 76, 100
Royal Humpy, **12,** 28, 114, 115, **116, 131, 133**
Royal Lime Trude, **29**
Royal Parachute, 76
Royal Stimulator, 76, **103,** 135
Royal Trude, 76, 106, **135**
Royal Wulff, 13, 29, 31, 76, 100, **106-109, 136**
rubber, round (rubber hackle), 23, **25**
Rubber Leg Stimulator, **102**
rubber legs, 122, 132
Rusty Spent Spinner, 28

S

saddle hackle, 25, **50, 52, 56**
salmonfly, 103
Sanchez, Scott, 11
Santiam River, Oregon, 137
Sapphire Lake, California, 64
Scarlet Ibis, 12
Schroeder, Ed, 92
Schultz, Otto, 137
Schwiebert, Ernest, 11
scissors, **15,** 125
securing materials, **35-36**
securing thread, 32, **33**
Seducer, 103, **105**
Seducer, Green, **135**
Seducer, Orange, **135**
selecting hackle, 50, 53
Selective Trout, 11, 12, 80, 94
setting up tying bench, 16
shank, hook, **17**
Shimazaki Caddis, **135**
Shimazaki Fly Wing, 23, **25**
Shimazaki, Ken, 135
shuck, **26, 28,** 62
Sidewinder, 80
Sierra Mountains, **40, 67, 111,** 115, 120, **127**
silhouette, 102
Silver Creek, Idaho, 42, 90
single hackle, **56, 57**
single downwing, **80**
single upright flared wing, 31, 46
single upright wing, **30-31,** 60
Siphlonurus, 70
Siphlonurus occidentalis, 70, 91, 136
Skues, 100
Slow Water Caddis, Gray, 30
Small Green Drake Sparkle Dun, **46**
Smedley, Harold Hinsdale, 76, 134

smooth-nosed pliers, 15
Snake River, Idaho, 103, 106, 115
sneezeweed, orange, **64**
Sofa Pillow, **13**
Sofa Pillow, Improved, **132**
South Island, New Zealand, 113
Sparkle Dun, **13**, 20, 21, 23, **26**, 31, **46-49**, **135**
Speckled Wing Spinner, **135**
speed tying, 124-126
Spent Partridge Caddis, **135**
spent spinner, 12, 13
Spent Spinner, Hen, **135**
spent wing, **26**, **27**, 30, **31**, 82
split tail, **27**, 47, 82
spring creeks, 42
stacker, **15**, 47, 125
Stalcup Adult Damsel, **98**
Stalcup, Shane, 11, 46, 47, 129
standard-style hackle, **29**, 45, **56**, 65
steelhead, 115, 120
Steeves, Harrison R. II, 43
Stenonema canadense, 72, 132
Stenonema vicarium, 133
Steenrod, Roy, 72
stillborn, 13, 46, 62
Stimulator, **13**, 30, **102-105**, **135**
Stimulator, Peacock, **135**
Stimulator, Royal, **135**
Stimulator, Tan, **102**
Stimulator, Yellow, **136**
stoneflies, 10, 13, 26, 88, 102-103, 114, 118
storage cases, 16
Strategies For Selective Trout, 11
strike indicator, 92
stripped peacock, 72
Superfine, **22**, 25
surface film, 42, 80, 106
surface flies, 80
surface impression, 102, 115
Swisher, Doug, 11, 12, 80, 94, 132, 133, 135
synthetic dubbing, **21**

T

tag, **26**
tail, **26-27**, **45**, 82
Tan elk Hair Caddis, **100**
Tan Stimulator, **102**
tanned hair, 24
Tarantula, Turck's, **13**, **136**
Tasmania, 42
teal, **22**, 25
tent downwing, **30**, 92
terrestrials, 10, 26, 68, 114
The Dry Fly, New Angles, 11, 106, 115
The Fly Fisher's Entomology, 42
The Trout And The Fly, 130
thermal drafts, 68
Thompson vise, **16**
thorax, **26**, **27**, **29**, 62, 68, 82, 84-87, 96
Thorax, Blue-Winged Olive, **136**
thorax flies, 21, 81, 84, 85
thorax hackle, **29**, 84-87
thorax patterns, 21, 81, 84, 85
Thorax, Pale Morning Dun, **136**
thorax-style wing, **29**, 85

thread, 21, 25, 125
thread head, **27**, **33**
thread rib, 60
threader-cleaner, 16, 125
three-part body, **29**
tie-in, 32
tie-off, 32, **37**
tied-down, 32
Tiemco ceramic bobbin, 14
Tiemco hackle pliers, 15
Tiemco hooks, 17-19, 20
Tiemco threader, 16
tinsel, 25
Tipulidae, 88
tools, **14-16**
trailing shuck, 47
translucence, 76
traveling sedge, 102
Trichoptera, 96
trico, **85**, 90
Tricorythodes, 84
timmed hair head, 118
trimming hair, 112-113, 121
Troth, Al, 100, 118, 130, 132
Trout, 12
Trout And The Fly, The, 130
Trout Fishing and Trout Flies, 70, 114
Trude, **13**, **29**, 76, 106, **134**, **136**
Trude, A. S., 134
Trude, Lime, **136**
Turangi, New Zealand, 41
Turck, Guy, 136
Turck's Tarantula, **13**, **136**
turkey biot, **23**, **25**, 82
turkey flat (shoulder), **23**, **25**, 86
turkey quill, **23**, 25
turkey tail, 25
turle knot, 18
turned-down tapered eye, 18
turned-up tapered eye, 18
Tying And Fishing Terrestrials, 42
Tying And Fishing The Caddisfly, 11
tying bench, **16**
tying case, **16**
Tying Flies for Spring Creeks and Tailwaters, 11
Tying Flies with Jack Dennis and Friends, 11, 114
Tying Flies with CDC, 11
tying materials off, **37**
Tying Western Dry Flies, 11
Tying Western Trout Flies, 11
tying with speed and efficiency, 124-126

U

ultra-violet light, 115
Umpqua Feather Merchants, 43, 68, 84, 100, 103, 106, 110, 114, 115, 118, 120, 122, 128, 129, 130, 133, 134, 135
Umpqua River, Oregon, 102
underbody, 73
undersize hackle, 58
Understand fly Tying Materials, 11
underwing, 118
uni-midge thread, 24
untying flies, 137
up-between-the-fingers technique, **35**, **44**, 55, 74

upright-divided duck wings, 31, 76
upright-divided feather wings, 31, 73, 76
upright-divided hackle tip wings, **27**, 31
upright-divided hair wings, 31, 115

V

V hackle, 85
V tail, 80, 82
V wing, 92
videos, 11
vinyl cement, 15
vise, **16**

W

Waste-Trol, 16
water beetles, 10
waterfowl, 22
water repellency, 76
wax, 16
web, hackle, 53
West Yellowstone, Montana, 114
Western Trout Fly Tying Manual, Vols. I, II, 114
whip finish, 34
White Wulff, 106, **136**
whiting hackle, 50, 51, 53
Whitlock, Dave, 120, 130
Williams Lake, Oregon, 98
Williams, Taylor "Beartracks," 134
Williamson River, Oregon, 102
wind currents, 68
Wind River Mountains, Wyoming, 110
winding hackle, 54-59
window of a trout, 80, 85, 115
windward shore, 60
wingcase, **28**, 62, 98
wings, **26**, **29**, **45**, 82
wire, 25
wire diameter, 17
woodduck wing, 31
Wright's Royal, 76
Wulff, 12, 23, 106
Wulff, Lee, 106, 136
Wulff, Gray, **136**
Wulff, Irresistible, **132**
Wulff patterns, **106**, 107
Wulff, Royal, **136**
Wulff, White, **136**

X

X Caddis, **136**
X design wing tie-in, 108
X rib pattern, 95
X system, hooks, 17

Y

Yakima River, Washington, 103
yellow drake, 94
Yellow Humpy, **132**
Yellow Royal Humpy, **114**, **115**
Yellow Stimulator, **29**, **102**, 103, **136**
Yellowstone National Park, Montana, 94
Yellowstone River, Montana, 94, 106

Z

Z-Lon, 23, **25**
Zap-A-Gap, 15